Occupying Power

STUDIES OF THE WEATHERHEAD EAST ASIAN INSTITUTE,
COLUMBIA UNIVERSITY

The Studies of the Weatherhead East Asian
Institute of Columbia University were inaugurated in 1962
to bring to a wider public the results of significant new research
on modern and contemporary East Asia.

A complete list of titles in this series can be found online at
www.columbia.edu/cu/weai/weatherhead-studies.html.

Occupying Power

SEX WORKERS AND SERVICEMEN
IN POSTWAR JAPAN

Sarah Kovner

STANFORD UNIVERSITY PRESS
STANFORD, CALIFORNIA

Stanford University Press
Stanford, California

An earlier version of Chapter 3 was published as "Selling Sex under Occupation: The American-Japanese Encounter after 1945," *Journal of Asian Studies* 68, no. 3 (August 2009): 777–804.

Library of Congress Cataloging-in-Publication Data

Kovner, Sarah (Sarah C.), 1973– author.
  Occupying power : sex workers and servicemen in postwar Japan / Sarah Kovner.
      pages cm. — (Studies of the Weatherhead East Asian Institute, Columbia University)
  Includes bibliographical references and index.
  ISBN 978-0-8047-7691-2 (cloth : alk. paper)
  1. Prostitution—Japan—History—20th century.   2. Sex-oriented businesses—Japan—History—20th century.   3. Prostitutes—Legal status, laws, etc.—Japan—History—20th century.   4. Japan—History—Allied occupation, 1945–1952.   I. Title. II. Series: Studies of the Weatherhead East Asian Institute, Columbia University.
  HQ247.A5K68 2012
  306.740952'09045—dc22

                                                                        2011014086

Typeset by Westchester Book Group in 11/14 AGaramond

To my parents

Contents

Acknowledgments

In writing this book, I learned from many people. Sheldon Garon's work on Japanese history remains to me a model of clarity and careful scholarship. David Howell is a terrific teacher and continues to inspire me with the range of his contributions and his keen sense of humor. I thank Henry Smith, who insisted on attention to detail but also encouraged creative use of visual sources, and Charles Armstrong, who helped broaden my scope to encompass East Asia. Greg Pflugfelder's multilingualism, imaginative thinking, and encyclopedic mastery of Japanese history are awe-inspiring. He listened to my ideas and then improved on them. My greatest scholarly debt is to Carol Gluck, who not only has a nuanced knowledge of Japanese history and historians but is a wordsmith without equal. She lives up to her own legend.

Other mentors, colleagues, and friends in the United States helped along the way. Among those who introduced me to new ways of thinking and pushed me to grow as a historian are Matt Augustine, Kim Brandt, Rob Fish, Darryl Flaherty, Christine Kim, Joy Kim, Dorothy Ko, Barak Kushner, Yasuhiro Makimura, Suzanne O'Brien, Scott O'Bryan, Maartje Oldenberg, Lee Pennington, Janet Poole, Kerry Ross, Miwako Tezuka, Lori Watt, Leila Wice, and Jon Zwicker. Special thanks go to those brave readers who read very rough drafts of the manuscript. Laura Neitzel helped me understand Japan's 1950s, while Atina Grossman encouraged me to make more of German comparisons. Andrew Gordon, William Johnston, and one anonymous reader reviewed the book manuscript, and their questions and suggestions made it much stronger. I also want to thank reviewers for the *Journal of Asian Studies*, including Jordan Sand, who helped sharpen my logic at a crucial early stage.

In Japan, I owe a great debt to the many people who mentored me, eased my way into archives, shared their memories, or simply let me stay in their homes—sometimes for very long periods of time. Ueno Chizuko, who sponsored my research at the University of Tokyo, is a force of nature. Her fierce intellect, intellectual courage, and personal drive are a model to me. Thanks are also due to Fujime Yuki, Muta Kazue, Nakano Rie, Satō Fumika, and Senda Yuki, who assisted me at several key junctures. It is hard to know how to thank Tom McDevitt, who hosted me for an entire year in Tokyo, and on several return visits, with dry wit and unfailing style. The Augustines let me stay with them in Kyoto on numerous occasions over many years. Much of the Sasebo section of this book could not have been written without the help of the Kawajiri family, who provided introductions, shared their memories, and graciously welcomed me into their home for weeks on end.

The University of Florida has been a wonderful place to complete this book, with colleagues who helped me learn about the big world beyond New York and Japan. In particular, I thank Sean Adams, Jeff Adler, Ida Altman, Juliana Barr, Michelle Campos, Nina Caputo, Mitch Hart, Sheryl Kroen, Helen Lee, Joe Murphy, Hikaru Nakano, Joe Spillane, and Luise White. I benefited in more material ways from a University of Florida Humanities Enhancement Grant, and also a grant from the Association of Asian Studies Council on Northeast Asia, which paid for a follow-up research trip to Japan, Australia, and New Zealand. This book also depended on librarians and archivists in the United States, Japan, Switzerland, Australia, and New Zealand. It would not have been completed without a fellowship from the Weatherhead East Asian Institute at Columbia University and a semester of research leave from the University of Florida. Dan Rivero, Jessica Walsh, and Carolyn Brown were of tremendous help in moving the manuscript through the publication process, and my expert editor, Stacy Wagner, displayed faith and confidence from beginning to end.

And most of all, I thank my family. I have been lucky enough to know three of my grandparents. Natalie Lieberman had both substance and style, and she showed me how to dream big. Don and Gloria Tassone always encouraged me in every endeavor. My sister, Anna Kovner, never refused to read, or reread, my many drafts. My daughter, Lily, gave me time to think but also let me know when it was time to stop working. Her father's daily admonitions to make history, unrelenting optimism, and unflagging support make every day better.

Since the time I began this book, my father, Anthony Kovner, tirelessly searched for typos, mailed me countless articles, and talked to me for hours about my work—and the world. My mother, Christine Tassone Kovner, inspires me every day to try harder, to work more, and to be a better person. This book is dedicated to my parents, with thanks and love.

A Note on Names and Nomenclature

The use of the term *prostitution* by authorities makes it impossible to avoid using it in this book, especially when referring to law and legal authorities. For instance, I refer to the law that stands at the heart of the study by its official translation, the Prostitution Prevention Law (Baishun Bōshi Hō). But in English, the word *prostitute* has clearly negative connotations: for example, "I prostitute myself to my job." Japanese has a richer vocabulary than English for sex workers, some specific examples of which are discussed in the following pages. Today, the general word signifying prostitution in the Japanese language is *baishun*, and *baishunfu* designates the women who perform sexual work. But these terms are mostly a product of the postwar era, when the phrase *baishun mondai* (prostitution problem) became commonplace.* The term *sex worker* is more neutral and therefore more appropriate in a study of how selling sex for money came to be seen as inherently illicit.

Although a few people who witnessed this history agreed to interviews, much of it was off the record, and none of them was herself a sex worker. As this book seeks to show, sex workers were ostracized and made to feel ashamed for what they did. The Japanese state made a deliberate attempt to reintegrate them into society, to the point that even their own spouses do not know their past. Out of respect for their privacy, all names of sex workers—with the exception of those already available through the mass media or the Diet debates—have been changed. I have also changed the names of interviewees I thought would prefer anonymity.

Japanese names are given in Japanese order (family name first). Macrons are omitted in cases of words commonly used in English (e.g. Osaka, not Ōsaka).

---

* See Yunomae Kazuko, "Baibaishun," in Inoue Teruko et al. eds., *Joseigaku jiten* (Tokyo: Iwanami Shoten, 2000), 643–644.

Occupying Power

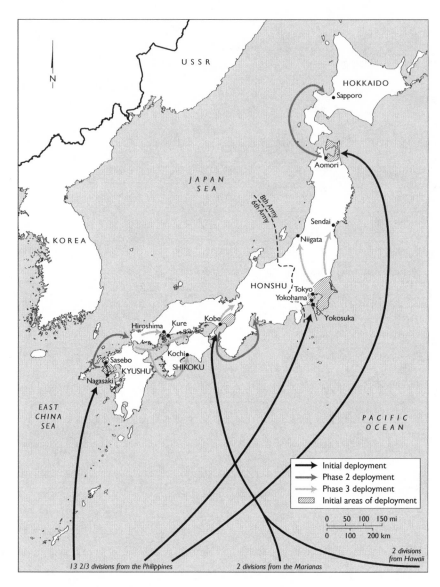

Occupying Japan

Introduction

A Special Business

In 1949, a reporter for the popular weekly *Sandee Mainichi* visited Kyoto's famed pleasure quarter of Shimabara and, after some investigation, concluded that geisha had become "living antiques." For centuries, formally trained and elegantly costumed geisha had embodied the height of fashionable dance, song, and wit. But the reporter believed that something was now missing. "They deal only with 'drinking,'" he explained, "so they are a kind of showgirl dressed in historical costume, performing historical plays. After that they only entertain clients while they drink or serve them tea. And that's all the business there is for them—they have nothing to do with the 'special business.'"[1]

That "special business" is the subject of this study. What made it appear new and special, even while the geisha came to seem quaint? For more than 300 years, Japan had tolerated and regulated the performance of sexual services for remuneration. Other more eclectic accounts have surveyed this earlier era, when authorities demarcated "pleasure districts," recognized debt contracts, and certified the health of sex workers. *Occupying Power* seeks to explain how and why the arrival of masses of foreign soldiers shifted the long-established landscape of the sex industry in fundamental ways. Together with the more generally democratizing policies of Allied officials, which gave greater voice to female political activists, the arrival of hundreds of thousands of servicemen struck Japan like an earthquake. The aftershocks produced a new political configuration that finally abolished licensed prostitution. Ironically, and tragically, abolition made sex workers less visible and more vulnerable.

The period of this study includes the most dramatic events in Japan's twentieth century, including total war, unconditional surrender, and foreign occupation. New buildings and whole neighborhoods in base towns and larger cities rose up to accommodate a veritable industry in sexual services. As the built environment changed, so too did Japan's psychological landscape. The visible presence of "objectionable" women served as a constant reminder of defeat. It was written on their very bodies, apparent to both the occupiers and the occupied. Dressed in brightly colored dresses, wearing pancake makeup and with cigarettes dangling from their lips, the *pan-pan*—or streetwalkers—seemed to embody both the fall of Japan's empire and the rise of something shockingly new. Decades later, the way Japanese talked about, or did not talk about, sex under occupation—above all, the experience of the "comfort women," under *Japanese* occupation—continued to show the influence of this singular, searing experience.

SELLING SEX UNDER OCCUPATION

Sex work provides a powerful subject to analyze social change. It can provoke troubling questions about the true nature of sexual partnerships and paid labor. Since the late nineteenth century, sociologists have cited prostitution to illustrate the problems that come with the commodification of the body through wage labor.[2] In the early twentieth century, sexologists and psychoanalysts helped create an enduring distinction, rendering male visitation to prostitutes as normal, even healthy, while pathologizing the sex worker.[3] Analysts reconsidered in the late 1980s and 1990s, when the issue became part of the feminist "sexuality debates." Some academics and activists suggested that commercialized sex could, under certain circumstances, actually be empowering.[4] Feminists argued that it was comparable to other kinds of service work.[5] For their part, sex workers and their supporters became active participants in such inquiries, drawing on this scholarship to lobby for recognition and decriminalization.[6] Although the "sexuality debates" were largely theoretical, recent work incorporates research among both sex workers and their clients.[7] Historians have drawn from and contributed to both approaches, at the same time expanding the scope of such inquiries beyond the Euro-American context. Some use cultural theory to investigate the symbolic meaning of sex work, while others use social history to describe how it has been structured.[8]

Japan under the Allied Occupation is a particularly revealing and important subject for such inquires. The firebombing of Japanese cities also incinerated centuries-old pleasure districts. Dazed survivors were utterly destitute. At the same time, hundreds of thousands of servicemen arrived from the United States and the British Commonwealth, including African Americans as well as white Americans, Aborigines, Maori, and Indians as well as Australians, New Zealanders, and Britons. Beginning in 1950, even more contingents would pass through Japan as part of the United Nations force fighting in Korea. The Japanese government first established official brothels, and even segregated black and white clients to please occupation authorities. But Douglas MacArthur soon ordered them disbanded. Even as they were deregulated, commercial sex markets proliferated. At the same time, the disgrace of militarists and the return of democratic politics meant that Japanese women would be given the vote for the first time. Female and socialist politicians could therefore exercise real power, but only within limits set by their American overlords. After more than a decade of activism, and critical compromises with their conservative opponents, they helped secure passage of Japan's first national anti-prostitution law in 1956.

This transition from regulated sex work, to outright deregulation, to criminalization—all in a period of unprecedented social upheaval—remains unique in the annals of the "oldest profession." Sex work in occupied Japan therefore permits us to grapple with fundamental questions about imperialism and individual agency, political economy and cultural change, and the political use and misuse of history.

Allied servicemen came to Japan with a good deal of historical baggage, including a set of policies and practices concerning sexual relations and venereal disease (VD). U.S. and British Commonwealth policies bore the imprint of particular notions of masculinity and manhood inflected by differences in race, class, and ethnicity. Comparing different policies in policing and public health, and the varied experience of African Americans, Indians, and others in segregated state-run brothels and more deregulated markets, enables us to address highly politicized historical questions more analytically. Examining both high politics and the everyday negotiations among servicemen, sex workers, and entrepreneurs, we will see how intimate histories and international relations are interconnected in ways scholars have only begun to explore.

Occupied Japan featured a proliferating array of different forms of sex work, as more—and more diverse—women entered and transformed the industry. They migrated from the countryside and cities to base areas, from Hiroshima and Osaka to Sasebo, from Tokyo to Yokosuka, and shifted sex work beyond regulated districts to public parks, port areas, and wherever else bodies could be bought and sold. Although sex work had always existed outside the regulated districts, women now sold sex openly on street corners near schools and other places where children played. They were difficult to dislodge because they occupied a crucial position in the postwar economy, earning precious dollars and black-market goods, while supporting a host of ancillary workers—from letter-writers to rickshaw pullers, from bar owners to bankers.

Many women became sex workers out of economic despair: former shop girls, office workers, or bus girls. Others simply moved positions within the larger entertainment industry, including geisha, cabaret girls, or beer hall workers. New sex workers who catered to servicemen tended to be more educated, ambitious, and entrepreneurial than women who worked in the established red-light districts. Exploring the variety of their experiences can help us understand how selling sex is like or unlike other kinds of labor, and how it changes under different regulatory regimes.[9]

The struggle over sex work can also illuminate the changing nature of Japanese politics in the postwar period. Government and society underwent dramatic legal changes after 1945, as regulators and regulations shifted. The legal system itself was transformed when Americans rewrote the constitution and the criminal code. Debates about prostitution occurred as women's groups, left-leaning politicians, and conservatives were jostling for power. Whereas conservative politicians contended that prostitution was a "necessary evil," activists and socialist politicians insisted that it was a "social evil." But even if it is clear only in retrospect, Japan was settling into what is known as the "1955 system," a pattern of one-party rule that persisted for decades and helped uphold a Cold War alliance with the United States. The weak 1956 law that criminalized prostitution punished sex workers but protected others who profited from the trade. And all along, American servicemen were shielded from prosecution, even in cases where they assaulted Japanese women. How did a reformist movement to improve the lives of women come to such an end? And how can this help us understand, more generally, the imposition of social order after a period of unprecedented change?

By granting equal weight to the experiences of the sex worker, client, and regulator, this book aims for a more sophisticated interpretation of the sex industry, one that is not limited to social history or women's history.[10] It will show how an influx of new buyers of sexual services, different sellers, and varied approaches to regulation shaped not just the larger political economy of Japan, but also the politics of memory and national self-perceptions.

The response of the Japanese people to the Allied Occupation was mediated through the bodies of individual women, as the nation was transformed from a conquering power to a conquered people. This provoked a reevaluation of sex work and gave a new and urgent credence to movements dedicated to its abolition. Popular distaste for prostitution with non-Japanese clients not only ended three centuries of regulated sex work but also changed the way Japanese remembered their own roles as occupiers of foreign lands, with consequences that continue to roil international relations across East Asia and the Pacific.

CONQUERORS AND CONCUBINES: SEX WORK IN THE CONTEXT OF OCCUPATION

Understanding this development requires an analysis that can relate race and gender to geopolitics. Military occupation, like colonization, is a situation of explicit political inequality. It is precisely within such a context that racial and sexual oppression can be taken to extremes. If occupied Japan provides a uniquely powerful lens to analyze the nature of sex work, examining sexual regulation and sexual relations affords a new perspective on the collapse of Japan's empire. The object of this study is not just the Allied Occupation, the specific historical event that supposedly ended in 1952 with the San Francisco Peace Treaty. It explores the broader concept of "occupation," a condition of compromised sovereignty resulting from a foreign military presence. In this latter sense, occupation may be said to have lasted in Japan through the Korean War years and continuing on until 1972, when Okinawa reverted to Japanese control. It persists in the form of permanent American bases operating on Japanese territory today. They form some of the oldest elements of what some analysts consider a new form of empire: a network of overseas bases and informal spheres of influence, virtually unprecedented in scope and expense.[11]

The occupation of Japan has often been held up as a model of what American power can achieve, quite literally in the case of U.S. military operations in the Middle East. Former occupation officials themselves wrote many of the earliest, most favorable accounts. The image of a beneficent and enlightened regime—particularly for Japanese women—still informs popular understanding of this period in the United States. But Japanese scholars were offering a very different view in the 1950s and 1960s. They emphasized how Cold War priorities led U.S. officials to "reverse course" on many progressive reforms, and they used Marxist theory to analyze the imperialist motives behind U.S. policy.[12] In the 1970s and 1980s, both U.S. and Japanese historians—most prominently John Dower in the United States and Eiji Takemae in Japan—began to write accounts of the complex interplay between occupation policy and Japanese politics based on newly available archives in both countries.[13] American and Japanese scholars soon began to work in cooperation.[14] By the 1990s, the focus of new scholarship was shifting to issues of race and gender, work that examined not just policy-making and high politics, but also the social and cultural history of the U.S.-Japanese encounter.[15] In Australia and New Zealand, scholarship has followed a similar course, though most U.S. historians do not take into account the British Commonwealth forces in the Occupation.[16] Even for the Japanese, the U.S. role is still the central preoccupation.

On the subject of sex work, the perception of remaining under U.S. occupation pervades the accounts offered by most Japanese historians. Yuki Tanaka, for example, compares the panpan to the military comfort women in wartime Asia. He points to the way Japanese authorities set up brothels in both cases, as well as the similarities in the predatory and racist behavior of servicemen.[17]

For Tanaka, as for scholars such as Fujime Yuki and Hirai Kazuko, the U.S. military's VD policy was no less egregious.[18] U.S. commanders typically identified the source of disease as Japanese women, not U.S. servicemen. They implemented humiliating contact-tracing methods, closely questioning women about their sexual partners. And they provided American servicemen with medications such as penicillin, while denying treatment to Japanese nationals.

This history helps explains why, fifty years after the end of the Pacific War, accusations of sexual assault by servicemen resonated so powerfully in U.S.-Japan relations. Military bases—in Japan as in other countries— create many sources of friction, whether nuclear weapons, toxic waste, or noise pollution. But Japanese activists chose to make rape cases their rally- ing point in a movement that continues to seek the expulsion of the U.S. presence. Okinawans, who have long felt marginalized from mainland Japan, have in this way become central in the fight to regain national sover- eignty, if only as victims.

But if sex work during the Occupation needs to be situated in a broader context, in both the larger history of East Asia and the longer history of U.S.-Japanese relations, it should not necessarily begin with the comfort women and end with the most recent rape cases in Okinawa. We must also look for continuities—as well as change—in how the Allies had dealt with sex work and sexually transmitted disease before World War II. There al- ready had been a long history of identifying VD with women, beginning with medieval European references to "diseases of the yard," and how they were contracted by lying with a woman.[19] Specific policies and practices varied tremendously, however, and tracing their development over time can help explain how Allied officials conducted themselves when they arrived in Japan. Few scholars have noted, for instance, the intensity of the efforts that U.S. and British Commonwealth commanders devoted to policing and punishing the sexual desires of their own men, including suspension of pay, off-limits postings, and denial of promotion. Nor do they note that policies such as contact tracing were implemented in the United States on U.S. citi- zens. And although it is true that servicemen were the first to receive peni- cillin, putting the needs of soldiers over civilians was standard practice for both U.S. and Japanese authorities. What is harder to explain is why VD rates among occupation troops remained staggeringly high, though here again examining what happened before they arrived in Japan provides im- portant clues.

In part because of the spread of disease, the network of institutional- ized sexual-service centers, the Recreational Amusement Association (RAA, Tokushu Ian Kyōkai), proved unacceptable to Allied military commanders and was disbanded after fewer than seven months. The arrival of British Commonwealth Occupation Forces in 1946—often ignored in accounts of the postwar period—meant that millions of Japanese would live under a

different regulatory regime, one dedicated to eliminating all forms of fraternization. For more than a decade after the beginning of the Occupation,
Allied servicemen, sex workers, proprietors, and an array of politicians continued jostling to negotiate new terms of exchange and new relations of
power. The parallels historians draw between comfort women and the women
who worked for the RAA therefore provide only a partial portrait of sex
work during the Occupation.

How does the picture change when we expand the time frame to take in
this longer, more complex history? Any convincing account of sex work in
the context of military occupation must address the question of agency. By
defining all sex work as oppression, we cannot begin to answer it. Selling
sex may not have been the first choice of many women. But it needs to be
understood in relation to their immediate economic and other interests. If
only for lack of good options, they voluntarily participated and were paid
for their efforts, unlike the Korean and Chinese women who were enslaved
by the Japanese military. And, faced with difficult choices, Japanese women
went on to work in ways that surprised and unsettled both their countrymen and occupation authorities.

Occupying Power will compare Japan to the occupations of Germany and
Korea. In both cases, women selling sex to foreign troops were scorned or
even subjected to violence—just as in Japan.[20] Sex workers were seen as
symbols of foreign occupation. But in Japan, unlike in Germany, sex work
had been accepted, regulated, and even planned for in wartime. It was not
selling sex for money that was problematic, but the awkward clientele. If sex
workers were symbols, what did these symbols mean? How did these
women define themselves, and how did this experience affect the way Japanese remembered their occupation of other countries?

OCCUPATION WITHOUT END?

Both in principle and in practice, the Allied Occupation of Japan was quite
unlike earlier military occupations, though it can be usefully compared to
the way imperial powers—including the United States—had ruled colonial
territories. Military occupation normally refers to the seizure and control
of an area by foreign military forces for a limited period of time. Since the
Hague Conventions of 1899 and 1907, international law has specified the
responsibilities of occupying states, seeking to protect occupied territories

so that "sovereignty may not be alienated through the use of force."[21] This is what distinguishes occupiers, who are temporary guardians over occupied territories, from imperial powers, who seek permanent settlements. The Americans, however, claimed exemption from the Hague regulations because of Japan's "unconditional surrender."[22] They rejected the law of military occupation in order to implement wholesale change in Japan, at the same time setting up permanent bases for servicemen and their families, complete with schools and shopping malls.

Even more than how the Americans defined their role, we can recognize the real nature and import of U.S. power in Japan by examining the actions it authorized. The ambitious program of the American authorities invites comparison with other political entities that have sought to reshape societies, ones usually characterized as empires. If empire is understood as "effective control, whether formal or informal, of a subordinated society by an imperial society," as Michael Doyle has usefully put it, then the U.S. role in Japan certainly qualifies.[23]

In occupied Japan, it was in the realm of social relations that effective control of a subject people was unmistakable. Whether attending to sex work, women's rights, VD, or miscegenation, the concerns of U.S. officials were strikingly similar to those of their Dutch, French, and British counterparts. As Ann Stoler has argued, regulating sexual relationships was essential in shaping the development of colonial societies.[24] In European colonies, authorities managed both marriage and extramarital relations. So too did American authorities in Japan, proscribing fraternization and prohibiting marriage to Japanese nationals. And at the same time they presented themselves as protectors of women against backward social practices, like the British in India and the French in North Africa.

American authorities also insisted on a legal system that accorded special status to U.S. nationals, both during and after the formal occupation, much as colonial codes discriminated between citizens and subjects. Shielded from Japanese local justice—whether for mundane traffic accidents or more serious crimes—American servicemen have benefited from a form of extraterritoriality. A Status of Forces Agreement (SOFA) assigns jurisdiction over the vast majority of legal cases involving servicemen and Japanese citizens in military-base areas to the military authorities. In 1953, land extending over 245,000 acres remained in American hands. Much of the territory on which troops lived and performed maneuvers still has not been returned to the Japanese, creating continuities in time and space.[25] Japanese citizens in base areas lived—and continue to live— in the modern equivalent of treaty ports, where foreign nationals enjoy privileged legal status.

But if the Occupation of Japan can be usefully compared to imperial dominion, it can also serve to remind us that power is never absolute. Just as French, British, Dutch, and other imperial authorities required collaborators and often ruled indirectly, U.S. officials also found Japanese partners indispensable—as bureaucrats, as policemen, but also as guides, interpreters, and confidants. All this raises more questions about the role of sex workers in the Allied Occupation. If we do not assume that servicemen were always conquerors and Japanese women their permanent victims, how do the power dynamics of occupation shift? How might we understand this as a process of negotiation and not just oppression?

FROM THE FLOATING WORLD TO THE MODERN WORLD

To appreciate the revolutionary transformation of sex work during the Occupation requires understanding how, for centuries, law in Japan had sanctioned different kinds of female entertainers. It is now the subject of a large scholarly literature, which has revealed a tremendously complex system. What contemporaries called the "floating world" had many different realms, with different rules, written or unwritten, for cities, castle towns, and remote villages all across the archipelago.

In 1589, Toyotomi Hideyoshi established the first regulated "pleasure district" (*yūkaku*) in Kyoto. The Tokugawa shogunate that ruled Japan from 1603 established other licensed quarters: Shinmachi, in the commercial city of Osaka, in 1610, and Maruyama in the port city of Nagasaki in 1642. The most famous district of all, the Yoshiwara, was approved by the shogunate in 1617. It opened in the city of Edo, now Tokyo, in 1618. By this point, sex work had already begun to assume myriad forms and constitute an elaborate hierarchy, including courtesans, streetwalkers, maidservants, and military camp followers.[26]

Within these licensed districts, a tiny proportion of sex workers held elite jobs. They were regarded as the female celebrities of their time. They were ranked in guidebooks, depicted in woodcut prints, and celebrated in literary works. Reaching this position required much hard work. Often sold by poor families, girls had to rise from the position of attendant (*kamuro*), performing the duties of a maidservant, and might suffer considerably. But they also gained the opportunity to learn performing arts, dancing, and manners critical to rise in the status world of the pleasure districts. After their training and debut, they could ascend through a variety of hierarchal distinctions to reach the coveted top-class designation variously denoted as *tayū, tayū kōshi, or yobidashi.* Most never did. Should the journey prove unsuccessful, the fall was rapid—debts soon piled up, and moneylenders crowded the doors.[27]

All but invisible next to the most elite sex workers, many more women who sold sexual services for money populated the pleasure districts. Together with proprietors, they had to operate under the watchful eye of samurai officials. Many other people profited from the trade, including fruit sellers, fortune-tellers, and hairstylists. And outside these districts were hot-spring geishas, bath attendants, maids, and post-station maidservants and waitresses. Part-timers of all sorts—musicians, actors, and dancers—worked beyond the city walls.[28] Female entertainers and maidservants easily moved in and out of the trade. For most, especially outside castle towns, the Yoshiwara experience was atypical. In the mining town of Innai, brothels were limited to a certain quarter, while other economic activities were assigned to different areas. In Niigata, authorities allowed sex work with no regulation whatsoever. Freedom of movement also varied: in Fukuoka, like Yoshiwara, women were limited to the quarter. In Mitarai and Takehara, they worked on boats.[29] The regulation of sex work in early modern Japan therefore created a patchwork pattern. Not only did sex workers have their place, but they also had many places to practice their trade.

Following the arrival of Commodore Perry's Black Ships, the collapse of the Tokugawa shogunate, and the restoration of the Meiji emperor, licensed sex workers, like many others in Japan, saw their lives change. Fujime Yuki, Japan's most prominent historian of the subject, has emphasized how the encounter with the West would lead authorities to reorganize sex work. Sheldon Garon has highlighted the role of social activists and middle-class reformers in persuading the state to adopt new methods to manage public morals. Both are critical of the motives as well as the consequences of these regulatory and reformist efforts.[30]

In re-regulating sex work, government officials sought out European models to emulate, much as they did in modernizing other aspects of Japanese society. They studied and adopted a variety of new regulations in the 1870s, including mandatory medical examinations. These were highly invasive, unpopular with sex workers, and—as it turned out—mostly ineffective in preventing the spread of VD.[31] They also planted the idea that, instead of being glamorous and alluring, sex workers were a source of disease.

But while seeking to initiate reforms, the Japanese government sometimes had to react to outside provocations and pressures. The most famous incident occurred in 1872 and involved the *Maria Luz*. When the Peruvian vessel stopped for repairs in Yokohama while carrying indentured Chinese laborers, some of them jumped ship and swam to a British ironclad. A special Japanese court convened and declared the laborers free. The Peruvian captain's lawyer asked why foreigners should be denied the right to buy and sell laborers when, after all, Japan's licensed quarters engaged in the same practice. Sensitive to foreign perceptions, the Japanese cabinet issued a proclamation liberating indentured prostitutes.[32]

One week later, the Ministry of Justice lacked similar sensitivity when it issued an infamous order excusing geisha and licensed prostitutes from repaying their debts. It argued that if farm animals could not be expected to be responsible to creditors, neither could the women. The order did not void the practice of prostitution, only indenture contracts—and these were reinstated by 1875.[33] In 1902, the Supreme Court confirmed that sex workers were required by law to pay back advances, even if they had escaped. Six years later, the Home Ministry ruled that unlicensed prostitutes (if caught) would be committed to penal servitude.[34] Though the indenture contracts that remained common among licensed sex workers might now be considered exploitative, these contracts were for a limited term and not for life. Families entered into them because they were often the only available source of credit during emergencies, such as failed harvests, which were all too common in prewar Japan.[35]

At the end of the nineteenth century, a movement arose to abolish sex work altogether.[36] The Freedom and People's Rights Movement (Jiyū Minken Undō) laid the groundwork for the abolitionists by calling for a popularly elected Diet and a democratic constitution. But it was not until 1880, when Christian activist Yuasa Jirō and others submitted to the Gunma prefectural assembly a petition to abolish prostitution, that any true Japanese anti-prostitution movement could be identified. The prefecture, which adopted an ordinance against prostitution in 1891, soon emerged as the center of operations for the National Prostitution Abolition League (Zenkoku Baishō Dōmeikai) and the abolitionist movement more generally. By this time, explicitly Christian groups had also begun to organize against prostitution. In

1886, the Women's Christian Temperance Union (WCTU; Nihon Kirisutokyō Fujin Kyōfūkai) began operations in Tokyo, joined by the Salvation Army (Kyūseigun) in 1900. After fires razed the Yoshiwara licensed district in 1911, the Purity Society (Kakuseikai) joined the anti-prostitution coalition.[37]

But the abolitionists could not thwart a flourishing commercial sex market. In fact, it had begun to spread to the countryside, where paid sex had previously been rare.[38] Nor could they dissuade public authorities from continuing to regulate it. For instance, although the Gunma ordinance may have stopped the licensing of prostitutes, taxation of sex-work businesses and mandatory VD examinations continued.[39] Activists' efforts did little to discourage the sale of sex or to improve the work conditions of women in the licensed districts.

Starting in the 1880s, Japanese sex workers formed part of a larger, transnational market that included port cities across Southeast and East Asia. They were among the more than 100,000 Japanese women who emigrated over the following fifty years.[40] Known as *karayuki-san*, they fled impoverished communities, particularly in northwest Kyushu, to seek work in such places as Rangoon, Hong Kong, and Singapore. Although many women were unaware of the kind of work that awaited them, others, especially those from Shimabara or the Amakusa Islands, knowingly entered the profession.[41]

For a newly powerful Japan, deeply concerned with its image and markets abroad, the *karayuki-san* were an embarrassment. Beginning in 1899, the Foreign Ministry instructed consuls to induce Japanese women to return. Other colonial powers assisted by declaring that Japanese sex workers were no longer welcome.[42] By 1919, the acting Japanese consul general in Singapore, Yamazaki Heikichi, began to pursue and repatriate Japanese women. With the cooperation of local authorities, he abolished Japanese prostitution houses.[43] From 1918 to 1920, Japanese consuls in Manila, Rangoon, and Hong Kong joined in efforts to send sex workers home. But an informal economy in sex work remained in these and other port cities.[44]

At the same time that the state sought to prevent Japanese sex workers from operating in foreign territories, it extended the system of licensed prostitution to its colonies. Licensed prostitution was introduced in Taiwan after the 1895 Treaty of Shimonoseki.[45] Even though the Japanese did not gain control of Korea until 1905, the Treaty of Kanghwa in 1876 had given them extraterritorial status, and Japanese-run brothels in Pusan and Wonsan soon followed. After Korea became a protectorate, prostitution was permitted in restaurants, and prostitutes began to be licensed in 1916.[46]

In the 1920s, as Japanese sex workers—and Japanese style-regulation—followed the expansion of empire across Southeast and East Asia, sex markets and the struggle for abolition in the home islands entered a new phase. As in other countries, the phenomenon of the "modern girl" inspired new notions of independence and sexuality. In the popular press, commentators focused on café waitresses, who worked in a highly eroticized atmosphere and received their wages from tips. Although evidence suggests that sexual labor was not mandatory and occurred outside the café premises, many women probably engaged in extra-hours activities.[47] Moreover, unlike most sex workers, they had control—albeit negotiated—over their bodies and their choice of clients.[48]

Despite sporadic crackdowns, café culture continued to be popular into the 1930s. By 1936, there were twice as many registered café waitresses nationwide as licensed sex workers. Abolitionists exploited the coming of war to fight new types of sex work, imposing restrictions on cafés and bars. For the first time, licensed brothels began to work with them, since eliminating unregulated sex work served to limit competition. Authorities continued to license sex workers, but other women still sold sex outside regulated areas.[49]

But the most important new development of the wartime period was not the beginning of more informal, less regulated forms of sex work, nor was it the first sign of a de facto coalition of anti-prostitution activists and brothel owners to stop such practices. Instead, it was the creation of a vast system of sexual slavery establishments for the Japanese military. Unwitting women from countries including Korea and China, as well as interned Dutch civilians, found themselves compelled to provide sexual services to Japanese servicemen, enduring the most appalling conditions. Estimates vary, since so much of the official record was destroyed, but as many as 200,000 women may have been consigned to this fate. In this way, the military hoped to control sexual violence against occupied peoples and contain the spread of VD in the ranks.[50]

In the first postwar decade, Japanese politicians would therefore have many histories to draw upon as they sought models upon which to base national policy. Conservative politicians, for example, could argue that sex work had long been accepted and regulated and that complete prohibition was unrealistic. Female activists could argue that the abolition movement had deep historical roots and the government had already begun to limit prostitution in particular prefectures and among Japanese expatriates. But the most immediate precedent was the system of comfort stations the state had created in occupied Asia.

This book begins with the arrival of U.S. troops in Japan in 1945. The first chapter, "'To Transship Them to Some Suitable Island': Making Policy in the Midst of Chaos," analyzes the differing responses—regulation, punishment, and preventive measures—that U.S. and British Commonwealth forces used to combat a purported VD epidemic among both their own forces and Japanese women. Japanese officials set up the RAA, modeled on the comfort stations they had established overseas. But this proved unacceptable to Allied authorities. They were alarmed about the spread of VD and also had to worry about critical reactions in the United States and Australia. The abolition of the RAA, along with all laws that permitted licensed prostitution and indentured contracts, amounted to the de facto deregulation of sex markets.

As complex cultural relations developed between sex workers and foreign servicemen, Allied and Japanese authorities struggled to impose some sort of regulatory system. Chapter 2, "Violence, Commerce, Marriage," examines the range of encounters between servicemen and Japanese women. In the first weeks, Japanese authorities stoked fear of sexual violence. But over time, both Japanese and Allied officials became more concerned about long-term relationships and biracial children. Chapter 2 therefore considers not just the ensuing changes in official policy, but how they were interrelated with the realm of intimate relations between servicemen and Japanese women.

The third chapter, "When Flesh Glittered: Selling Sex in Sasebo and Tokyo," maps the changing topography of the sex markets with the influx of servicemen and the delicensing of the commercial sex industry. Confusion reigned in districts where prostitution had long been regulated and tolerated. Streetwalkers became a vivid and contentious symbol of the American Occupation. In military-base areas, such as Sasebo, a flood of new sex workers forced Japanese men, women, and children to confront a changed physical and social landscape, reconfigured to accommodate the occupying forces. As the commercial sex market expanded, its representatives became increasingly unpopular: sex workers were widely disliked—and discriminated against—as men and women discovered in this a way to display an abiding nationalism.

The fourth chapter, "Legislating Women: The Push for a Prostitution Prevention Law," turns to the female activists and legislators who worked locally and nationally to pass laws against prostitution. Even as the Allied Occupation made some women victims, it gave other, newly enfranchised women the tools to fight back. Female legislators such as Fujiwara Michiko, Ichikawa Fusae, and Kamichika Ichiko inspected military-base towns and protested in the popular press. Politicians and critics refigured prostitution as a crime against children to appeal to Japanese patriotism. Women's organizations formed local and national networks, and local governments passed more than sixty prefectural and municipal ordinances against prostitution.

The fifth chapter, "The High Politics of Base Pleasures: Regulating Morality for the Postwar Era," explains how a national anti-prostitution law finally passed in 1956, when Liberal Democratic Party legislators made the cause their own. Different politicians had distinct perspectives on sex work. Although some saw it as emblematic of a moral crisis, others argued that men would always need an outlet for their sexual desires. For Prime Minister Hatoyama Ichirō, the sex industry constituted a political conundrum. Brothel owners were important contributors, but their support had become embarrassing. He solved this dilemma by securing passage of a government bill that did not actually threaten the business of brothel owners. Where activists had fought for a strong law that punished prostitution as criminal exploitation, Hatoyama refigured prostitution as contrary to morals. Although the law was a narrow institutional triumph for female legislators, it actually safeguarded a sex industry that left men in charge.

Chapter 6, "The Presence of the Past: Controversies over Sex Work Since 1956," surveys the consolidation of new sexual markets that persist to this day. The 1956 law hastened a process that had begun ten years earlier, leading to the demise of licensed sex work and, with it, a whole way of life. Other changes became evident in the built environment, as proprietors evaded legislation by creating businesses they dubbed "Turkish baths," then "soaplands." In the military-base areas, bars continued to predominate, even if Japanese characters replaced the English lettering when the Japanese Self-Defense Forces began to patronize the same establishments. With no contracts to guarantee the terms of work, labor conditions worsened. Thais, Filipinas, and eventually Eastern Europeans gradually took the place of Japanese women. In the 1990s, the worldwide campaign against sexual trafficking led the Japanese government to change its visa policies. Now illegal immigrants, sex workers became more invisible and more vulnerable, completing the transformation that started in 1945. Sex workers are marginalized, even while remaining essential to defining nationalism and defending international norms.

Power abhors a vacuum, which is why the period immediately following Japan's defeat was so chaotic and tumultuous, with fierce struggles between farmers and landlords, women and men, and Left and Right. What remains remarkable about postwar Japan is how, if only for a brief period, those who are usually thought of as the most powerless and most victimized—people who sell their own bodies—were suddenly in a pivotal position. They were potent symbols of defeat, but they were not just symbols. They could actually negotiate the terms of their own relationship with the occupiers. As we shall see, it was not an unconditional surrender.

ONE

"To Transship Them to Some Suitable Island"

Making Policy in the Midst of Chaos

When American troops disembarked in Japan just after the surrender, they found something none of them had anticipated. Some had feared they would encounter die-hard defenders. After all, these men of the Sixth and Eighth Armies had fought a brutal ten-month campaign to retake the Philippines. At the very least, they expected the defeated enemy to show hostility. Instead, the reporter for *Stars and Stripes* happened upon an incredible scene. "Jap welcomers on the street were directing every lonesome looking American to the grand opening"—the grand opening of what appeared to be a USO club.[1] "Inside, young Japanese hostesses with their polite bows, giggles and broad smiles waited to serve large milkshake glasses full of beer for five yen." Soon the Americans discovered something even more astonishing. Such establishments were intended to satisfy not just the thirst of U.S. servicemen, but also their erotic desires.[2]

Hundreds of thousands of American servicemen and civilians would work, drink, and play in Tokyo, Osaka, and more remote regions of Japan as part of the Allied Occupation. In 1946, tens of thousands of Australian, New Zealand, British, and Indian troops would join them as part of the British Commonwealth Occupation Force (BCOF). The Allied Occupation of Japan included commissioners, delegates, and war crimes judges from eleven countries, even if the supreme commander for the Allied Powers (SCAP), General Douglas MacArthur, preferred to ignore them. But no one, not even the imperious MacArthur, could control the complex and often chaotic relations among the people who came together in this crowded archipelago, whether soldiers and settlers repatriated from overseas, Korean and Chinese laborers who had come to work in war industries, orphans and widows wandering through bombed-out cities, or an eclectic assortment of civilians and servicemen from several nations. They included Aborigines from Australia, Maori from New Zealand, and Punjabis from India.

The number of Allied servicemen would peak at 430,000 in late 1945 and early 1946. It gradually declined until 1950, when most of the BCOF forces had departed and just 115,000 Americans remained. During the Korean War, it would more than double again, to 260,000.[3] Many thousands more Allied servicemen would stream through Japan on their way to or from the war in Korea. They trained, performed maneuvers, and came for R&R (rest and recreation) trips. As customers, they possessed unusual power because of their privileged position in occupied Japan. Local economies and whole neighborhoods were transformed to satisfy their desires, which reflected the longer history of Euro-American perceptions of the Orient. The "geisha girls" or *panpan*, dangling cigarettes and garbed in bright dresses, catered to their fantasies. And the Japanese also created new social spaces where they could be given free rein, far from the traditional, regulated sex-work districts. In 1955, it was estimated that one in every twenty-five women between the ages of fifteen and twenty-nine worked in the commercial sex industry.[4]

As the first to arrive in Japan, the Americans would have to decide what to do with the Recreational Amusement Association (RAA, Tokushu Ian Kyōkai) Japan had established for Allied servicemen. U.S. commanders came with a set of policies and practices—formal and informal—that had developed over decades to deal with sex work and sexually transmitted diseases. Most military bureaucracies have acknowledged, explicitly or implicitly, that some soldiers, sailors, and airmen pay for commercial sex.[5] Such behavior, particularly before the discovery in 1943 that penicillin could cure syphilis and gonorrhea, was a major threat to military efficiency.[6] In nineteenth-century colonial India, for instance, on average no fewer than one in five British soldiers was hospitalized each year for VD.[7] This was no less a problem for the U.S. military. In the Civil War, almost 20 percent of those fighting were infected. During World War I, U.S. troops missed

7 million days of active duty because of VD. It was the second most common illness after influenza.[8]

As a result, military commanders focused on keeping their troops healthy. They faced the choice between trying to prevent prostitution altogether or regulating it to reduce the risk to troops. The resulting policies ranged from strict prohibition to laissez-faire to limited regulation to actual sponsorship of brothels. The United States often regulated—rather than prohibited—sex work, especially in overseas possessions, such as Puerto Rico, the Philippines, Hawaii, and the Panama Canal Zone.[9] During General John J. Pershing's campaign against Francisco Pancho Villa from 1916 to 1917, sex work was also regulated on both sides of the Mexican border.[10] Concerned at the incidence of VD among his troops, Pershing had the Army Medical Corps inspect and treat both sex workers and their clients. During World War II, some local commanders in central Africa, India, the Middle East, France, and the Caribbean also cooperated with brothel owners despite official disapproval.[11]

Closer to home, U.S. management of sexual behavior took a different approach. In the late nineteenth century, some local governments had regulated sex work by selectively enforcing prostitution laws. But incarcerating and rehabilitating sex workers became increasingly common, finally coalescing during the progressive era and World War I into what became known as the American Plan. Social activists and the military provided positive recreational facilities, stepped up police enforcement, and supplied prophylactic treatment to servicemen—but not to sex workers. This initiative would persist through World War II, when military authorities considered the moral threat to servicemen in base areas so serious that officials pushed for national legislation.[12]

In 1940, a meeting of the military medical services, the Public Health Service, and the American Social Hygiene Association produced the Eight-Point Agreement, which called for a ban on prostitution and medical care for the afflicted. The plan also recommended that infected individuals provide names of sexual partners so that public health officials could track them down. But contact tracing tended to be ineffective, since many were reluctant to disclose their sexual history. Even when their partners could be positively identified, it was difficult to bring them in. The military did little to implement this program, and in response Congress passed the 1941 May Act, which legislated "moral zones" free of prostitution near military installations in the United States. The act also gave the Justice Department the legal authority to supersede local police in prosecuting violators.[13]

Different state models of regulation and prohibition were therefore available to U.S. officials when they arrived in Japan. But there was no precedent for a system of official brothels. In fact, there was a clear trend in policy to prohibit prostitution altogether.

Japanese policy and practice displayed a very different tendency. Commercial sex work had been tolerated and regulated in Japan for more than three hundred years. In Japan, as in other places, venereal diseases were considered prostitutes' diseases, and therefore disease-fighting focused solely on this population. With the opening of treaty ports, this included lock hospitals that confined those found to be infected. The British helped to establish the first such institution in Yokohama in 1868. Beginning in the 1870s, Japanese authorities also adopted the French practice of making medical exams compulsory. The Japanese National Hygiene Bureau gathered statistics on the percentage infected, and Western-style newspapers reported the results.[14] The state's focus on the health and welfare of the Japanese nation and especially its army brought even more restrictions on sex workers, although no similar measures applied to the general population. In 1927, the Law for the Prevention of Venereal Disease provided for weekly examination of licensed prostitutes, the establishment by the Ministry of Welfare of clinics to treat and examine prostitutes and anyone else who had VD, and the punishment of affected persons. Those who procured customers or owned brothels and knew that their prostitutes had VD were also subject to punishment under the 1927 legislation.[15]

But the regulation and examination of these women did not provide an effective method of fighting VD. Poorly trained doctors pronounced sick women well. Sanitary conditions and inaccurate tests prevented even the best doctors from properly diagnosing disease or treating it appropriately. Even if diagnosed with VD, sex workers often were unable to afford expensive medicine. Bribery was also a factor, whether brothel keepers paying off doctors, or a sex worker doing so herself.[16]

Beginning in 1933, the Japanese military overseas turned to more authoritarian methods to organize sexual services while also containing disease. They established what they called comfort stations, which, in fact, became sites of sexual slavery. Although many Japanese sex workers volunteered to go to the front—they may have either had little taste for factory labor or suffered from onerous debts—few likely understood the conditions they would face. And there is no question that women from Korea, China, the Netherlands, and elsewhere were forced to serve. The organizers intended the system not only to contain the spread of VD but also to reduce the incidence of attacks on civilians in China. Rapes occurred as early as the first Shanghai Incident in 1932, and on a larger scale with all-out war in 1937.[17] This experience overseas led Japanese officials to fear that occupying forces would engage in mass rapes of Japanese women, so they took it upon themselves to organize comfort stations for U.S. troops.[18]

The arrangement of sexual services for Allied servicemen was rapid and well-funded. It was overseen by future prime minister Ikeda Hayato, at that time director of the Tax Bureau of the Ministry of Finance.[19] The first meeting took place just a week after surrender and before the arrival of occupation troops. By August 18, 1945, Tanaka Yūichi, Home Ministry Security Division chief, had already telegraphed the governors and police chiefs of each prefecture about establishing special comfort stations as a bulwark (*bōhatei*) against the danger posed by foreign servicemen. The Tokyo Metropolitan Police Board met that same day and assigned the task to the Tokyo Restaurant Association (Tōkyō Ryōri Inshokugyō Kumiai), which included representatives from the geisha union as well as restaurateurs. On August 21, 1945, military envoy Lieutenant General Kawabe Kōjiro discussed the "needs" of the incoming Allied forces before an audience of the most powerful statesmen in Japan. He spoke at the prime minister's residence in Nagata-chō, still the center for political power-brokering in Tokyo.[20]

The planners of the RAA thought big, even if they were not able to enact all their ideas. And they received lavish funding, with an eventual budget of 33 million yen provided by the Ministry of Finance through a loan from Nippon Kangyō Ginkō (Japan Industrial Development Bank).[21] Management hardly bothered with bookkeeping. Many of them came from wealthy families. They decided to set up the first bars and brothels for foreign servicemen in Tokyo. The RAA worked with former brothel owners to renovate hotels and staffed them mainly with experienced sex workers.[22]

One RAA official, Watanabe Yasuo, later recalled that, with so few job opportunities in the immediate postwar chaos, the RAA was a good place to work. Whether these brothels and bars were a good place to work for the women—or even whether what they did can be called "work"—has become a subject of burning controversy. Historians such as Hirai Kazuko and Yuki Tanaka have argued that the RAA's establishments can be compared to the wartime military comfort stations.[23] Certainly the rhetoric surrounding the creation of the RAA would support this view. In a ceremony held outside the imperial palace, a government statement noted that it would require the "hardening of determination for selfless patriotic service (*messhi hōkō*)," nationalistic language familiar from the war. The statement continued: "We have become conscious of a foundational undertaking for the inauguration of the reconstruction of a new Japan and the protection of the chastity of all Japanese women."[24] The women who staffed RAA facilities in the hot-springs resort of Atami were even called female kamikaze (*onna no tokkotai*).[25] The policy of operating official brothels presumed that sex workers would protect other Japanese women who were deemed more worthy of protection.[26]

But even if Japanese officials had wished to replicate the comfort-women system, they could not have. The Japanese state was no longer an imperial power at war. Regulators could not forcibly procure colonial subjects to staff the brothels. Therefore, the RAA had to advertise for sex workers, placing ads in the major Tokyo newspapers and recruitment posters in Atami, the port of Yokohama, and the Ginza district of Tokyo.[27] And unlike the military comfort women from Japan's colonies, RAA workers were paid.

Continuing to work in the brothels would indeed have required self-sacrifice, even if nationalistic rhetoric is not what actually induced women to become employees in the first place. The first such establishment, Komachien (Babe Garden), featured as many as thirty women at a time dressed in the thin silk undergarment normally worn under a kimono, the *nagajuban*. Though they entertained clients behind screens, privacy was minimal and turnover was heavy. A short-time visit cost a soldier just 30 yen, or $1.56.[28] In Atami, some reportedly had to take in twenty to twenty-five clients in three hours.[29]

One cabaret, likely an RAA establishment, provided GIs a quart of beer for 10 yen and the opportunity to dance with Japanese women for 2 yen per dance. Open between three and five in the afternoon, the cabaret hosted five hundred troops on a typical day. Private Wright Young of Dallas, who served on MP duty outside, observed that "guys really like this. It's a shame they don't stay open longer."[30] In November, Sergeant Robert Cornwall described the Oasis of Ginza as "a vast room filled with a high percentage of pulchritude and a minimum of gold-and-buck teeth, and servicemen carrying out their roles as conquerors."[31] Here the powerful metaphor of "gold-and-buck teeth" stands in for the Japanese men so notably absent from the Oasis.

But focusing on the RAA as it appeared in the pages of *Stars and Stripes*, and later in critical histories, provides a quite limited, even misleading view of what sex work was like under the occupation. Some RAA facilities, such as Cabaret New Atami, served Japanese as well as GIs. Others quickly transitioned into private establishments.[32] Although it is unclear how many women the RAA employed—some estimate as many as 70,000—far more participated in the sex-work industry outside these establishments.[33] For example, it is estimated that in Tokyo in 1945–1946, 30,000 women worked in the sex industry, just 1,360 of whom were in the RAA.[34] Moreover, most occupation authorities did not have such a tolerant (or even applauding) attitude toward the RAA or to the less institutionalized sexual-service industry that supplanted it. In fact, most U.S. military commanders considered prostitution an endemic problem that plagued their troops.

For all their power as occupiers, U.S. officials would find it impossible to mount a unified or even coherent response. Prostitution and VD fell under two jurisdictions: the U.S. Far East Command, responsible for all servicemen in East Asia, including their health, and the Public Health and Welfare (PH&W) Section, civilian officials in charge of the physical well-being of the Japanese population. Sex work would become "a source of constant conflict," as a later report observed, "resulting in a lack of cooperation and coordination in venereal disease control activities between these agencies."[35] Even if there had been total harmony between the Far East Command and the civilian officials, there were also differences of opinion among local army, navy, and air force commanders. The long distance between Japan and Washington limited and delayed communications, making it all the more difficult to resolve these conflicts.

The subsequent development of patterns of interaction between Allied servicemen and local sex providers was influenced not only by the Far East Command's official attempts to promote abstinence, but also by PH&W's more pragmatic efforts to combat VD. PH&W was responsible for preventive medicine, nutrition, sanitation, and medical training among the Japanese. Until 1951 it was headed by Dr. Crawford Sams, a career military surgeon from Illinois. PH&W used public health control techniques to treat VD as a disease that endangered everyone living in Japan. As one directive put it, "[Venereal disease] is a communicable disease and from the public health standpoint we believe that it is no more of a crime to have venereal disease than it is to have smallpox, typhus fever, cholera, plague, measles, or any of the other communicable diseases."[36]

PH&W policy sought to bring VD treatment out of Japan's floating world into the modern world. They had to contend not only with the military's skepticism, but also with long-standing Japanese beliefs and practices. Previously, Japanese public health authorities had considered VD an illness transmitted by sex workers that chiefly affected men who visited the pleasure quarters. PH&W sought to show that sex workers were not solely responsible for disease, and at the same time raise sanitation and public health standards for all of society. O. M. Elkins, a consulting physician for PH&W, was scornful of the on-site brothel inspections he witnessed during a tour of commercial sex districts in Tokyo. "To my mind, the International Palace is an example of the complete worthlessness of examining prostitutes. The set-up is elaborate and might impress a lay person, although its uselessness is immediately obvious to persons with medical training."[37] Venereal disease hospitals were no better: "The Yoshiwara Hospital is in a filthy and disorderly condition." Exams were insufficient, and worse, "much worthless laboratory work is being done on prostitutes who have taken douches just previous to the examination."[38] The system of examining prostitutes itself was at fault, with physicians using "mechanized, stylized, methods of examination, as if the patients are not people . . . [displaying almost a total] pre-occupation with the diagnosis and treatment of infected women with no attention being given to infections in men."[39]

PH&W officials agreed with Elkins. They had even more damning observations on the way VD was treated. Drugs were administered only until the patients became symptom free. "Clinical standards are poor. Treatment methods are totally inadequate. The number of chronic gonorrheal infections are probably too appalling to contemplate." The doctors themselves were no better: "the extreme disinterest and lack of energy and enthusiasm of the medical profession can be accounted for only by the lack of education."[40]

U.S. officials were largely oblivious to the challenges their Japanese counterparts faced: medicine shortages, miserable working conditions, and an overwhelming caseload. Staff and patients in Yoshiwara Hospital, for instance, were crowded into a single floor, since the second and third floors had been destroyed by American incendiary bombing. But for all the failings of the Japanese public health system, the reported case rate of VD infection in Japan was much lower than in the United States—at least at the beginning of the Occupation. According to Sams's own statistics, there were 1.7 cases of gonorrhea for every 1,000 Japanese in 1946, compared to 2.7 in the continental United States. The rate for syphilis was 1 in 1,000, whereas in the United States it was two and a half times higher. The U.S. rate would have been higher still were it not for the massive use of penicillin, which, as we shall see, Washington refused to give to the Japanese.[41]

Nevertheless, limiting testing and treatment of VD to sex workers was a flawed practice. Contemporary statistics indicate that more men than women were infected with VD, and many of the women who visited clinics sought treatment because they had been infected by their husbands, not because they were sex workers. Some of them wrote to General MacArthur. Hara Endo, for instance, urged him to help find a cure for syphilis. She had lost four children to the disease and had to have an abortion because of it.[42]

The observations that Sams, Elkins, and other officials made of VD inspections and treatment would prove crucial in their construction of a new policy, one premised on the idea that VD was a public health problem rather than a moral failing. The primary goal would be to "find and isolate all infected persons and treat them to the point of cure before they can spread their diseases to others."[43] In October 1945, occupation authorities issued a Potsdam Order, using their power to make policy without having to consult the Diet. SCAPIN-153 bound both Japanese and U.S. authorities to new standards for examination and treatment, required that all VD cases be reported, and called for the provision of necessary drugs and personnel.[44]

Sams knew that at least some commanders would support this more pragmatic approach. He reported that one senior military commander believed that the American soldiers from the Sixth and Eighth Armies—who had suffered 47,000 casualties in the Philippines, including 10,400 battle deaths—were now entitled to enjoy themselves.[45] Some officers therefore turned a blind eye to a serviceman's night out on the town.

MacArthur's headquarters may have even designated parts of Tokyo as places where servicemen could buy sex. American ideas about race would shape the way sexual services were regulated, since Japanese officials willingly complied with their preferences. The head of the Tokyo Bureau of Epidemic Protection, Yosano Hikaru, later explained to the *Asahi Shimbun* how this happened. He recalled that he was summoned to headquarters on or around September 14 or 15, 1945.

> When I went to see what it was about, they took out a large, aerial photograph of Tokyo and said that the real reason that they had summoned me was about the women who took care of the soldiers. They had carefully examined the areas and put points on portions of the picture separating it into areas. They wanted my advice about where it would be good for officers to go, where white soldiers should go, and where black soldiers should go.

Yosano decided to put the black soldiers in "an area that was beyond help."[46] His account is credible considering that at the time, the U.S. military itself was segregated. Not one African American serviceman worked in Mac-Arthur's headquarters, and he would later resist orders to desegregate.[47] Other reports confirm that RAA establishments, such as the Oasis, were whites only, whereas the Paramount catered to black servicemen. Still others had different hours for whites and blacks. Subsequently, the Americans asked the RAA for additional facilities in the hot-springs resort towns of Atami and Hakone.[48]

A month after U.S. troops landed, the First Cavalry Division had set up four prophylactic stations in "major prostitution areas of Tokyo"—Senju, Mokojuna, Yokohama Road, and the First Brigade area—where servicemen could obtain free condoms. By the end of September, a senior medical officer reported that this division was providing 7,000–10,000 prophylactic treatments a week, and it was just one of three divisions plus a regiment stationed in Tokyo alone. He was already running short of supplies, including sulfa drugs and even paper towels. Told that some favored re-regulating prostitution, the officer "offered to cooperate in every way possible with any plan which might be adopted."[49] The Navy also created military huts marked with *prophylaxis* in red letters.[50] The commander of the U.S. Army Air Force in Japan, Major General K. W. Wolfe, complained that his MPs could not keep troops from entering brothels because the Army MPs were letting them though.[51]

Other commanders would continue trying to suppress prostitution altogether, at least when it was publicly visible. In March 1946, Lieutenant General Robert L. Eichelberger, the commander of the Eighth Army, issued orders banning public displays of affection. "The sight of our soldiers walking down the streets with their arms around [a] Japanese girl is equally repugnant to most Americans . . . as well as to most Japanese," he explained in *Stars and Stripes*. "Such action in public is prejudicial to good order and military discipline and will be treated as disorderly conduct."[52] Military police were supposed to take offenders to the stockades, but Eichelberger's order was never consistently enforced.[53] Even as military superiors looked on with disapproval, the lack of a clear policy allowed different kinds of fraternization between U.S. servicemen and Japanese nationals to proliferate.

These contradictions were already apparent to the U.S. press in November 1945, when Lawrence L. Lacour, the first navy chaplain in Japan, provided a detailed account to his local paper, the *Des Moines Register*. He noted that despite the Navy's public anti-prostitution stance, he had observed a long line of enlisted men who would "pay the 10 yen to the Japanese operator and then go with the girl to her room." Afterward, Navy corpsmen registered them and administered prophylaxis. *Newsweek* published a report based on Lacour's findings, prompting American politicians to lodge their objections to sailors' conduct in the *Congressional Record*.[54]

Secretary of the Navy James Forrestal quickly responded to congressional concerns. His reply attested to the Navy's efforts to suppress prostitution and to reduce VD—and to their failure.[55] He explained that the incident Lacour had observed was the result of "group pressures, sudden release of inhibitions long pent up by many months of hazardous sea duty, cessation of hostilities, and the general let-down in morale and stamina of all personnel, all occurring during the confusion incidental to the occupation of Japan by American forces." Forrestal claimed that unity existed in both opinion and directives issued by the policy-making bodies of the Army, Navy, and Public Health Service that prostitution be suppressed. But, as Forrestal also explained, "there is a wide divergence of opinion on the matter among the rank and file of the services."[56]

Servicemen's letters published in *Stars and Stripes* substantiate the second part of Forrestal's assessment. Some considered the Navy's interference, not prostitution, to be the real problem. Sailor R. J. Porter wrote:

> Allowing the [Y]oshiwara house to operate was one of the most sensible things the Navy has ever done. Despite the way some people try to delude themselves into believing that servicemen are poor, misled, evil-tempted angels, it's a fact that as long as there are women around they are going to attempt to have relations. . . . Closing the houses never has and never will prevent men from seeking an outlet somewhere else. . . . Why don't some of these people who are so blasted interested in our morals watch their own morals and the kids' morals and let us alone. I'm sick of some sap I've never seen or heard of telling all about my morals and how to protect me from the mean old world like I was a three year old.[57]

Debate over Lacour's accusations—and the Navy's reaction—illuminates several inconsistencies in U.S. policy. Officially prostitution was morally wrong, and men were told to refrain from sexual contact.[58] Through newspaper articles and other means, military brass trumpeted the risks of VD. *Stars and Stripes*, the main source of news for service personnel, ran stories on the rise in infections, including spurious claims that "Japan's V.D. Rate

Is World's Highest."[59] An Army pamphlet quoted in *Time* magazine issued this stark warning about Japanese women:

> They do as their men tell them, and many of them have been told to kill you. Sex is one of the oldest and most effective weapons in history. The Geisha girl knows how to wield it charmingly. She may entice you only to poison you. She may slit your throat. Stay away from the women of Japan—all of them.[60]

Yet free condoms and mandatory inspections of sex workers conveyed a very different message.

Commanders consistently pressed MacArthur for a clear directive banning fraternization between servicemen and Japanese women. But MacArthur refused. Local commanders were therefore left to make their own policy. In southern Honshu and Shikoku, for instance, a Sixth Army directive placed known houses of prostitution off-limits to American servicemen in December 1945. In Hiroshima, U.S. commanders wished to go further, completely shutting down all brothels. Conferences held later that month with local authorities revealed some of the challenges in implementing such a policy. Hiroshima, devastated and desperately poor after the nuclear attack five months earlier, had a thriving sex-work economy. There were 566 registered sex workers in seven houses in the city and its environs. But police considered the growth in "amateurs" and returning professionals who would work "in the hills or in private houses" a still greater threat to controlling VD.[61]

Like police in the rest of Japan, those in Hiroshima were few in number and poorly paid. In this context, commanders and local officials alike doubted the efficacy of an outright ban. Captain Rogers, the Kure Base provost marshal, argued that "cutting off of the legitimate source of women would cause an increase in cases of rape with their resultant police problems." The prefectural police chief for Hiroshima requested that brothels be kept open. Because of the American demand, he complained, no women were left for the Japanese. But Colonel Pence, provost marshal of the X Corps, replied that this would contradict the new regulation. Even so, he worried that enforcing it would be unpopular with troops and that other crimes would increase.[62]

Police investigations in greater Hiroshima revealed that when houses were shut down, sex workers remained where they were or simply moved— mostly to homes owned by their employers. In Kaitachi and Otake, women moved to hotels. In Fukuyama, they remained in the quarter along with an additional forty refugees from neighboring Yano. In Kure, a former Japanese naval base, 537 women remained at the houses of employers or their relatives.

A few women returned home, but they were in the minority. Most had nowhere to go and remained with their employers, in all likelihood continuing to sell sex for money.[63]

Notwithstanding these failures, in January 1946 SCAP issued a sweeping order that abolished all laws licensing sex work. It was "in contravention of the ideals of democracy," the order avowed, "and inconsistent with the development of individual freedom throughout the nation."[64] The order abrogated all debt contracts and forbade brothel owners from holding women in bondage, and placed RAA establishments off-limits.[65] All servicemen and officers were forbidden from entering, and Army personnel painted "VD" in large letters across the outside of RAA buildings. Two months later, SCAP went further and decided to ban the organized sexual service centers outright.[66]

But the order did not outlaw sex work when individuals acted "of their own free will and accord."[67] And while abolishing the RAA, U.S. officials did not move against the many other, unofficial brothels that had begun to proliferate, much less take on all the thousands of streetwalkers who solicited U.S. servicemen. Even to have enforced off-limits regulations around brothels would have been impossible with the numbers of military police available. In February 1946, there were an estimated 926 houses of prostitution in Tokyo and 328 more in Yokohama. Enforcement of off-limits regulations would require a guard in front of each one for at least eighteen hours daily, requiring thousands more military police at a time when force levels were already being drawn down.[68]

In April 1946, MacArthur decided to begin segregating Japanese and Americans, and in June, Japanese women were banned from Army billets. Later that summer, Japanese women as well as men were forbidden to enter American mess halls. Restaurants and bars open to servicemen were off-limits to Japanese. GIs rode in first-class cars on trains, Japanese in unheated, windowless coaches. In some public buildings, there were separate entrances and even separate bathrooms. These regulations left few legitimate places where Americans and Japanese could meet. And unlike Germany, where restrictions were less severe and largely abandoned within five months, in Japan they became increasingly comprehensive and rigid.[69]

These anti-fraternization measures may not have been intended to imply racial inferiority. But whether it was racism or unreasoning fear of VD, they reflected commanders' belief that their troops had to be protected at all costs from the Japanese. In the first three months of 1946, there were already 233

Occupation authorities forbade servicemen from fraternizing with Japanese men and women, and kept Japanese from entering establishments reserved exclusively for the Allies. The policy proved impracticable. Courtesy of City of Kure

cases of VD per 1,000 U.S. occupation troops.[70] This was significantly higher even than rates recorded among U.S. troops in occupied Italy, which had shocked commanders.[71] In November, Army Air Force Major General Thomas White wrote that VD was a "serious and immediate health menace" to his command. According to White, Japan was a particularly risky environment. He went on: "Experience during the past year indicates that there is an extremely large and virulent reservoir of venereal disease in the Japanese civilian population."[72]

Why were so many U.S. troops in Japan infected with VD? Though never acknowledged by commanders such as White, many were already infected when they arrived. In January 1945, the rate of infection among U.S. Army forces in the Pacific was 5 cases per 1,000, virtually the same as reported in the general population in the continental United States. But by June, two months before any troops arrived in Japan, it had soared to 97 per 1,000. The Army Medical Department found that, as military operations wound down in the Philippines, there was a post-combat "letdown" and "increased leisure." These same troops in the Philippines had two more months of "leisure" before they embarked for Japan, while others came from Hawaii and the Marianas. Even if the rate of infection had not increased, the level recorded in June suggests that tens of thousands of infected U.S. soldiers were about to land in Yokohama, Yokosuka, Sasebo, and dozens of other Japanese seaports and landing fields. This was a "reservoir" of disease that would soon begin to wash over an unsuspecting people.[73]

In November 1946, Sams reported that there had been 200,000 new cases of VD among the Japanese, which he said were mainly in prostitutes. He attributed this entirely to improved reporting, rather than the influx of U.S. servicemen.[74] But the rate of infection among Japanese continued to climb, from 2.71 to 4.63 cases reported per 1,000 in 1947, though it was still substantially lower than in the continental United States. The number of syphilis cases had almost doubled, from 74,609 to 147,853, and there were 212,108 cases of gonorrhea, up from 128,845 in 1946.[75] Though some portion of this increase may be attributable to better reporting, which included random inspections of women suspected of being sex workers, it seems unlikely that this alone could account for the scale of increase.

Of course, along with hundreds of thousands of Allied troops with high rates of infection, millions of repatriated Japanese soldiers and colonists may well have contributed to the spread of disease. Many of the women had been sexually assaulted after the surrender and were widely suspected of being infected.[76] But when infection rates are broken down by prefecture, they provide good reason to believe that Allied servicemen were indeed a major source of infection and would remain so. In 1949, three years after the bulk of repatriates had returned, Nagasaki, Fukuoka, and Kanagawa had the highest rates of VD. All had U.S. military bases and large numbers of servicemen. Nagasaki, with Sasebo Naval Base and the Thirty-Fourth Infantry Division, had 7.41 cases per 1,000 compared to a national rate of 4.46. Fukuoka, a short train journey away, was a popular R&R destination for both U.S. and BCOF troops, and also hosted Itazuke Air Base. Its rate was 9.36. And Kanagawa, with Yokosuka Naval Base and Atsugi Naval Air Station, had a VD rate of 11.9 cases per 1,000. During the Korean War, Kanagawa and Fukuoka continued to have the highest reported disease rates in the country.

They were followed by Nagasaki, Hiroshima—with Kure Naval Base—and Yamaguchi, with the Marine Corps Air Station at Iwakuni.[77]

Nonetheless, U.S. authorities continued to blame Japanese women and resorted to increasingly draconian measures to identify and detain those suspected of spreading VD, drawing on longstanding practices in the United States.[78] They used contact tracing, raids, compulsory examinations, and involuntary detention, techniques previously imposed on women who lived near military bases in the United States.[79] Even those serving in the Women's Army Corps were compelled to submit to monthly exams to detect VD, a practice that aroused resentment and protests.[80] Rather than a particular animus toward the Japanese, the determination to "protect" servicemen and presume that women were responsible for any rise in the incidence of disease was part of a longer history that went beyond the Occupation.

The dominant tradition of the U.S. military held that abstinence was the best form of prevention. It emphasized character-building, moral guidance, religious instruction, and physical education.[81] Concern with servicemen's morale started with the selection of troops and basic training. Even before World War II, psychiatrists and social psychologists worked with military leaders to develop a set of strategies to help servicemen cope with combat. Surveys had shown that the "most well adjusted trainees" had dated girls and played on sports teams in high school. These indicators of adjustment became the norm for servicemen.[82] The American military also had a long history of providing its troops with "wholesome entertainment," attempting to occupy young men with recreational activities or exhaust them through athletic activity.[83] The Navy stressed VD education and instituted athletic and recreation programs to discourage sailors from seeking out sex workers.[84] Commanders came to believe that sex work thrived when other forms of entertainment did not exist. For example, in Okayama prefecture in November 1945, authorities noted that sex workers provided the only entertainment and amusement option for Americans. Although movies might have been an alternative, they lacked a projector.[85]

In 1946, General White himself conducted a VD prevention program for his own Army Air Force personnel. His suggested program included "intensification of education and training programs, quarantine of infected individuals, and the provision of wholesome recreation to the existing limits of the present facilities." Servicemen infected with VD were confined to base and denied promotion.[86] Similarly, the Women's Army Corps compelled those who went AWOL to undergo a pelvic examination. If found to be infected, they were subject to dismissal.[87] It was not, therefore, just Japanese women who were now under close surveillance.

White's educational program, at least, may have been necessary in a service comprising young men, many of whom were probably uninformed about VD. A U.S. questionnaire about VD shows that medical authorities believed servicemen required very basic instruction: "What is by all odds the ordinary means of acquiring venereal disease?" soldiers were asked: "A. Kissing B. Sitting on dirty toilet seats C. Sexual intercourse D. Using dirty drinking cups."[88] Educational materials also stressed the dire consequences of infection, with graphic images of open sores around the mouth and penis.

Until treatment with penicillin became common, alarmist VD warnings contained a certain amount of truth—momentary pleasure with an apparently healthy woman could mean a lifetime of gonorrhea or death from syphilis. Most women infected with gonorrhea do not realize it, and even those who do have symptoms, such as a burning sensation when urinating, vaginal discharge, or bleeding between periods, can mistakenly believe they have a bladder or vaginal infection. In women, gonorrhea can lead to pelvic inflammatory disease, a serious infection of the uterus that may cause infertility. So too can chlamydia, which was not even widely recognized until the late 1970s. Men with gonorrhea, on the other hand, usually experience immediate and obvious problems, including painful or swollen testicles, or a white, yellow, or green discharge from the penis. Infection could also cause epididymitis, a painful condition that, like pelvic inflammatory disease, may lead to infertility.[89]

Syphilis is far more serious for both men and women, though it too can be spread unwittingly. Primary-stage syphilis is marked by the appearance of a single or multiple sores, but not until ten to ninety days after initial contact. Without treatment, the infection progresses to its secondary stage, characterized by a non-itchy rash, and sometimes fever, sore throat, headaches, and weight loss. Without treatment, the infection either becomes latent or—for 15–30 percent of the infected—progresses into tertiary syphilis. The bacteria continue to reproduce for years, causing pockets of damage to internal organs, including the heart and brain. Infection of the central nervous system leads to mental and emotional changes. Some of the afflicted exhibit immediately identifiable signs of the disease, such as a characteristic shuffling gait or a bobbing of the head. After a time, others are struck with dementia, gradual blindness, or paralysis. The damage can sometimes lead to death, as was demonstrated with unsuspecting black men during this period in the notorious Tuskegee study.

Because many people infected with syphilis are asymptomatic for years, they remain contagious and at risk for the serious complications that occur in later stages of the disease. As stated above, gonorrhea is mostly asymptomatic in women, and occasionally asymptomatic in men. Infected men and women could therefore easily transmit it without knowledge of the infection.

These risks help explain why at least some servicemen were willing to submit to painful prophylactic treatment to prevent infection, which required injecting a disinfectant directly into the urethra and holding it for five minutes before urinating it out.[90] But although some military commanders pursued policies and preventive measures based on fear—and continue to do so today—they were undermined by changing medical technologies. The discovery of penicillin and its efficacy in fighting venereal diseases on a mass scale discredited the threat upon which these old-style campaigns depended.[91] "Why shouldn't we take chances?" asked U.S. servicemen in Iran in 1944. "We don't lose our pay and one can be cured of gonorrhea in one day and syphilis in one week." The Persian Gulf Command decided to fight this perception by putting infected Iranian sex workers on display, pointing out their genital lesions to a shocked audience.[92] In Japan, commanders continued to paint "off-limits" and "VD" on the sides of known prostitution establishments. But many servicemen and officers persisted in patronizing them, confident that they could avoid the worst consequences.

By 1947, Air Force, Navy, and Army commanders agreed that, rather than merely abolishing state-run brothels and laws that licensed sex work, they needed to outlaw prostitution altogether to have any effect on the spread of VD. R. L. Eichelberger, commander of the Eighth Army, complained:

> I have utilized every facility at my command within the Army and firmly feel that a reduction of venereal disease in the civilian population is the only remaining factor which will contribute materially to further reductions. It appears only logical that control of prostitution, whether licensed or unlicensed will reduce the high incidence of venereal disease in the civilian population, particularly that small portion of the population so highly infected and which is so easily available to the troops.[93]

But the American military command did not determine policy for the civilian population. SCAP's Public Health and Welfare Section was responsible for the physical well-being of the Japanese, and the section was against any such ban. One of MacArthur's closest advisors, Chief of Intelligence Charles Willoughby, backed this position: "A law making prostitution a crime has never anywhere in the ancient or modern world stamped out or seriously approached the eradication of venereal disease." Willoughby also judged that "public sentiment in general is non-committal or in favor of prostitution."[94] In 1947, MacArthur rejected a proposal for another SCAPIN. In 1950, he again made it "emphatically plain" that he would not issue a SCAPIN to direct the Japanese government to outlaw prostitution or solicitation.[95] As he explained in a 1967 *Esquire* profile, "My father told me never to give an order unless I was certain it would be carried out. I wouldn't issue a no-fraternization order for all the tea in China."[96]

It is interesting that, reflecting on his time in Japan, MacArthur conflated a law that would have banned prostitution with an order prohibiting fraternization—as if they were the same thing—so central did sex work become in relations between the occupiers and the occupied. But it is no less striking that in 1947, the chief of intelligence considered the Japanese public to be either noncommittal or opposed to outlawing prostitution. As we shall see, though providing sex workers to U.S. servicemen was no longer an official government program, a large segment of the population had come to depend on this business.

There can be little doubt that MacArthur was correct in his assessment that an outright ban would have been unenforceable, as the experience of the BCOF demonstrated. If anything, the Australian commanders—who led BCOF—and the public they answered to were even harsher toward their charges. Thus, they were even more concerned that servicemen were having sex with Japanese women.

The problems began almost immediately upon the arrival of the Australians in Kure, their new headquarters, in March 1946. Shortly after Sydney papers reported—incorrectly—that "geishas" had met the first Australian ship to arrive in port, Lieutenant General John Northcott sent a personal instruction reminding each and every serviceman that the Japanese were "a conquered enemy" who had "caused deep suffering and loss to many thousands of homes throughout the British Empire." They were not to "enter their homes or take part in their family life," and must obey all instructions that placed certain establishments out of bounds.[97]

U.S. forces occupying the same area around Kure and Hiroshima had already tried, and failed, to close down brothels. But Australian governmental

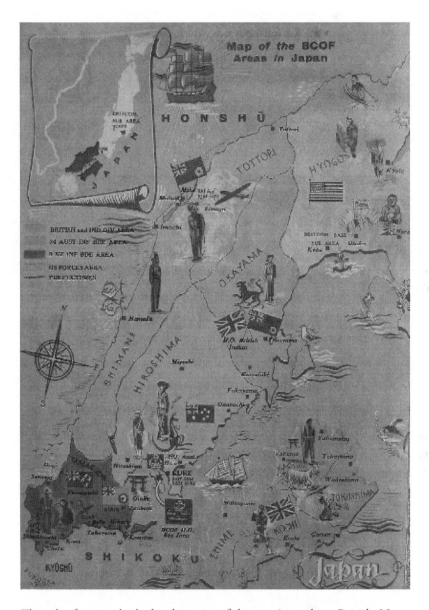

Though often overlooked in histories of the era, Australian, British, New Zealand, and Indian troops were responsible for a large part of western and central Japan. Courtesy of City of Kure

and public attitudes toward Japan gave Northcott little option but to insist publicly on non-fraternization, even while he privately reported to London that a formal order necessary to give the policy force and effect was "impracticable."[98] Memories of the wartime invasion threat and the atrocious treatment of POWs remained strong, and London, Wellington, and New Delhi all approved the policy. When Northcott became governor of New South Wales in July 1946, his successor in Japan, Lieutenant General Horace Robertson, carried on in the same spirit. At a 1948 ceremony in Hiroshima, Robertson told his Japanese audience that the atomic bombing was their own fault and had fighter jets fly overhead to underscore the point. For Robertson, the Australian troops who had sex with Japanese women were victims. "They live lonely lives and the fraternisation and consequent evils are more or less forced on them."[99]

Despite general approval from the public—such as the Melbourne housewife who wrote that "the Japs were dreadful enemies and Australians should remember the atrocities"—the non-fraternization policy also brought criticism. In a 1946 *Sydney Morning Herald* article, a salesman named J. Alexander pointed out that Australians had to dance with someone. K. Todd, the mother of an airman in the Royal Australian Air Force, agreed: "If women were just entertaining there was no harm—Japanese women didn't start the war."[100] Many Australian servicemen felt that, as long as they had to live in barracks with no fresh meat or vegetables, no organized sports, no heat, and few blankets, fraternization was unavoidable. As one pointed out, "Hell, the only way we can keep warm is to shack up with a Jap Sheila."[101]

A New Zealand serviceman agreed. Strictly enforcing non-fraternization "would not prevent the blokes from getting what they want and would only encourage them to engage 'free-lancers' who are almost invariably diseased." He continued:

> No matter how much the public at home in New Zealand may imagine it, the Kiwi overseas is no angel, and a considerable percentage will have women whether they are in brothels or not. It is the army's responsibility to protect the health of the soldier and it is logical [to] do that by the most direct and effective means, even if those means do not bear too close an investigation.[102]

Other skeptics criticized the non-fraternization policy on principle: it went against SCAP policy and contradicted larger goals of democratization. Japanese were not even permitted to attend Australian church services.[103]

SCAP policy, on the other hand, was initially limited to placing private homes out of bounds to Allied personnel, so the Australian position risked causing a rift. The commanding officer of the Second New Zealand Expeditionary Force Japan (J-Force), Brigadier General Leslie Potter, argued that Northcott's order was too categorical.[104] Potter thought that commonwealth forces could interact with Japanese, as long as the Japanese were men or members of the right social classes. Members of the "depressed classes," on the other hand, should be avoided because of their "staggering" incidence of VD. For Potter, "the only alternative was to limit associations to that part of the Japanese population where the women invariably were chaste and moral."[105] Still other skeptics pointed out that BCOF servicemen constantly interacted with Japanese nationals and employed them at bases and in homes as house girls and houseboys. By December 1946, the commonwealth forces alone would employ 41,000 Japanese.[106]

Like their American counterparts, the Australians had a history of different ways of regulating sex work. Most recently, Australians had operated brothels in the Middle East to prevent VD, so the idea of setting up regulated zones for prostitution had an immediate historical precedent.[107] Provost Marshal Henderson pointed out that Kure was a former naval base with a system of medical inspection and control, and proposed setting up a semi-official red-light district where women could get checkups. Although Henderson thought he had approval from Base Commander Brigadier Wilson, at the last minute his plan was shot down and he returned to civil occupation.[108]

It was almost immediately apparent that BCOF's stricter non-fraternization policy was not effective in controlling the spread of VD. By May 1946, two months after their arrival, the VD rate had more than doubled. About one in twenty Australian servicemen had an active case and required an average of six days in the hospital for treatment. The rate of infection fell, but the average hospital stay increased, since men were coming in with more serious types of VD, such as syphilis. By September 1946, the rate of new infections had risen once again to 4.26 percent, about a third of them soldiers infected for a second or third time. By this point, almost 17 percent of Australian troops in Japan had been infected by VD at least once.[109]

Unlike their American counterparts, some BCOF commanders blamed servicemen for the spread of VD. The nature of the Australian commitment precluded sending draftees to Japan, so volunteers had to be formed into new units. Officers were therefore unfamiliar with their men, and units were thought to contain many undesirables. Some junior officers were also considered "not of the right type," and morale had suffered before deployment during a long wait at Morotai. Though they had to stay in poorly heated barracks with few amenities, strong drink was readily available. Officers also pointed to the devastation and destitution of Japan, which they considered particularly acute in the area under BCOF command. For example, Kure and Hiroshima faced a dire food shortage. At a June 1946 conference at Britcom base, the commander of the Thirty-Fourth Australian Infantry Brigade attributed rising crime to the "slum environment.[110] Others blamed Kure itself. Since it was the main embarkation and disembarkation point for Japanese army and naval forces since the Russo-Japanese war, it had higher VD rates than any other locality—nearly 100 percent among prostitutes, some alleged.[111]

But servicemen—who also had high rates of infection—ignored off-limits regulations, leaving some commanders to suggest putting entire towns out of bounds.[112] An undated cartoon from a New Zealand servicemen's magazine suggested that a new radio station announce the arrival of MPs to an out-of-bounds area.[113] When commanders discovered that troops were stealing condoms, they turned a blind eye. As captain R. J. Rowe pointed out in October 1947, "The discrepancy must be accepted as such, it being better to lose pounds worth of condoms than to run the risk of a lover going short at the crucial time."[114]

Still other BCOF commanders attributed high VD rates to the ineffectiveness of the Japanese civilian police. Local government officials, including the mayors of Hiroshima and Kure, supported the police in their contention that lack of personnel and prevalence of crime meant they could not make prostitution a priority.[115] Although dishonest police had been removed, new ones were not yet trained. Their members were poorly paid and sometimes subject to abuse by BCOF troops. They argued that nothing besides more pay would work: a low salary of 3,000 yen per month—less than some sex workers—was barely enough (or not enough) to live on.[116]

Australian and American officers concerned about crime focused on the non-white units under their command. Both blacks and Indians were more likely to be blamed for criminal activity. In December 1945, one U.S. commander told the Hiroshima police chief, who was alarmed by what he considered a rise in black crime, that headquarters would "call to attention of base command" that "rigid law enforcement is necessary to curb outbreaks by colored troops."[117] BCOF observers were quick to criticize Indian units: "In practically every case we were much struck by the appearance the detached Indian units gave us of indifferent morals, slack discipline and lack of initiative in regard to improving their own living accommodation."[118] A 1946 report of a visit to Japan by Cyril Chambers, Australian minister for the army, offered a confusing explanation, though one that clearly expressed his unease about how the occupation was disrupting racial boundaries: "It is certain sections of the Indian troops who, in the commander's opinion, might go wrong, as in India they are not permitted to visit white houses and to them, the Japanese are white."[119]

Both SCAP and BCOF measured VD rates by race, as if racial differences could explain the pattern of infection: New Zealand measured Maori and European cases separately, as did SCAP VD statistics for white and black servicemen.[120] BCOF commanders argued that Indian troops were more likely to be infected, with some officers claiming that they neglected to use condoms, which would explain their higher syphilis rate.[121] In fact, Indian troops had much lower rates of infection, usually half or less that of the Australians.[122]

In the end, most commanders would decide that, whoever was to blame, Japanese women had to be the focus of disease control efforts. In an evaluation of BCOF in 1946, Major General S. R. Burston considered "excessively high" VD rates a "natural consequence of having a concentration of troops, many with low moral standards, in an area where there is a high Venereal Disease rate amongst a large number of Japanese women, also of low moral standards, as in the Kure area. The main radical line of attack is to reduce the amount of Venereal Disease amongst the women."[123] Starting in June 1946, infected servicemen were closely questioned about their sexual partners, sexual practices, and the amount paid.[124] The idea was to track down sex workers who were spreading disease. But many Japanese were homeless or transient, making it difficult to find someone even if they could be positively identified.

At the same time, BCOF began using a blunter instrument. Military police launched raids to round up sex workers for compulsory pelvic examinations. Those who tested positive would be detained for treatment. SCAP officials were initially critical of the practice, arguing that it violated human rights. But over the following years, the American-occupied zones also witnessed innumerable raids—for example, in Atami, Tokyo, Kanagawa, Kyoto, and Iwakuni—eliciting increasing rancor among the Japanese.[125] Without adequate treatment facilities, such raids would have little effect on the spread of VD. A June 1946 raid in Yanai was typical. Of the twenty women taken to the hospital, seventeen had VD. A Japanese civil policeman was posted at the hospital to prevent them from leaving, but there was no permanent doctor, and only a nurse.[126]

The most famous roundup occurred in Tokyo in November 1946, when as many as three hundred women were taken to Itabashi Police Station. Most of the women were released when the Japanese police realized they were innocent. Some had been taken from their husbands, and one was only fifteen years old. But among the seventy women forced to go to Yoshiwara Hospital for mandatory VD examinations were two women on their way home from a trade union rally. Even after the women showed their membership cards and insisted they were not prostitutes, MPs subjected them to humiliating accusations. "You must have had intercourse with several men," the Americans insisted. The Japanese police apologized to one woman, even while urging her to go with the MPs, explaining that "we were defeated by the war." One girl was beaten when she tried to escape. Most insulting of all, they were made to pay 5 yen for their own exams.[127]

Several female Diet members, most notably Katō Shizue, had already received complaints about such episodes and decided to help the women lodge protests. A former baroness, Katō had wed a labor organizer during the war and joined the Socialist Party. Some 2,000 people, including both union representatives and members of middle-class reform groups such as the WCTU, came together in a rally to demand the end of these indiscriminate roundups. They focused their ire on the Japanese government, both for its subservience to the United States and its failure to improve economic conditions. The *Women's Democratic Newspaper* (Fujin Minshu Shimbun) published "Protest of a Virgin," in which one policeman was quoted claiming that "we cannot treat prostitutes as human beings." And since they could not discriminate among the many they rounded up, he insisted that the police had to treat all of the women in the same way.[128]

Female officials in SCAP joined in efforts to investigate these abuses, and conveyed the Diet members' complaints to the Public Safety Division and Government Division.[129] Yet this cooperation produced scant results. Two years later, even after Army circulars forbade MPs from participating in forcible entries in Japanese homes without warrant or probable cause, they were still working with Japanese vice squads in Kyoto to kick in the doors of unsuspecting civilians.[130] A public health officer witnessed a case in which they broke in after midnight, awakened the occupants, and dragged five young women to be inspected at Heian Hospital. Such raids could be made simply because a "pom-pom girl" was suspected of living there, had lived there before, or had simply associated with the occupants. In response, the public health officer felt obliged to recommend that vaginal examinations not be carried out on virgins.[131] As Dr. Isamu Nieda, a Japanese-American who served as chief of venereal disease control of the Preventive Medicine Division of PH&W, argued, "The indignities forced upon these women and the injustice done to them have given the venereal disease program a black eye in the eyes of the public."[132]

For those found to have VD, penicillin would have been the most effective treatment. It was clearly superior to the former treatment, drugs from the sulfonamide group. These "sulfa" drugs were increasingly ineffective as bacteria became resistant. But in 1945, a shortage of penicillin for U.S. civilians caused Washington to prohibit the use of U.S. penicillin on Japanese and Koreans.[133] They also forbade sharing technical literature on how to mass-produce penicillin, deeming such information a state secret.[134]

American officers requested an end to temporary restrictions on the use of U.S. penicillin.[135] They suggested the Japanese might at least receive penicillin that had passed its expiration date, since it was not even being used by U.S. troops.[136] But in June 1947, faced with continuing shortages of penicillin, U.S. policy dictated that none would be available for Japanese hospitals, and Japanese would also have to pay for sulfa drugs.[137] Not only would Japanese women and men be denied effective treatment, but disease would also continue to spread. New Zealand medical officers, commenting on the arrest of sex workers infected with VD—apparently transmitted in the barracks—warned of the danger to troops in light of the new drug policies.[138] They complained that Japanese women could not be admitted into hospitals and that clinics were not properly equipped. Several reports described how women escaped quarantine.[139] The rate of active cases among New Zealand troops mounted through 1947 to 3.3 percent in November, almost doubling by the following May.[140]

Among the Australians, the total of new cases never again exceeded 3 percent of the average troop strength. But hospital stays became ever longer. Soldiers were spending an average of eleven or twelve days in the hospital with each new infection. The actual proportion of troops affected was probably even higher, because so many men did not present symptoms. Another reason may be that they were obtaining treatment from Japanese doctors using locally produced penicillin. In late 1947, Brigadier General B. S. Wetzel of the Australian Air Force determined that this was the real reason the rate of infection had declined in the previous year. Many of those who came in for treatment—and thereby risked punishment—required increasingly large doses of penicillin because they had developed resistance.[141]

In May 1948, the brigadier general of the Australian Medical Services found that some 30 percent of the hundreds examined were infected. He ordered that all men be investigated for chronic VD, such as gonorrhea and latent syphilis.[142] Even when servicemen were permitted to bring their families to Japan—which commanders expected to reduce contact with sex workers—it appeared to make little difference in the rate of infection. On the other hand, the presence of Australian women and children in Japan made the public more aware of the prevalence of sex work in base areas.

By May 1947, there was once again quiet consideration among Australian officials of "the practicability of segregation of brothels into an 'out-of-bounds' area," where it could be more easily controlled.[143] But instead commanders simply ordered sex workers to leave base areas, and professed surprise when these policies did not work. As J. S. Thompson noted in 1947, "They have disappeared for a few days only to return like the 'bad penny' after a short interval of time. In many cases it has been proven that they have returned due to encouragement from the troops."[144]

A few commanders argued that attitudes toward sex workers were too harsh, especially when compared to the indulgence shown toward servicemen. One officer in the New Zealand medical service said in 1947 that he felt that a "greater measure of punishment should be meted out to the soldier who contracts the disease as it seems out of all proportion to that given to the female"[145] But such men were in the minority.

Brigadier General C. Scales, for one, thought sex workers deserved harsher treatment. He insisted that—in line with Australian tradition—"the only practical suggestion would be to transship them to some suitable island and charge the Japanese government with the task of providing adequate guard measures to prevent their return until declared free from disease." For General Scales, the mainland would not suffice: "only absolute segregation as offered by a natural perimeter—the sea—would be effective in keeping them in one location." Although BCOF never instituted the policy, its serious discussion underscored the frustrations of commanders and the inefficacy of banning prostitution.[146]

Commanders had to cope with an Australian government that was acutely sensitive to publicity about the VD program. Press interest reached its height in 1948, when Cyril Chambers, minister for the army, called for a public inquiry after the federal president of the Australian Legion of Ex-Servicemen attacked Australian troops for their immorality and black-market activities. In April 1948, three chaplains general, Major General C. E. M. Lloyd, and the journalist Massey Stanley spent three weeks in Japan investigating the charge and considered BCOF's VD infection rate—already reduced from 1946 to 1948—excessively high.[147]

On June 10, 1948, Chambers instructed that servicemen who contracted VD be returned to Australia. Commander in Chief Robertson concurred but asked whether the policy would apply to the Royal Australian Navy and Air Force. The minister for the navy said no, explaining that penalties on personnel who contracted VD would lead to concealment and that those who wanted to return home would simulate VD. The minister of the air force agreed that servicemen would suppress information, leading to heightened danger. John Dedman, the defense minister, told Robertson that the policy would not apply to the Navy and Air Force, only the Army.[148]

Cabinet-level discussions revealed the extent to which adverse press influenced policy. Chambers was forced to defend BCOF troops by claiming that the high VD rate resulted from postwar conditions in occupied countries, that British and American rates in Japan were low compared to those of troops in Europe, and that the BCOF's VD classification was more inclusive than the American one, leading to higher infection estimates.[149]

BCOF commanders—like their U.S. counterparts—urged MacArthur to pass laws against prostitution and solicitation. Up to this point, voluntary sex work was still regulated by a 1908 Home Ministry Ordinance.[150] But in May 1948, nominally even this was allowed to lapse. Although various local ordinances prohibited solicitation and other related practices, Japan now had no national law governing sex work. Authorities who wanted to prosecute sex workers were forced to use a new VD law enacted in 1948, requiring physicians to report the existence and location of every patient to the district health office, and to give to the prefectural government the exact name and address of anyone who could infect others. In the case of non–sex worker patients, these details generally were not reported.[151] The law included provision for premarital and prenatal examinations, as well as examination of all contacts and suspects for VD. Police therefore could no longer arrest someone for prostitution under national law except when they were thought to be spreading disease.

On May 6, 1948, the lieutenant general commander in chief of BCOF asked SCAP to "instruct the Japanese government to re-proclaim the offences

Military police organized patrols of entertainment districts that catered to Allied servicemen, such as this one in Kure City. They also rounded up women, subjected them to compulsory medical examinations, and detained those found to be infected with VD. Chūō Shimbun, April 28, 1953. Courtesy of City of Kure

of prostitution and soliciting."[152] In the meantime, both BCOF and U.S. commanders stepped up raids on red-light districts. That summer, Japanese police—on instructions from the provost marshal's office—indiscriminately rounded up girls suspected of being streetwalkers. In October 1948, MPs in Tokyo assisted in arresting sixty streetwalkers and forty-seven touts, that is, hawkers who helped bring in customers.[153] All of the women had to submit to a medical exam.[154]

SCAP civilians continued to criticize BCOF behavior on legal and human rights grounds, but did not stop their own commanders from launching similar raids. The National Rural Police complained that American MPs were detaining prostitutes.[155] Others were outraged that even middle-class women were swept up in the raids. BCOF authorities argued that VD Law 167 was inadequate and that there should be a national law against prostitution and solicitation. After all, they argued, it "could not conceivably infringe on personal liberties and human rights. . . . Most civilized states, including—it is understood—the U.S.A. have such laws." SCAP's response was that the VD law was adequate.[156]

MacArthur seemed inclined to go in the opposite direction. In 1949, he relaxed almost all restrictions on fraternization between U.S. servicemen and Japanese. U.S. servicemen and Japanese would in principle have the same relationship as U.S. servicemen and American civilians.[157] A debate ensued in Canberra. Commander in Chief Robertson, with the support of the Defense Committee, sought to relax BCOF policy, but the government decided against such a recommendation.[158] As Defense Minister John Dedman explained to the House of Representatives, "The Australian Government does not believe in a policy of fraternization with the Japanese people."[159] By this point, 29 percent of Australian troops sent to Japan had been infected with VD, and more than one hundred of them had been infected at least five times.[160]

Despite all the debates about sex work since the arrival of Allied troops, regulatory practice in many places had changed little. What had changed was the massive increase in the reported rate of VD infection among the Japanese. In 1948, there were 436,360 new cases of syphilis and gonorrhea, or 5.46 per 1,000. The "reservoir of venereal disease" that U.S. commanders blamed for infecting their troops had finally risen to the same level as in the population of the continental United States, though it was still far below the astronomical rates among both U.S. and BCOF servicemen.[161]

By 1948, the Japanese government had begun to publicize VD as a threat to the general public through posters, exhibitions, loudspeakers, and radio programs. Men and women would see dramatic warnings in propaganda films, such as *Body and Devil* and *A Thing That Will Ruin Japan*. PH&W had been pushing for such a campaign, though the Japanese still were not permitted to mention the particular menace posed by Allied servicemen.[162] Local medical and police authorities continued to act as if sex workers were the source of VD. They were subject to mandatory inspections and detention, and hospitals for prostitutes were run like prisons, surrounded by barbed wire and guards.[163] Activists complained that these women were kicked, beaten, and treated like "worms."[164] For increasing numbers of Japanese, the mixed messages could mean only one thing: sex workers themselves were a symptom if not the cause of the pathologies that plagued postwar Japan.

Faced with the unprecedented problems posed by occupation, both Japanese and Allied officials fell back on earlier practices, including official brothels, de facto regulation, and prohibition. Preexisting ideas about race, class, and masculinity informed these policies, but the implications were contradictory: racism could justify strict prohibition, or celebration of the subservience of Japanese women. Class prejudice led Japanese officials to procure prostitutes on behalf of servicemen, but the same prejudice led Allied officials to prefer the supposedly chaste company of middle-class women. And contrasting notions of masculinity could make a sexual outlet seem essential, or support programs to discipline the bodies of servicemen.

As a result, sex work could not be controlled by Japanese officials—in the form of the RAA—or banned outright by Occupation authorities. Deregulated markets would therefore develop their own dynamic through the everyday interaction of sex workers and servicemen. Even as officials from each country looked on with disapproval, base cities throughout Japan were fundamentally reshaped as contacts between Allied servicemen and Japanese nationals multiplied.

Violence, Commerce, Marriage

On August 16, 1945, women together with their children crowded Tokyo's main train stations, for fear that U.S. soldiers would rape those remaining in the city.[1] Over the following week, reports from around Japan signaled mounting panic. In Kure, near Hiroshima, and Hachinoe, in Aomori prefecture, residents worried that Allied troops would rampage through their cities.[2] In Fukuoka City, an army officer advised that women and children should flee, and female government staff were instructed to evacuate.[3] In Kanagawa prefecture, to the south of Tokyo, where Allied troops were expected to land at the port cities of Yokohama and Yokosuka, local authorities warned councils to evacuate women and children inland.[4] Neighborhood associations planned to establish vigilante corps, and anxious parents spoke of disguising their daughters to look like men.[5] Major national newspapers tried to dampen fears, but some, such as the *Yomiuri Hōchi Shimbun*, still discouraged Japanese women from walking alone down quiet streets.[6]

Japanese authorities had issued such warnings before. In the Caroline Islands, the Japanese military told women that they would be raped when the Americans came.[7] In Saipan, warnings of rape and murder led hundreds of civilians on the island to kill themselves and their families rather than fall into the hands of the Americans.[8] The same warning was given to hundreds of student nurses who cared for injured soldiers in caves in Okinawa, the Himeyuri Butai, or Star Lilies Corps. Japanese commanders insisted they leave rather than risk capture. Wandering without shelter, most died from bombing or took their own lives.[9]

Contemporary Japanese reports show that veterans spread rumors about how Allied servicemen would engage in rape and pillage.[10] It is not surprising that they would expect their former enemies to perpetrate the same kind of sexual violence, or worse, that Japanese men had committed in occupied areas. It also echoed wartime propaganda and served to explain—and perhaps excuse—why national authorities had chosen to continue the war long after hope of victory was lost.

But for some women, fears of rape would prove well-founded. On August 30, when MacArthur flew into Atsugi and American planes landed every three to four minutes—4,200 troops would land by air alone that day—Japanese police reported at least two rape cases in Kanagawa prefecture.[11] In the first few weeks of the Occupation, rapes were reported nearly every day.[12] Kanagawa prefecture offers the most complete records from August 1945 to January 1946, with fifty-eight rape cases out of a total of 1,900 crimes committed by GIs.[13]

Some of the rapists made a point of humiliating both victims and their families, and the incidents read like a catalog of horrors. In Yokosuka, marines raped both a thirty-six-year-old mother and her seventeen-year-old daughter.[14] Drunk GIs raped a disfigured forty-seven-year-old woman. In Yokohama, four or five U.S. marines gang-raped a twenty-six-year-old woman, and servicemen took a photograph of her vagina—all witnessed by an eleven-year-old boy. In Hiratsuka City, GIs broke into a private home, and while one soldier holding a gun watched outside, other GIs raped an eighteen-year-old as her parents protested.[15]

When British Commonwealth Occupation Force (BCOF) troops landed beginning in 1946, more incidents soon followed. Even a year later, in Hiroshima, twenty Australian soldiers were reported to have gang-raped a Japanese girl.[16] In February 1947, an occupation employee accused two Indians of raping her after she received a ride home with them. In March 1947, in Okayama prefecture, a BCOF truck driver giving a Japanese base employee a ride demanded sex, and when refused punched her several times in the face, then kicked her with such force she fell into a roadside ditch.[17] In Kaitachi in April 1947, a sixteen-year-old Japanese girl was accosted by three Indian soldiers. One held her down, one pulled off her clothes, and the third held off her two brothers, then all three soldiers raped her.[18]

From the earliest days, Japanese girls and women reported that some of their attackers would offer them money or material goods in recompense. In September 1945, a GI offered tobacco and candy to a fourteen-year-old girl and ordered her at gunpoint to perform oral sex.[19] That same month in Chiba prefecture, near Tokyo, three soldiers showed "something like a 10-yen bank note"—most likely B-yen notes, military currency distributed to U.S. forces before landing—to a housewife. She was raped when she refused payment.[20]

For some historians, such evidence only goes to prove that even without use of physical force, even when Japanese women solicited sex from service-men, the power imbalance between them meant that such liaisons could not be considered consensual. After all, if rape by Allied servicemen was an ev-eryday reality, could women who asked for compensation really be called sex workers? Were they not simply victims, no less than the women who were forced to work in Japan's wartime military comfort stations?

Feminists have long argued that rape can best be understood as an asser-tion of power, not sexuality. Susan Brownmiller's 1975 *Against Our Will* argues that rape was an expression of generalized male violence toward all women, citing evidence from the Vietnam War as well as U.S. society.[21] In the late 1980s, other feminists, such as Catharine MacKinnon and Andrea Dworkin, pushed the argument even further, arguing that heterosexual sex can never be truly consensual because the oppression of women under pa-triarchy is so prevalent.[22]

Although Brownmiller's analysis is widely credited with bringing war rape to the attention of scholars, the media, and activists, it has been criti-cized for being overly broad. Her book posits the same causal explanation with no allowance for historical variability between cases.[23] According to this view, women play no role in this history except as victims, with no room for the possibility that women can be on opposing sides, or that some might even sanction rape.[24]

In the 1990s, as widespread rape was reported in Bosnia, some feminists began to argue that, rather than being simply an expression of patriarchy, rape could sometimes be an instrument of genocide, aiming at a particular ethnic or racial group. Scholars point to cases such as Nanjing in 1937, Ber-lin in 1945, Bangladesh in 1971, Bosnia in 1992–95, and Rwanda in 1994.[25] By impregnating enemy women—and in some cases preventing them from having abortions—an invader or occupier can create "ethnically cleansed" children.[26] Others have argued that this kind of rape by soldiers is a way to assault the honor of enemy combatants by showing that they cannot protect their women.[27]

The historian who has most closely investigated the particular episode of rape by occupation troops in Japan is Yuki Tanaka, and his work on the subject has been accepted by leading scholars.[28] One of Tanaka's more provocative arguments is to compare the behavior of the Allies to that of the Japanese when they occupied China. As Brownmiller notes in her foreword to Tanaka's book, *Japan's Comfort Women*, Tanaka describes these cases as part of a larger pattern of "worldwide male aggression."[29]

But using occupied Japan to illustrate worldwide male aggression may not help us to explain the particularities of what happened there, and how and why this case was different from—say—Nanjing in 1937, or Berlin in 1945. If one does not consider all forms of heterosexual sex coercive, it becomes important to determine the degree of women's agency. The context for commercial sex is crucial, clearly, but it is no less important to consider whether individual women—and individual men—were able to make different choices. This requires looking into the range of relationships that developed among them.

There is little contemporaneous reporting or other evidence that U.S. servicemen carried out large-scale attacks on the Japanese. Tanaka acknowledges that "the mass rape and murder of civilians, like that committed by Japanese army troops in Nanjing in December 1937 (and that the Japanese political leaders and civilians feared would occur when the Allied troops landed), did not take place."[30] Conversely, whereas in other cases— including Nanjing, Berlin, and Bosnia—rape received official sanction or even encouragement from senior commanders, in Japan U.S. and BCOF forces recorded rape accusations and began arresting servicemen during the first few months of the Occupation.[31]

Therefore, in determining how oppressive and dangerous the Occupation was for women, one can examine crime statistics from Japanese as well as Allied sources. In published accounts, figures vary widely. The historian Fujime Yuki reports 30 rapes for all of 1946, where Duus, for example, reports 165 rapes for March–September 1946 in just the Tokyo-Kanagawa area.[32] As for Tanaka, he freely admits that accurate statistics are not his main concern. In *Hidden Horrors*, for example, he misread a set of crimes that included robberies and assaults as only rape cases, leading him to vastly overstate the true number.[33] Similar factual errors also raise questions about his account of sexual violence in *Japan's Comfort Women*. For instance, Tanaka says that in 1946, 38 percent of crimes in Hiroshima were rapes, but that figure refers to extortion—rapes were 2.8 percent of crimes. In the same city, there were fourteen, not eighty-four rapes in 1945.[34]

Tanaka acknowledges that the number of rapes reported fell off dramatically in Kanagawa prefecture after September 19, 1945, though the daily toll was not as high as he claims (on September 1, 1945, for instance, the police reported two cases, not twelve). He suggests that people may have simply given up on the police, who appeared powerless even to defend themselves. This is very plausible, considering reports of servicemen stealing their swords and even pistols.[35] And statistics also do not measure other kinds of sexual harassment that occurred between servicemen and their Japanese employees. A list of BCOF "commandments" intended as a joke suggests how common such harassment may have been: "thou shall not love thy house-girl better than thy wife."[36] House girls were sometimes subject to mandatory VD examinations, and some found the examinations so objectionable that they quit.[37] BCOF orders stated employers could do nothing if women objected or refused examination, but encouraged their dismissal.[38] VD exams fed public suspicion that house girls were prostitutes. Shitamoto Hichibei of Koyo, on Eta Jima, for example, stated that her mother told her to resign her job for this reason.[39]

Nevertheless, some Japanese women continued to report rapes to the police, as revealed by case files and crime statistics collected by both U.S. and BCOF commanders. Because they include Japan as a whole, these figures should be much more complete. Instead, they are much lower than the number of rapes reported in Kanagawa prefecture, though it is not clear why. But they show the same pattern: a higher incidence of rape when occupying forces first entered an area, with fewer rapes reported in the months that followed. In the Eighth Army, which occupied Hokkaido and northern Honshu, eleven rapes were reported in September 1945, ten in October, seven in November, and five in December. Similarly, after BCOF forces arrived in southern Honshu and Shikoku, taking over from the U.S. Sixth Army, eight rapes were reported in July 1946—the first month for which data is available—seven in August, and four in September. The same pattern was apparent when U.S. forces entered Germany: more than 250 cases of rape were reported in April 1945, with fewer and fewer in the months that followed.[40]

This pattern is consistent with how scholars have come to understand the prevalence of rape in wartime. The nature of the incidents described in the occupation of Japan, including exhibitionism, gang rape, and underage victims, has become all too common in contemporary conflicts. Moreover, it has been found that even apparently "normal" men engage in this behavior, and the usual psychiatric diagnoses of rapists do not apply. Instead, it is the very conditions of war that lead to this kind of aggression, including the constant fear and stress of combat, and the way this can lead tight-knit groups of men to behave like gangs.[41] When servicemen first arrived in Japan and fully expected to meet hostility, it seems likely they would have felt and acted as they would have on a battlefield. With time, this perception would change, which helps explain why reported sexual violence diminished.

Of course, it is also possible that women simply gave up reporting sexual violence when they despaired that anything would be done to stop it. For example, Christian anti-prostitution activist Satō Kimiji complained to occupation authorities in 1949 that rape was happening incessantly and perpetrators were rarely brought to justice. He described one case in which a woman waiting for a friend in Meiji Park was kidnapped and raped by three servicemen. When she reported the incident, she was treated as a prostitute and put into a guarded VD hospital.[42]

And yet many reports of sexual violence did result in the arrest of the accused servicemen. In 1947, 144 rapes were reported, leading to 77 arrests; in 1948, 140 rapes were reported, with 83 arrests; in 1949, 171 were reported, with 146 arrests.[43] But in the end, most of these men did not face trial for this offense. Figures are not available for Japan, but in the Far East Command as a whole—of which Japan accounted for the vast majority of cases—just 104 of the 422 arrested between 1947 and 1949 were court-martialed. Of them, 53 were convicted.[44]

The small number of servicemen tried and convicted after rape accusations raises the obvious question of whether military authorities disregarded the testimonies of the victims or were unduly lenient to the accused. But this was not a situation unique to Japan. Much the same thing occurred in the United States, where prosecutors often disbelieved victims and deemed rape accusations to be "unfounded."[45] Moreover, commanders were not predisposed to dismiss all rape complaints against American servicemen. African Americans were more likely to be tried and convicted than white servicemen. During World War II in the European theater, blacks received a disproportionately high number of life sentences and death sentences for rape. In Britain, 56 percent of those executed for rape were black men, and in France it was 86 percent, even though blacks accounted for fewer than 10 percent of the American contingent.[46] The same pattern continued in the Far Eastern Command, to the point that in 1951, the NAACP dispatched Thurgood Marshall to investigate. The Eighth Army had the largest all-black unit in the U.S. Army, the Twenty-Fourth Infantry Regiment, and Marshall found a pattern of unequal treatment.[47] Twice as many blacks as whites were court-martialed for various offenses, even though there were six times as many white servicemen.[48] It is clear from U.S. military documents that authorities closely tracked numbers of alleged rapes by blacks in Japan. BCOF commanders, for their part, took a keen interest in rape allegations against Indian soldiers.[49]

Of course, Japanese complainants would have been most struck by the unfairness of Allied military justice to victims. U.S. servicemen were tried by U.S. officers, not Japanese officials. But court-martial procedures could also be quite tough on the accused. Military courts were designed to maintain discipline, and soldiers were jailed until trial, denied due process, and usually did not have a trained attorney to defend them. Instead, an officer or other personnel was appointed. Military courts were criticized for uneven and severe sentencing, and for command influence on sentencing.[50] Most important, the rate of conviction for rapes committed by servicemen in the United States was comparable to that in Japan: 57 percent versus 51 percent.[51]

Nevertheless, in postwar Japan perhaps even more than the United States, the 140 to 171 rape accusations each year between 1947 and 1949 only suggests the amount of sexual violence that must have occurred. Reporting rape to police often resulted in the stigmatization of the victim instead of prosecution of the perpetrator. Rather than accepting these statistics as a reliable guide to how many rapes were committed by U.S. servicemen, we can interpret them as indicators of underlying trends. If anything, they suggest that there was a decline in sexual violence after the first months and that rape accusations were increasingly likely to lead to arrests. In a nation of 83 million, it therefore seems unlikely that fear of rape by Allied servicemen was so pervasive that no sex could be considered consensual—not unless we are willing to look at relations among Japanese men and women in the same fashion. After all, there were six times as many reports of rape by Japanese men in 1947. Moreover, the number rose dramatically, doubling the next year and totaling 3,558 in 1950. And it is not clear that women would have been more, rather than less, likely to report rapes by Japanese men, especially if they were committed by close acquaintances.[52]

It is therefore possible—and necessary—to examine the range of relationships that Japanese women entered into with servicemen without assuming that they were merely a way to avoid sexual violence or that contractual sex and marriage constituted rape by other means. This also allows us to listen to the testimony of the women themselves—albeit mediated through judicial proceedings, Diet hearings, and press reports—and not just assume that they were powerless victims.

As we have seen, both U.S. and BCOF commanders discouraged even consensual relationships, and all unofficial contacts came under the rubric of "fraternization." Although the term was sometimes used positively, more often it connoted servicemen's relations with local inhabitants that contravened military discipline—typically a private relationship with a Japanese woman. Some American women who served in the civilian section of the Occupation consorted with Japanese men, but these relationships appear to have been rare.[53]

Sexual relationships between men serving in the occupying forces and Japanese men undoubtedly occurred, although they were infrequently reported. One rare exception shows how the provost marshal sometimes plea-bargained sex crimes rather than risk public exposure—one more reason for the low rate of court martials and convictions. The incident occurred when a Japanese man complained to U.S. authorities about an encounter with two corporals on or about April 23, 1950. The Japanese national, who was reported to have been drinking, performed oral sex twice with one serviceman and once with the other. According to the investigators, the Japanese man claimed he was not forced and submitted voluntarily. The first corporal admitted participating but later said the confession was involuntary. The report recommended trial by general court-martial, with the option of dishonorable discharge "for the good of the service" in exchange for a signed statement.[54] However idiosyncratic, the incident suggests that at least some Japanese felt they could complain to U.S. authorities even when it would bring embarrassment.

Far more common were sexual relationships between servicemen and Japanese women. In Japan, servicemen's relationships with women included short-term sexual encounters, long-term affairs with one exclusive client (known as *onrii*, from the English word *only*), and relationships that servicemen and women sought to have recognized by the state in marriage. The simplest to analyze is the short-term sexual encounter, and it is that liaison into which Allied servicemen most commonly entered. By engaging in sexual commerce, servicemen participated in a publicly availably practice involving two transacting parties: a buyer (the serviceman) and a seller (the sex worker).[55] The commodity exchanged was a sexual act, with money or other means of payment changing hands. Because these clients and sex workers were nonexclusive, their relationship formed part of a larger market.

In a wide range of memoirs, letters, and archival evidence, observers often noted how large and how free this market had become. As one reporter for Armed Forces Radio later recalled, what servicemen "most enjoyed [was] sex without nonsense, sex without guilt, sex without preliminaries, the way the prostitutes and night-club girls gave it to them."[56] But it was not only the availability of the Japanese women (as the servicemen saw it) that was of interest. It was also the characteristics the servicemen imagined the women to possess. In 1951, the American Leonard Forman produced a not untypical account of servicemen's attraction to Japanese women in the major Japanese periodical *Kaizo*. "Whatever Japanese men say about the women of their own country," he ventured, "one of the biggest reasons why American men like Japanese girls is . . . [that] Japanese girls, whether it is a boyfriend or a customer, completely obey American men."[57]

The quality of submissiveness was one frequently associated with the Japanese geisha, and many Americans persisted in calling sex workers geisha girls. Geisha are by profession not mainly providers of sexual services, though sexual services are in some instances available. Geisha are instead known for their training in the arts of conversation, poetry, singing, and dancing. Yet since army personnel generally assumed that any Japanese woman wearing a kimono was a geisha, many women working in the sex industry found it a successful marketing strategy, advertising themselves as geisha girls regardless of their backgrounds. Photographs of Tokyo bars promoting "geisha girls" accompanied articles in *Stars and Stripes* and in the American mass media. Authorities blamed Japanese women's purported attitude of subordination outright for high VD rates, since they supposedly did not insist that the men wear condoms.[58]

American press coverage also used another, contrasting stereotype of Asian women. Geisha girls were portrayed as wily oriental seductresses who lured innocent GIs. One 1947 article in the *New York Times* explained: "She is a waitress, factory hand or oriental bobby soxer who had borrowed her

Many Japanese women sought to appeal to servicemen by playing on their fantasies. Even if few had actually trained to be geisha, the "geisha girl" was a common sight in entertainment districts. U.S. Army Medical Service

betters kimona [*sic*] and gone out to show the unsuspecting American precisely what the real geisha is not."[59] The most popular "how-to guide to Japan and Japanese women" was Bill Hume's *Babysan* cartoon, which originally appeared in the *Navy Times* and was later collected in a book published simultaneously in Japan and the United States. Hume's pinup-style portrayal of the panpan played to American male fantasy, but many of the cartoons rendered Babysan as getting the better of her GI patrons—two-timing them while taking their money.[60]

It was in the base towns that servicemen most frequently entered into liaisons with women who fully acted out these imagined roles, with some developing into longer-term relationships. An onrii-type relationship also took place between two transacting parties, a buyer and a seller (the onrii), but the services performed included companionship, cleaning, and cooking. Money or other means of payment changed hands. In this case, however, the woman had in principle only one client, even if some onrii worked for more than one serviceman.

Euro-American men in foreign ports, especially in Asia, had a long history of keeping "local wives." In some cases, sophisticated subcultures developed. Japanese and other Asian women served as negotiators between local cultures and foreign men. In colonial sites such as Batavia (modern Jakarta), local wives occasionally achieved considerable standing.[61] This practice was less common in Japan, where, with the exception of a licensed quarter for Dutch and Chinese men in Nagasaki, few foreign men had contact with local women. It was only in the late nineteenth century that a growing number of foreign men began to associate with Japanese women, providing fodder for Euro-American literature and opera. Tōjin Okichi, who was said to be the mistress of Townsend Harris, the first U.S. consul general in Japan, was the most famous. In the 1950s, social critics sought to cast a glamorous light on these women (some of whom, like Tōjin Okichi, may not have been consorts). In 1953, Ōya Sōichi, one of Japan's most prolific and insightful culture critics from the 1920s to the 1960s, noted in *Kaizō* that courtesans in Nagasaki had been the very first Japanese women to wear rings and bracelets and to carry parasols.[62] Yet the fame of women such as Tōjin Okichi highlights how few consorts there really were.

In the first postwar decade, some servicemen began to lay down deeper roots, forming common-law relationships or even marrying Japanese women. The onrii lived in a tenuous position, accepted fully neither by Japanese society nor by the Allied authorities. Some Japanese authorities fully acknowledged

"Joe-san! I think you have duty tonight!"

Bill Hume's depiction of Babysan showed how servicemen with Japanese onrii sometimes did not realize they could be just one of several partners. Courtesy of David Hume

the onrii as belonging to a separate category from ordinary sex workers by giving them identification cards that excused them from compulsory medical examinations.[63] The American authorities were not as understanding: though some commanders tolerated sex work, they were unwilling to acknowledge the range of relationships that existed between Japanese women and American servicemen. Long-term relationships could result in demerits on conduct sheets or blocked promotions. Commonwealth authorities, who mostly turned a blind eye to sex work when they could not stop it, forbade long-term relationships.

Both Allied and Japanese authorities tended to condemn as prostitutes all Japanese women found consorting with servicemen, as a rare series of reports of women caught in a police raid reveals. The 1950 raid in Iwakuni caught sex workers specializing in short-term encounters, but also onrii and women who were merely in the area. Thirty-six-year-old Yasui Mitsuko, a three-year employee of the base, was an onrii. In her case, two MPs approached her residence and that of three colleagues, also onrii. Yasui and the others thought they would be immune from police action, but their residences were searched. The net also dragged in two women who claimed to no longer be in the business.[64] Twenty-one-year-old Tanaka Yuko told the police, "Since coming here I have not had any relations with soldiers as I have not had enough time. I will take a medical examination since it is an order from the M.P. and if any disease is found I intend to take medical treatment by myself. I desire to live with a soldier as his girl in Iwakuni if it is possible." Thirty-seven-year-old Kitamura Yasuko, who admitted to having been a sex worker, had been previously caught and hospitalized for VD. But she had come to Iwakuni with her nine-year-old child, and therefore denied any intention of selling sex.[65]

Most commonly, women caught in police raids or otherwise arrested were charged with the 1948 VD law. Until 1949, they appeared before provost courts, set up to try cases involving occupation personnel and Japanese citizens. Some prosecutors opposed this treatment in light of the negative attitude of GHQ and Eighth Army command, and not least because servicemen were responsible for solicitation, not the women. Therefore, not all VD cases would be prosecuted, and the records are rarely available due to archival restrictions.

One surviving series from 1949 nevertheless provides other examples of how even short-term encounters could be varied and complex.[66] Rather than exhibiting abject submissiveness, these sex workers negotiated the terms of exchange, even if in VD trials they insisted servicemen were to blame for the consequences. Takeda Michiko, for instance, was accused of infecting U.S. Private First Class Grady L. Freeman with VD. At twenty years of age, the five foot, one inch, 115-pounds Takeda had originally been a typist at the Daiken Building. She became an onrii and then took other clients to pay school expenses. She admitted receiving 1,000 yen for sex with Freeman but insisted that she had gotten VD from another client, Private First Class Pedro J. Montano, from whom she had received 600 yen. Takeda claimed she had unknowingly transmitted gonorrhea and blamed the servicemen: "Whenever I had sexual intercourse with any person, I requested him to use a prophylactic, but none of them used it at all." Nevertheless, the court concluded that she had given both servicemen gonorrhea and illegally engaged in prostitution. Takeda was sentenced to three months of confinement, to be suspended if she could show she was cured of VD.[67]

Similarly, Nakano Sumiko, known as "Betty," was brought before the court on charges of transmitting VD to U.S. Private George C. Edwards. The tiny, twenty-four-year-old Nakano (four feet, eight inches, ninety-five pounds) was "light-skinned and good looking" but had a checkered history. An occasional sex worker between 1945 and 1949, Nakano had previously lived with three different servicemen and also had experience running a dressmaker's shop. When Edwards realized he had symptoms of gonorrhea, he told investigators where to find Nakano. On June 9, 1949, the vice squad picked her up and confined her to the Kyoto VD hospital. Nakano pled guilty but protested that servicemen never used condoms. She was sentenced to six months' confinement, which was suspended when she produced a medical certificate showing she was free from VD.[68]

Thirty-one-year-old Fujiwara Misako received goods rather than cash— one can of shoe polish and one bag of soap powder, plus the promise of a shirt—for having sex with an Australian serviceman, which suggests it was meant to be the beginning of a longer relationship. Shortly after being convicted, Fujiwara was readmitted to the VD hospital with gonorrhea. She was fined 2,000 yen for infecting him with syphilis, but soon she could be seen soliciting once again. Prosecutors therefore argued that 2,000 yen was an insufficient deterrent.[69]

Veneral disease prosecutions were rare and ineffective. Nevertheless, relationships that spread VD presented a simpler problem for authorities than those that resulted in marriage. Marriage was discouraged even between American men and American women working in the Occupation.[70] Most commanders were hostile to the idea, and immigration law also stood in the way of long-term relationships. Barring exceptional cases, Asians were prohibited from moving to the United States, and Australia completely excluded them.

Nevertheless, some U.S. and Australian servicemen wed Japanese women in Shintō ceremonies, not considering them real marriages because they were not Christian nuptials.[71] Under Japanese law, a marriage was an agreement between participants, and no license or ceremony was required—it became legal when they notified the Japanese registrar. Other servicemen merely set up households with Japanese women without any intention of marrying them, much less bringing them home to the United States. Some hoped to marry their Japanese girlfriends but were unable to complete the necessary paperwork before their commanders transferred them to a new post—in many cases, precisely in order to break up such relationships. Still other servicemen were deeply committed to repatriating with their wives or girlfriends.[72]

BCOF policy flatly prohibited servicemen from marrying Japanese. The "White Australia" policy banned the entry of Asians into Australia, regardless of whether they were born in the United States or only one parent was Asian.[73] A Japanese-American remained Japanese, but any white person could be Australian. British and New Zealand authorities also had a racial understanding of rights: what was important was descent, not citizenship. For example, New Zealand Command forbade the marriage of New Zealander James Carnegie to Clarice Higashida, a Japanese-American who was a U.S. citizen.[74] Indian marriages to Japanese were also strongly discouraged.[75] Any BCOF servicemen wishing to wed needed the written authority of the commander in chief of BCOF. Marriage could be performed only by the British consul general in Yokohama. And as the 1946 BCOF administrative instruction No. 39 said, "Under no circumstances will approval be given for marriage between a member of BCOF and a Japanese national."[76] It was official policy that marriage by a civilian clergyman or under Japanese civil law would bring disciplinary action, and that dependence and marriage allowances would be withheld. Even so, many BCOF members wed Japanese women informally.[77]

The Australian press frequently reported on the question of marriage between Japanese women and Australian servicemen. In February 1947, after widespread press reports of Australians marrying Japanese women and supplying them with money from the black market, the Australian cabinet took

up fraternization. In March 1948, the minister for immigration, Arthur Calwell, said in the House of Representatives that in light of wartime actions,
"it would be the grossest act of public indecency to permit a Japanese of either sex to pollute the Australian shores."[78] After Calwell's announcement
that no Japanese wives would be allowed to enter Australia, a debate raged
in the editorial pages of the *Sydney Morning Herald*. The majority of letter
writers opposed allowing Japanese women to immigrate, either because of
war memories or fears of biracial children. One woman wrote, "No Australian mother whose devoted son, no Australian wife whose decent Australian
husband lies buried in some Pacific battlefield will have her feelings outraged by an Australian flaunting a Japanese woman before her."[79]

Others disagreed on grounds of racial equality or personal liberty. On
March 12, Mary M. Jackson wrote that the policy "smacks of the superior
race doctrine." She continued, "This assumption that all Japanese are to be
lumped together and condemned outright is as stupid as it would be to suggest that because we are both Australians, Mr. Calwell and myself are similar in all respects."[80] Another reader wrote that Australians should remember that "the essence of democracy is observance of the principle of the
'liberty of the individual.'"[81]

But some Australian and American servicemen were determined to marry
Japanese women, no matter what obstacles were placed in their way. The
most famous of them was the Australian Frank Weaver, whose adventures
were reported in Australian newspapers in the early 1950s. Weaver, who
preferred to be known as Tetsuichiro Kitagawa, had been a soldier in the
BCOF before his discharge in 1948. He reportedly married Sachiko Kitagawa
in a Shintō ceremony in August 1947, and again in a Christian ceremony in
November 1950. He tried to renounce his Australian citizenship and swore
he would never return to Australia. Weaver was ultimately deported eight times
from Japan for illegal entry, and his adventures included an escape from immigration jail with a hacksaw blade stolen from the prison plumber. Weaver
blamed "Australian interference" for losing his wife, who by his seventh attempt to enter Japan had remarried. He had to beg the Australian government to help him return home and was billed for the seventy-five pounds
required for passage.[82]

The more common problem for both Australian and American servicemen was securing visas for their Japanese brides. U.S. law precluded large-
scale emigration to the United States. However, some women were able to
gain entry after the war ended. Special riders attached to congressional

legislation by senators and representatives allowed for individual exceptions. For instance, in 1949, New York Representative Jacob Javits wrote to occupation authorities saying he planned to introduce legislation waiving immigration restrictions for Nobuko Maeda, fiancée of Lieutenant George Asai.[83] By 1952, U.S. servicemen had taken advantage of a grace period in immigration law to register more than 5,000 marriages with U.S. authorities in Japan.[84] The passage of the McCarran-Walter Act that year ended the blanket exclusion of Japanese immigration into the United States, though they were still subject to a quota allowing just 185 per year.[85]

Australian policy also changed in 1952, with the widely publicized case of Cherry Parker, the first Japanese woman who was permitted entry after marrying an Australian serviceman. Gordon Parker was the son of the mayor of Ringwood, Victoria, a Melbourne suburb, and he and Cherry had two children. The policy change did not mean that all Japanese wives could immediately enter: the *Sydney Morning Herald* explained that each case would be judged on its merits and that only about twelve women were being considered.[86] The newspaper editorialized that the government policy had been correct: that there were strong reasons against allowing all marriages—soldiers might regret their action and Japanese girls away from home might also be unhappy. But by this point, after marriages had taken place and husbands were sent home, the government could not force couples to stay apart.[87]

After Cherry Parker's arrival in June 1952, more Japanese wives soon followed. For the most part, the Australian press portrayed the story positively, with flattering photographs and interviews. In 1953, Australian immigration policy changed again, and approximately two hundred war brides entered Australia. According to the Hiroshima newspaper *Chugoku Shimbun*, women who wanted to emigrate faced a complex process. To be eligible, men first applied to their commander. Then military authorities and Japanese police authorities conducted an investigation. If the initial investigation was positive, authorities looked into the bride's knowledge of English, her education, and her physical condition, as well as the opinion of her relatives on the marriage. In January 1953 the Australian Army established a bride school with classes on how to dress and prepare meals. By 1956, some 650 Japanese women had emigrated to Australia.[88]

The release of the 1952 motion picture *Japanese War Bride*—and the widespread posters that advertised the film—made Japanese wives increasingly visible in the United States.[89] Other films such as the 1956 *Teahouse of the August Moon*, based on the 1951 novel by Vern Sneider, or the 1957 *Sayonara*, presented American audiences with sympathetic examples of interracial couples.[90] As Naoko Shibusawa has argued, fiction and film about marriages between Americans and Japanese helped to create a national discourse about the need for racial tolerance.[91]

The most successful of these films, *Sayonara*, was based on a novel by James Michener, who would himself marry a woman of Japanese descent. The movie told the story of an American airman's love for a Japanese performer and how it forced him to reckon with U.S. military prejudices. The film illustrates several issues of fraternization: the tension between commanders and servicemen, the difference between officers and enlisted men, and the variations between casual relationships and marriage. The film juxtaposes the pageantry of the military against the "exoticism" of Japan: the stark lines of the base barracks against the elaborate kabuki theater and *tatami*-matted house; the military uniform against the elaborate kimonos; the clear American English of the military men against the heavily accented English of the Japanese women, Hana-ogi and Katsumi. But the relationships it portrayed between servicemen and Japanese women put racial binaries in a new and unflattering light. After one character's plans to marry a Japanese woman are thwarted by an unsympathetic commander, he chooses suicide rather than accept transfer.[92] Another, played by Marlon Brando, is shown in Japanese dress and finally succeeds in consecrating his relationship in marriage. Even Brando's jilted girlfriend, Eileen Webster, finds consolation with a kabuki actor. All of these figures are depicted negotiating the space between the two states, rejecting the racial identities that were supposed to define and separate them.

But although *Sayonara* has a Hollywood ending, most relationships between servicemen and Japanese did not end so happily. The plight of abandoned Japanese women—those left before immigration policy changed, or even afterward—contributed to a growing perception among their countrymen that relationships with Allied servicemen had created a social problem of major proportions. For many Japanese men and women—who had been subject to wartime propaganda on the superiority of pure Japanese blood—biracial children fathered by white or black servicemen were even more troubling than mixed marriages.[93] They were most commonly known as *ai no ko*, a pejorative term meaning literally "child of mixture" that also meant love child. The term *konketsuji* (mixed-blood children) emerged in the 1950s and was originally more neutral, but became linked with illegitimacy and other social problems associated with the occupation.[94]

The issue had emerged early in the Occupation. In March 1946, *Stars and Stripes* ran an article reporting that police anticipated "fourteen thousand G.I. babies by June."[95] The birth of the first biracial child was announced on June 28, 1946, close to nine months after occupying forces had arrived. The journalist who initially relayed the news was fired.[96] By 1948, the Australian and New Zealand press would report 2,000 BCOF babies in the Tokyo/Yokohama area.[97]

Many of these babies suffered abandonment or neglect and became the subject of sensationalist reporting in the United States. Sawada Miki, the daughter of a wealthy diplomat, claimed that the cadaver of a mixed-race baby literally fell into her lap when she was riding in a train in 1946. She went on to found the Elizabeth Saunders home—naming it after the first benefactor—to shelter abandoned GI babies, and became an important source for foreign journalists covering the issue.[98] "Babies with un-Japanese pigmentation are found dead in refuse heaps," Darrell Berrigan reported in the *Saturday Evening Post*. "More are found alive in crowded railway stations, in the park in front of the emperor's palace, and in public baths." The homes he visited were "dirty, shabby places, where ten or fifteen babies are kept with government assistance." Berrigan claimed that the owners enriched themselves and in one case even conducted experiments with biracial babies.[99]

One reason so many feared large numbers of biracial children was that abortion remained illegal, though Berrigan reported that at least one practitioner was mainly employed aborting the offspring of servicemen.[100] The treatment of women who returned from Manchuria provided a precedent for a different policy. Many worried that, after being raped by Soviet soldiers, they would give birth to mixed-race children. Japanese staff and volunteers at repatriation centers therefore asked them whether they had been subject to violence and gave them the option of having an abortion.[101]

In 1947, the Diet took up a bill that would make Japan one of the first countries in the world to legalize abortion. Women would be able to petition to end a pregnancy in cases of rape, if the mother's life was in danger, if the mother was ill, was poor, or had many children, and on eugenics grounds. The bill would also have legalized contraception. But it was subsequently revised to restrict birth control and remove the financial hardship provision for abortion, at the same time emphasizing sterilization, both voluntary and involuntary.

The main sponsor of what would become the Eugenic Protection Law, Taniguchi Yasaburō, sought to give obstetricians a monopoly in abortion services (he later became chairman of the Japan Medical Association). But he told fellow Diet members that the main purpose of the bill was to prevent a decline in the quality of the Japanese population because of the higher fertility rates of lower-class people. He was especially concerned about panpan.

> I want public health centers to round up those who do not have the ability to live by themselves, or those who are sometimes indigent. And if women are found to be pregnant, they should be examined. I have heard that there are many *panpan* girls and beggars who have mental disabilities, so I hope the health centers can find the mentally retarded among the *panpan* and the beggars, and perform eugenic sterilization on them to prevent them from having babies.

According to Keio University professor Takashi Hayashi, by legalizing abortion, "80 percent of our prostitutes and delinquent youths will be eradicated twenty years from now, and Japan will then become a country with people of good quality."[102]

Press reporting on the Eugenic Protection Law focused on the problem of overpopulation, and it is hard to know whether other proponents were aiming to prevent mixed-race children. Open mention of the issue was prohibited by occupation authorities—Berrigan was deported because of his *Saturday Evening Post* article.[103] SCAP's Civil Censorship Detachment collected and studied all material before publication, and between 1945 and 1949, the largest group of deletions from fiction concerned fraternization.[104]

As it was finally enacted in 1948, the Eugenic Protection Law (Yūsei Hogo Hō) did not provide funding for birth control clinics. Instead it set up Eugenic Protection Commissions, which gave permission for abortions to protect the mother's health or to prevent transmission of hereditary defects. The following year, women could petition on grounds of economic hardship.[105] These commissions could also order sterilization. Between 1950 and 1959, there were 8,408 cases of compulsory sterilization.[106] Some sponsors, such as Katō Shizue, had been longtime supporters of women's access to birth control and were embarrassed that it gave these commissions such power without providing public financing for contraception. Other women's rights activists known for their interest in eugenics, such as Ichikawa

Fusae, who became a Diet member in 1953, were instrumental in linking what they called the *konketsuji* problem and prostitution in public minds.[107]

In fact, most sex workers likely would have willingly aborted unwanted offspring. They would have paid a heavy price for continuing their pregnancies.[108] Nevertheless, many Japanese continued to blame panpan for orphaned children and failed to distinguish them from the large number of women in long-term relationships with servicemen. By 1952, authorities familiar with the issue estimated 200,000 biracial children had been born.[109] More informed estimates placed the actual number at closer to 100,000.[110]

Statistics from the Elizabeth Saunders home demonstrate the variety of nationalities represented: children had fathers from the Philippines, Australia, and Russia, as well as the United States. A range of factors explained why mothers gave up their children: 18 percent thought the child would have a better future, 17 percent worried they would have a negative environment, and 15 percent explained that the father had returned to his home country. The largest percentage of children—30 percent—were simply abandoned.[111] Nationality was a key concern for these children: until 1985, paternal blood determined citizenship in Japan. Therefore, none of them was a Japanese citizen. They were stateless, except in the unlikely case that their fathers had registered them at their consulates.[112]

In the Diet, debate on the issue began as early as 1946 and reached its height in 1952–1953, when members considered whether biracial children should be permitted to remain in Japanese schools. In March 1950, the Ministry of Education had declared that they were indeed Japanese and should attend Japanese school.[113] Some Diet members were sympathetic, others expressed fear, and still others accepted that biracial children should be considered Japanese, even while acknowledging their differences.[114] A consensus agreed that they needed financial support but disagreed about how to provide it. Some argued for approaching the United States, though others thought it should be left to the Japanese social welfare system.[115]

Occupation authorities avoided taking any responsibility. Colonel Crawford Sams of the Public Health and Welfare Section ordered that the children be treated as Japanese to avoid the creation of a Eurasian minority.[116] This had been a perennial concern for colonial officials in the Netherlands East Indies, French Indochina, and India.[117] Interracial unions and their offspring destabilized the boundaries upon which their authority rested. Reporting on biracial children in Japan was therefore censored, and Sams also prohibited the Japanese government from conducting research on the subject.[118]

For the Japanese women involved, bearing biracial children with foreign servicemen could have terrible consequences. Such women often would have to disappear from their communities or give up their babies to orphanages in major cities nearby.[119] Children who remained with their mothers faced prejudice in the towns in which they were reared.[120] Attitudes toward dark-skinned biracial children were especially harsh: writer Nogami Yaeko argued that because dark-skinned children had not previously existed in Japan, they attracted attention, were subject to discrimination, and would be happiest "sent back" to the States. Sawada Miki, founder of the Elizabeth Saunders home, went further in her book *Konketsuji no haha* (Mother of a Biracial Child), arguing that dark-skinned children should be isolated in an institution, ostensibly to protect them from discrimination.[121]

In 1952, a special issue of the women's magazine *Fujin Kōron* focused on the biracial children question, with letters between Pearl Buck and Nogami Yaeko, and articles by Sawada Miki and Furuya Yoshio of the Ministry of Health and Welfare. Buck praised biracial children, while Sawada claimed they were inferior to Japanese children. Furuya, who headed up a Ministry of Health and Welfare task force on biracial children, distinguished between two kinds of biracial children: mixed close race, such as Japanese/Chinese, and mixed far race, such as Japanese/African American. He also claimed that biracial children tended to cause problems.[122]

Not all Japanese voiced strong opinions against biracial children. A 1953 *Mainichi Shimbun* article explained that the children were happy playing together—it was the adults who were prejudiced.[123] A number of literary and film representations dramatized the discrimination dark-skinned biracial children faced. Sekigawa Hideo's 1956 *Konketsuji* (Mixed-Blood Children)—based on Takahashi Setsuko's 1952 novel—and Imai Tadashi's 1959 *Kiku to Isamu* (Kiku and Isamu) testify to the widespread public interest in the phenomenon. The author Ariyoshi Sawako's 1964 novel, *Hishoku* (Without Color), was the first to focus on a mother of biracial children.

But even though some accounts were sympathetic, reporting on biracial children suggested that prostitution was not a victimless crime. In a 1953 article for *Fujin Kōron*, social critic Kanzaki Kiyoshi used the issue to argue that most Japanese men and women thought bases were a negative influence, and maintained that an anti-prostitution law was the only solution.[124]

The widespread interest in biracial children presented an opportunity for opponents of regulated sex work, who could now argue that prostitution endangered children and—by implication—the nation's future. According to the popular press and surveys by the Ministry of Labor, mothers worried about how their children engaged in panpan play. They reported that they were imitating prostitution transactions; girls acted as panpan and boys as pimps or clients, trying to buy or sell their playmates.[125]

By 1953, most Japanese were aware of military-base sex workers, according to a survey by the Women and Minors Bureau. Sixty percent felt antipathy toward them, and only 21 percent sympathized with their situation.[126] Their aversion derived in large measure from protective feelings about Japanese children. When asked what harmful influences sex workers might cause, 33 percent cited children's education, and 21 percent pointed to other related factors, such as negative moral influences on young girls.[127] Such results suggest that many, if not most, Japanese men and women considered the primary ill effects of the military-base sex workers to be the creation of an undesirable moral climate or more specific harm to (full-blooded) Japanese children. In the early 1950s, after censorship lifted, intellectuals, Christian activists, and Diet members played to these concerns in making a case to Japanese women that anti-prostitution legislation was essential to their well-being and that of their families.

As we shall see, politicians agitating in the Diet for anti-prostitution legislation would concentrate on the issue of biracial children. They framed the discussion as part of the wider threat that prostitution and bases presented to mothers throughout Japan. Although they may have had genuine concern for the very real problems the children faced, they were also using them to appeal to mothers who wanted their schools and neighborhoods clear from sex workers and their children. In 1952, Ichikawa Fusae suggested a solution. In a special issue of the intellectual journal *Tōyō Keizai*, she wrote, "As for the *pan-pan* problem, let's cooperate with the U.S. armed forces and make as many of them marry as we can, and send them to the United States." The problem of biracial children had an equally easy solution for Ichikawa: "We will walk in hand with the occupying forces and the United States about the *konketsuji*. We will have the United States take charge of them. The children will probably also be happier that way."[128]

In fact, U.S. immigration law would prevent mass adoption. Although the McCarran-Walter Act lifted the blanket exclusion of Japanese, it still sharply limited immigration from Asia. The 1953 Refugee Relief Act was supposed to provide a means for orphans to enter the country. But by 1955, only fifteen biracial children had been sent to the United States under its provisions. As Yukiko Koshiro has argued, the way government and society in both the United States and Japan abandoned these children shows the "consensual toleration of shared racism under the veneer of U.S.-Japanese friendship."[129] Japanese welfare authorities, and many Japanese men and women, concluded that the "GI baby" problem was one best left to charity, even if that meant an orphanage like the Elizabeth Saunders home and a woman like Sawada Miki.[130]

In Australia, as in the United States, even orphanages seemed out of the question. A 1948 article in the *Sydney Morning Herald* defended BCOF men against charges that a recently established shelter was for their children. It was for orphans of the bomb, and no children were under age two.[131] Responding to an article on Japanese wives, reader Barbara Britten explained that the problem with such marriages was the children they produced: "the unfortunate children would be the real sufferers." Some Japanese writers agreed with Britten. Christian social activist Uemura Tamaki suggested that perhaps the children would be better off not being born at all. In a 1953 article in *Fujin Kōron*, "Towards a World Without Prostitutes," she quickly got to the heart of the matter:

> Obviously, the mixed Japanese, black, and white children born from the *pan-pan* are small now. But what will happen when the children of mothers born from normal (*jōshiki*) relationships look down on the fallen mothers? Must the children consciously suffer? Without understanding the reason why, the children are naturally dyed by their mothers' filth.[132]

When servicemen first landed in Japan, the pervasive fear was that they might act with the same brutality as Japan's own army when it took possession of conquered lands. But within a few years, the fear shifted to the future, as personified by the biracial offspring of Allied servicemen, and the sense that the Occupation might never end. Attitudes toward biracial children of sex workers—as well as the more specific provisions of the Eugenic Protection Law—show how Japanese society began to isolate sex workers because of the way some women consorted with the occupiers. A conservative vision of the Japanese nation, one that ostracized particular women and children, would shape the ostensibly progressive movement to end prostitution. But before such attitudes could assume the force of law and overcome the vested interests of the sex industry, it would require reconciling the different elements of the anti-prostitution critique—including reformers' concern to redeem "fallen women." In the meantime, a host of commentators would try to find order in the chaos of deregulated sex markets as they continued to evolve and grow.

THREE

When Flesh Glittered

Selling Sex in Sasebo and Tokyo

When in 1946 MacArthur directed the Japanese government to abrogate all laws that permitted licensed prostitution and nullified all contracts that committed women to the practice, it did not even begin to end the sale of sex. Nor did it free women from all forms of debt bondage. The action merely deregulated the market in sexual services. As masses of women moved to cities and military base areas in search of employment, many became sex workers, and many more people became dependent on the trade. Increasingly visible amid the rubble of shattered cities, sex workers loomed even larger in government surveys, literary accounts, and the mass media, all of which document growing animus and discrimination.[1] When Allied officials failed to control commercial sex, local and regional governments—including metropolitan Tokyo in 1949—passed some sixty local ordinances (*jōrei*) to prosecute sex workers.[2]

At the same time, sex workers, proprietors, and clients engaged in complex negotiations and compromises that were no less consequential. Deregulated sex markets shaped the built environment and economy of Japanese cities. But they also spurred many people to reimpose order: constructing elaborate taxonomies, cartographies, health regimes, and moral codes to give

The popular artist Rokuura Mitsuo drew panpan the way many Japanese imagined them: cold, unsympathetic, and predatory. But their business helped many others earn a livelihood, such as the vendor shown selling snacks.

meaning to this most conspicuous sign of their occupied status. Sex workers were active participants in this process, but their personal testimony shows how their lives defied categorization. When conservative members of the Diet finally agreed to intervene, it was merely the culmination of a long process involving every segment of Japanese society.

After 1945, Japanese politicians and journalists in the popular and elite press focused on what they portrayed as enormous growth in sex work. The data available are more uncertain and suggest that, although there may have been significant growth, it was not as dramatic as often portrayed. In 1925, it is estimated that one of every thirty-one young women between eighteen and twenty-nine worked in the commercial sex market.[3] Thirty years later, an even rougher estimate indicates that one in twenty-five women between the ages of fifteen and twenty-nine was so employed.[4] Although it is difficult to determine whether and to what extent the number of sex workers increased, the focus of their critics' ire is unmistakable. It was not prostitution per se, but the patronage of Allied servicemen.

After Allied forces landed in August 1945, no figures were more notorious than the panpan. They were the source of desire, debate, and derision. Dangling cigarettes or popping amphetamines, they were frequently shown extending arms languidly to invite servicemen away for a few hours. Ubiquitous photographs, newspaper articles, and literary descriptions proffer vivid images of heavily made-up women standing on street corners, posing on subway platforms, or lurking under bridges. Panpan wore the latest Western fashions, it was said, where ordinary women were still clad in wartime work trousers. Photographers and other visual artists most often portrayed the panpan looking away from the camera.[5] It may have been intended to protect their privacy, but the anonymity gave the impression that any Japanese woman could be a panpan.

Many Japanese today associate panpan solely with Allied servicemen, if only because the most common pictorial, literary, and filmic representations depict them in their company. But it is clear from the use of terms in the popular Japanese press such as *yōpan* ("Western *pan*"—in other words, panpan specifically for foreigners) and *wapan* (pan who took only Japanese clients) that panpan engaged in sexual commerce with both Japanese and foreign men. Among those who specialized in foreign clients, there were also *shiropan* (white pan) and *kuropan* (black pan). Sex workers were thus categorized according to their clientele, underscoring the overriding importance the choice of clients had for contemporary observers.

Panpan referred to any woman who sold sex on the street, and the new occupying American servicemen were simply their most conspicuous customers. One witty cartoon in the weekly *Sandee Mainichi* summed up the hypocrisy that panpan often elicited: upon seeing one with a serviceman, a Japanese onlooker remarks: "I can't stand seeing such fraternization," while pulling a package of Lucky Strikes from his pocket.[6]

Allied observers also commented about the omnipresence of the panpan: In Iwakuni, F. C. Bibby, an Australian Air Force Officer, complained that after he got out of his jeep, two Japanese women walked by and one poked what appeared to be an inflated white condom in his face, saying something in Japanese. Both girls laughed and proceeded on their way.[7] Another Australian, G. R. Gregg, noted that "it is impossible at any time, either day or night, to walk along the street without being accosted by prostitutes or being approached and mauled by elderly [women] or young men procuring for prostitutes."[8] The American popular and military press also displayed ambivalence about panpan culture. The *New York Times* pointed out that "geisha girls" were hardly real geisha, but rather were panpan, as the subtitle of one 1945 report emphasized: "She is not what Joe thinks she is."[9]

These observations point to something that made the panpan no less unsettling to Japanese men and women: even while embodying unwelcome changes in Japanese society, the panpan were also in a position to represent Japan to the occupiers. Early postwar journalists and others therefore devoted a great deal of time to analyzing the panpan, beginning with determining the origins of the term. Although the Japanese language continued to maintain a rich and precise vocabulary to refer to different kinds of sex workers, the coinage of a new word reflects the extent to which the panpan were viewed as a new cultural phenomenon, one specific to living in an occupied polity. And although the word's etymology remains ambiguous, a consensus early emerged on two points: that the word originated in the South Seas, meaning "sex worker" for the Imperial Japanese Navy, and that it was Japanese servicemen who brought the word home.[10]

Such a derivation is another example of how the Japanese interpreted the Occupation through their own imperial history. After all, the word reminded men of a time when they were the primary consumers of sex from colonial subjects in a foreign place. But ex-soldiers may have felt uncomfortable when it was Japanese women who sold their bodies to Allied servicemen.

In his examination of the anti-fraternization movement in the U.S. occupation zones of Germany and Austria, Alexander Biddiscombe points to the importance of wartime propaganda and the lack of immediate cultural inhibitions in the violent treatment of women who had relations with the occupying forces.[11] In wartime Japan, purity and purification were perennial themes in official propaganda. American and British values, such as materialism and money worship, were represented as lice that had to be purged from the Japanese body politic.[12] Given this, it is not surprising that there were similar instances of violent retribution by Japanese men against women who consorted with the occupiers.

In 1945, demobilized Japanese servicemen reportedly attacked women who consorted with GIs. One sailor, nineteen-year-old Risamatsu Masaharu, was taken to the provost marshal headquarters after allegedly striking a Japanese woman he found with an American soldier in Hibiya Park. Witnesses said he was one of nine sailors doing the same thing. In this case, the woman ended up in the hospital.[13] Japanese women who worked on bases faced similar insults and threats.[14] Men called house girls prostitutes and, in one incident in Tokushima, said they would beat them up once the Occupation was over.[15]

But such reports are not common, especially when compared to those of Germany. A more typical response among those Japanese angered by women who associated with GIs was to ostracize them. They were called "gaudy" and "disgusting."[16] Men and women avoided panpan in the street, gossiped with their neighbors, and made angry complaints to the Metropolitan Police. The toughness of sex workers and their sometimes tragic fates were perennial themes in postwar popular culture, especially in the "flesh culture" (*nikutai bunka*) literary movement of the late 1940s and in the films of directors such as Mizoguchi Kenji. Though censors would not permit the films to show GI clients, it is hard to imagine that they would not have been in the minds of filmgoers.

Threats and ostracism were not Japanese society's only reactions, and perhaps not the most significant ones. There was also a marked tendency to find order in the chaos panpan came to represent. The chaos, of course, was considerable. Panpan were among the 9 million men and women who struggled to find temporary shelter in the fall of 1945. The war years had wrought bewildering destruction. After Allied forces had finished their work, sixty-six of Japan's largest cities were devastated, with only 60 percent of built-up areas still standing. Almost a third of Japan's city dwellers were made homeless.[17]

In March 1946, one journalist tried to write about rocketing inflation and the extent of unemployment in a mainstream women's magazine, *Fujin Asahi*. The comments were stricken by a censor for "disturbing public tranquility."[18] The deleted comments give an idea of how bad things were. "With the upward swing of the price of commodities, it becomes absolutely foolish for a person to stick to natural, honest ways of living. This leads to degradation of morale; crimes increase. Day by day the social outlook becomes more threatening." The writer continued: "People engaged in acts that they might not have done otherwise. Criminals, robbers, and practitioners of *oihagi* [stealing clothing off the wearer by force] stalked the streets."[19] In the 1949 Kurosawa Akira police procedural *Stray Dog* (Nora inu), a pickpocket even manages to steal the gun from a homicide detective.

In Tokyo, where 65 percent of residences were destroyed, Ueno Park became a center for the poor and the homeless and the place best known for its high concentration of panpan.[20] Some even said that it was where panpan culture originated. Other people also flocked to the park to make their living—returnees from the former Japanese colonies, war victims, and widows and their children. They too sometimes became both buyers and sellers of sex.

The misery in Ueno Park, which was also the site of Japan's most important zoological garden, became fodder for articles in the popular press. Writers explained the social problem that plagued Japan with a style of "scientific" reportage full of charts, graphs, and maps. Their books and articles mapped out the park in laborious detail, providing diagrams that showed the hierarchies of panpan, what it meant to sell what kind of sexual services where, how much was charged, and even what sex workers wore. Elaborate studies by mainstream women's magazines as well as lowbrow weeklies explained for the concerned reader—as well as for the lascivious one—the postwar commercial sex market.

Kanzaki Kiyoshi, a social activist, reporter, and writer, quickly emerged as the leading "scholar" of the panpan in the postwar era. Kanzaki would soon skyrocket to national fame as an anti-prostitution crusader, writing countless articles in the popular press, publishing an astonishing number of books, and even testifying before the Diet. In 1949, Kanzaki published an article titled "The Zoo Without a Cage" in *Josei Kaizō*, a leftish women's monthly. In describing conditions in Ueno Park and its environs, Kanzaki conducted himself like a zoologist taxonomizing a lower form of life. He was clear early on to point out that these women were different creatures from the educated woman who read *Josei Kaizō*.[21]

A year earlier, investigators such as Ōtani Susumu had only found three classes of sex workers in the park.[22] Kanzaki claimed to have discovered a far more complex society, complete with status markers and intricate class relations among streetwalkers, describing the hierarchy based on the geography of the park grounds. He explained how clothes and accessories showed buyers "who was who." The lowest level of sex worker was called "*yama no pan*," or the panpan who lived in the heights of the hills in the park. In Kanzaki's hierarchy, the next group, *shita no pan*, the pan underneath, worked at ground level in the park, by the south exit of Asakusa Station. Kanzaki considered them more "modern," noting that "they wore garish western clothes, shoes, and some have kimono, but it is of low quality." Kanzaki also outlined another, less desirable category, which he called women of the three-mat room (*sanjō no heya*)—that is, rooms measuring just sixteen square feet.[23]

Kanzaki's anthropological style resembled the earlier work of Andō Kōsei and Kon Wajirō, who had published a best-selling explanatory map of cafés in the Ginza in 1931. Like Kanzaki, Andō and Kon had detailed what behaviors were considered erotic, and how clients met with workers (in this case, café waitresses).[24] But after the war, elaborate taxonomies like Kanzaki's regularly appeared in the popular press. Journalists writing for the intellectual weeklies also displayed a tendency to categorize sex work according to a moral system, rather than a merely taxonomic one. Thus, social critics such as Ōtani Susumu and Minami Hiroshi argued that toiling to save one's family from financial ruin was acceptable, but working out of personal choice was not. In his 1948 ethnography of Ueno Park, Ōtani tugged at readers' heartstrings by presenting the sad stories of women such as Katō Yoshie, who struggled to support her six younger siblings, and Okawa Katsuko, orphaned by the war and abandoned by her brother.[25] However, Ōtani sharply criticized those who worked for other reasons, and even those who spent money on their looks (not unreasonable, considering their trade). "While they say they cannot lead the lifestyle of war victims or returnees, they are devoted to extravagant color and to their appearance and spend huge sums on living expenses. Their ideas and lifestyles clearly have no balance."[26]

One year later, Minami Hiroshi, a professor at Japan Women's University, argued that, even worse, postwar sex workers articulated a social transformation from a prewar ideal of household responsibility to the postwar ethos based on personal choice. In a roundtable discussion published in the progressive journal *Kaizō*, Minami compared the sex workers of his own day unfavorably to their prewar counterparts, who had been loaned to proprietors by their parents "because of their families' poverty." As for postwar sex workers, Minami opined, "I think everyone chooses this kind of work out of their own way of thinking." Itō Akiko, a sex worker participating in the same panel, had a different perspective: "Some enter such society out of necessity, facing a dead-end; others enter out of vague curiosity; still others join in because of their extreme idolization of foreigners. . . . Also, there are those who are drawn into it, having been lured by someone."[27]

Surveys and other evidence suggest that the majority of sex workers in the early postwar period, like their counterparts at other points in the twentieth century, entered the profession for economic reasons.[28] A police report revealed that 60 percent of prostitutes said their motivation was the difficulty of making a living. Many had to pay for medical expenses for husbands or children or were war widows.[29] Sex workers tended to be relatively well paid. In 1949, a sex worker in Tokyo could make as much as 40,000 yen per month.[30] Such earnings would have been sufficient to support many others. The average citizen paid 54 yen per kilo for rice in 1949, and the price of admission to public baths averaged 91 yen.[31]

Six years later, the Women and Minors Bureau of the Ministry of Labor produced more detailed data. It carried out a large-scale survey, conducted by bureau employees, other ministry bureaucrats, and local officials. They assessed some fifty areas throughout Japan, including military bases. A total of 350 proprietors participated and some 600 sex workers took part in group interviews. The survey showed that most sex workers made between 20,000 yen and 30,000 yen per month. Few women saw monthly earnings of less than 5,000 yen or more than 70,000 yen. This income compared favorably with that of other female workers: a waitress could expect to earn on average 8,300 yen a month, a factory worker between 7,600 yen and 11,500 yen per month, and a textile worker 7,500 yen a month.[32]

The same survey, like many in the postwar period, distinguished between metropolitan and military-base sex workers. As we shall see, government officials sometimes made further distinctions, such as between "red-line" and "blue-line" sex workers in metropolitan areas, corresponding to the maps that demarcated the more and less officially recognized areas. In fact, even the division between military-base sex workers and the others was difficult to maintain. Servicemen patronized red-line establishments, and some military-base sex workers also had Japanese clients. Despite this overlap, there were significant and measurable differences between the two groups.

Sixty percent of military-base sex workers entered the industry for financial reasons, compared with 73 percent of other sex workers. The military-base women carried fewer debts: 48 percent owed money, compared with 82 percent of the other district sex workers. The same pattern held true for their visions of the future: 55 percent of the red-line district women preferred marriage, and 26 percent wanted to work for themselves. Among military-base sex workers, 25 percent preferred to marry, and 52 percent wished to work for themselves. Combined with other evidence, such statistics suggest that military-base sex workers demonstrated greater economic independence and entrepreneurialism.[33]

But reasons for becoming a sex worker were not always reducible to economic incentives. One 1952 survey in Kanagawa prefecture indicated that military-base sex workers serving Euro-American clients had complex motives. As with other local surveys of the period, it is not clear how it was conducted. But the author, Takahashi Fuyō of Kanagawa-Ken Women's Rehabilitation Center, reported that it included 1,352 women. Respondents cited a range of reasons for entering sex work: they were encouraged by friends and family, they had a previous relationship with a serviceman, they were deceived by a procurer, or they simply wanted to move to an urban area and saw no other means.[34]

Although the choice to become a sex worker depended on personal circumstances, financial or otherwise, the discussion in *Kaizō* suggests that even some knowledgeable critics were quick to make broad generalizations about the kind of women who were drawn into the trade. Panpan had become unpopular among another audience as well. For some Japanese males—particularly veterans, returnees from Japan's colonies, or the unemployed—condemning the panpan served as an oblique and effective way of criticizing the occupiers and expressing dissatisfaction with postwar life. Some Japanese men and women resented the panpan because of their (stereotypically) flashy clothes and bright makeup. A 1949 government survey revealed the extent of popular dislike for the panpan. A forty-six-year-old white-collar worker from Sendai said of the street girls, "They are gaudy and conspicuous, so they strike the eye," and a thirty-two-year-old farmer from Kumagaya City was harsher: "The panpan are disgusting."[35]

But most Japanese still found organized prostitution less objectionable. A forty-two-year-old housewife from Kawaguchi City said, "Organized prostitutes don't go out so much, they don't run loose in the streets. They are not as harmful as those panpan girls."[36] One Sendai farmer agreed: "There have been places like the Yoshiwara since a long time ago, so I don't particularly think they are bad." These comments reflected a difference of not only perception but also the actual behavior of regulated prostitutes compared to the panpan. Regulated prostitutes behaved in expected ways and mostly stayed in the former licensed quarters. In contrast, panpan could be found brashly strolling through the metropolis.

Groups from Iwakuni and Kanagawa prefecture were among the concerned citizens who complained to occupation authorities. A 1949 petition to BCOF from the Kawaraishi and Higashi-shioya-chō welfare committees pointed to the increase in house girls, interpreters, and prostitutes. Locals profited by renting their houses and rooms to occupation employees, and the petitioners complained about crowding in the streets. When troops visited, their cars would block the road and make it difficult for Japanese men and women to pass.[37]

In 1949, citizens' groups began to target more traditional establishments. In Kanagawa prefecture, they wrote to complain about four houses that were "hotbeds of venereal disease and are poisoning society." The letter testified that women were held in debt bondage, while masters live in "the lap of luxury," concluding: "it is a matter of grave significance to society that venereal diseases are prevalent through the aforementioned houses. These evil persons should be ostracized from society as early as possible, otherwise our society will never be bright and fair." An investigation revealed the complaints to be well founded. The owners were charged by SCAP with violation of Imperial Ordinance No. 9, which had abolished indentured contracts.[38]

The next year in Iwakuni, Yoshida Mitsuko, of the local branch of the Japan Christian Women's Moral Reformation Association, complained: "Recently we have been confronted with hundreds of misguided women who have found their way into Iwakuni encroaching upon the virginity of priceless youths. The ill effect suffered by the people in the town in general deserves as serious attention and there is little to be wondered but that it will entail a serious social question of no mean magnitude, if left alone."[39]

In an undated petition, most likely from that same month, the president of the Imazu Women's Association, Tanaka Mitsuye, complained about behavior in the public baths. She claimed that in violation of the rules, "questionable girls" had been using them to wash their linen. She also reported that a primary schoolteacher had seen a woman who clearly had VD, and the teacher was forced to go home without a bath. Children were also affected: a third-year primary school boy had been playing with a condom he found on the road, and others had engaged in panpan play.[40]

The press was also stepping up criticism: a 1950 article in the Hiroshima newspaper *Chugoku Shimbun* complained about the lack of attention to the panpan. "Public denunciation is getting intensified, much to the concern of local authorities on the question of street girls strutting down the street, not in the evening but in broad daylight with their painted lips and glaring neckerchiefs."[41]

The panpan visually transgressed the borders of what was acceptable, intruding into daily life where organized sex workers had not. In response, social critics sought to discern order in panpan culture and impose it where necessary. They argued that the panpan differed because their work was performed not out of filial duty but out of female choice. But these critiques were already expanding to the former licensed districts and the people who worked there.

After MacArthur's 1946 decree abolishing licensed prostitution, authorities struggled to maintain order with a series of new laws and regulations. Proprietors would have to register not as providers of sexual services but under new, more ambiguous classifications. Particularly in the Yoshiwara district, trade associations took advantage of public-health reforms to boast that their employees were disease-free. But even though proprietors underwent a complete redistricting and a transformation of their legal status, their greatest problem was from the panpan. Though proprietors worked with the police and legislators—and regularly bribed them—their struggle to keep sex work legal would become a losing battle.

In contrast to the self-employed panpan, the delivery of sexual services in brothels depended on several categories of workers, including recruiting agents (*keian*), touts (*ponbiki*), and rickshaw pullers. The agents procured sex workers, sometimes from the farthest and poorest reaches of the Japanese archipelago. Touts encouraged clients to visit sex-work establishments, and rickshaw pullers transported them there. All of these workers received a cut of the earnings, but proprietors relied most heavily on recruiting agents.

Recruiting agents had been essential to the market's functioning since at least the end of the nineteenth century. The work remained lucrative: one journalist concluded that it was the most profitable job in the commercial sex market.[42] Recruiting agents provided advance money to parents or guardians for women to enter multiyear contracts, most commonly with proprietors. Even though MacArthur's 1946 decree abolished indenture contracts, women could still be bound by debt contracts. According to a 1955 survey by the Women and Minors Bureau of the Ministry of Labor, a majority of sex workers had some sort of contract. They typically agreed to serve for a maximum term and could not stop working any sooner unless they repaid the principal.[43]

After the war, established proprietors had to rebuild more than just their recruiting networks. The firebombing that devastated Tokyo dispropor-

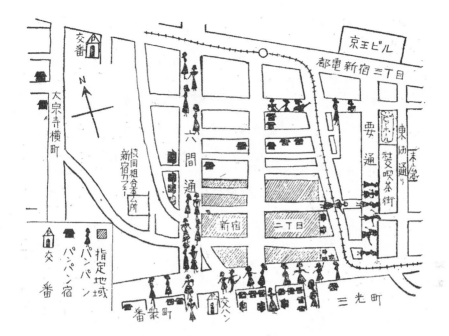

In the early postwar period, panpan expanded sex work outside former
licensed districts, indicated in the shaded area at the center of this 1948
map of Shinjuku by journalist Kanzaki Kiyoshi. New houses of prostitution, marked in black, were just across the street from police boxes,
indicated with a "P," at the top left and bottom center. Reprinted from
Kanzaki, *Musume o uru machi*, courtesy of Kanzaki Hiroshi

tionately affected metropolitan sex work districts such as Yoshiwara and
Tamanoi. In 1945, only an estimated fifty out of 3,000 sex workers were left
in the few remaining houses in Yoshiwara.[44] Japanese authorities impro-
vised a set of regulations to allow prostitution to continue. In Tokyo, beginning in 1946, Metropolitan Police Bureau guidelines created "special
eating and drinking shops" (*tokushu inshokuten*) limited to the former licensed districts, requiring proprietors to set aside one room as a café. Some
questioned why they needed even the trappings—tables, chairs, and the
like—since they would be conducting business as usual.[45] In their maps,
the police drew borders around these areas with red lines (*akasen*). But they
also demarcated other areas of Tokyo that had a significant population of
sex workers with blue lines (*aosen*).[46] In this way, even the Tokyo Metropolitan

Police recognized that their regulations could not contain the actual extent of sex work.

The "special eating and drinking shops" were just the first in a series of efforts by authorities to regulate the entertainment industry in a way that accommodated sex-work businesses without legally recognizing them. The 1947 Adult Entertainment Law (Fūzoku Eigyō Torishimari Hō), the Food Hygiene Law (Shokuhin Eisei Hō) passed that same year, and the 1948 Venereal Disease Prevention Law (Seibyō Yobō Hō), as well as many local regulations together created an ambiguous and transitory regulatory environment.

Trade associations would play an important role in responding to the new regulations and combating the growing competition outside red-line districts. They worked both on a local level and under a national umbrella group, the National Council on Venereal Disease Prevention (Zenkoku Seibyō Yobō Jichikai), which included 16,000 proprietors. At the top of the organization was Suzuki Akira, the chief director of the Yoshiwara Café and Teahouse Cooperative (Yoshiwara Kafe Kissa Kyōdōkumiai), and himself a café owner from Tokyo's Asakusa neighborhood. Although it included new businesses in base areas, the group was dominated by established proprietors.[47]

The police preferred that proprietors work together to create one big association and thus make it easier to regulate their activities and reduce the panpan problem. Sometimes police even allowed trade associations to open more establishments, such as the 1949 case of Shinkōkai and the first postwar association in the area, the Hanazonokai.[48] Similarly, in 1951, Japanese officials ignored protests from a town commissioner in charge of child guidance and allowed the reconstruction of a hotel destroyed by fire where sex workers catered to GIs.[49]

In 1949, the provost court system—the U.S. military court that tried Japanese—was curtailed, leaving it to the Japanese to prosecute sex workers. But the power imbalance between MPs and Japanese police produced confusion. SCAP's legal authorities continued to insist on proper police procedure and "human rights," though in practice many MPs were indifferent.[50] The whole Japanese criminal justice system, on the other hand, depended on extracting confessions.

A September 1949 conference of both U.S. and Japanese officials aimed at a clearer code of conduct for enforcing Tokyo's new prostitution ordinance. MPs would have the right to enter a Japanese house if they believed it was a brothel and off-limits. They could ask the Japanese police to accompany them, but not to enter or make any arrests without a search warrant. The Japanese could gather information to obtain such a warrant and then enter and arrest any woman engaged in prostitution. With reasonable evidence of habitual prostitution, they could examine her for VD. In Tokyo—and other jurisdictions with applicable regulations—police could also question suspects and apprehend those found to be engaging in prostitution.[51] If sex workers were found to be infected with VD, they would be taken to the public procurator's office—the Japanese equivalent of a public prosecutor. If no disease was found, then they would be charged with violating Tokyo's prostitution ordinance.[52]

Local police found the new directives confusing. The National Rural Police complained that they had too few patrolmen available in the area around Camp Drake, near Tokyo, and that MPs were unable to help. The local police chief was unsure of what actions to take, besides arresting sex workers for loitering. "The situation is out of hand and is rapidly becoming worse," one official reported. "Venereal Disease is skyrocketing and the Commanding Officer of the hospital had earnestly requested the Provost Marshal to control the G.I.s in a better manner."[53] Sex workers knew how to evade the police: they arrived by train from Tokyo at about 4:00 p.m., dressed in Japanese-style clothes and sandals, so as not to stick out, and changed into Western-style clothes only when they reached the street. And it was not only the women who patrolled and solicited in front of the base. Rickshaw pullers came from Tokyo and hung out at the main gate. GIs snuck out through rice paddies after hours, often with stolen goods, which they exchanged for a night with a sex worker.[54]

In 1950, the chief of the Public Peace Section of the Metropolitan Police clarified procedure in a step-by-step action plan. First, police were to determine whether the prostitute was "a conspicuous suspect of habitual crime." If so, then the officer was to bring her to VD officials and to relevant authorities. Second, police were to investigate and inspect houses of prostitution, and conduct a search after getting a warrant. If they found a flagrant offense, then the suspect could be arrested; if not, she could still be examined. Third, when some were found to be infected, a metropolitan VD official could also enter. Fourth, if a member of occupation forces were found, he would be arrested.[55]

Perhaps more important than the formal regulations was the attitude of the police who enforced them. They criticized sex workers as "nothing more than a sort of women who hate to make themselves busy about any honest calling, fond of leading an easy, dissolute life, wanting to make easy money. They are just the women belonging to the so-called 'pastwar school' [sic]."[56]

If panpan were emblematic of the postwar era, contemporary fiction and film show how at least some people still believed they were victims of circumstances. Kurosawa Akira's classic police drama, *Stray Dog*, depicts how police themselves struggled to find their place in this new era. In one scene, the older detective takes his young protégé into his confidence, explaining that he still cannot entirely understand—or even pronounce—the *"après guerre."* But he mentors the younger man and helps him pursue the murderous gangster who stole his pistol. For most of the film, it is portrayed as a Manichaean struggle. The gangster's girlfriend, brutal and heartless, finally breaks down and explains that she has become depraved because of suffering degradation at the hands of men. In the climactic scene, the young detective, wearing an immaculate white suit, must get down in the mud to disarm his nemesis.

This more complicated view of the moral ambiguity of the postwar period and the possibility of reform is also in evidence in one of the rare examples of sex workers organizing in their own defense. Most such organizations were fronts for proprietors, but the Hakuchō-kai (White Swans) claimed to be an organization of and for streetwalkers around Tokyo and Yurakuchō stations. By 1950, it claimed six hundred card-carrying members and garnered press coverage, at the same time distributing pamphlets asking for the public's sympathy. One such pamphlet explained that the women were "lost sheep" who were born from the "social evils produced by the postwar confusion." Deprived by the war of parents, brothers, and husbands, often homeless and hungry, they insisted that selling their bodies was their only choice. In the five years since the war had ended, "we were chased by the police," the pamphlet recalled, "put into the prison, and how often did we pledge to ourselves to go into a new life, looking at the moon through the bars of the jail weeping and thinking of our past happy days when we were all innocent girls?"[57]

Things were certainly no better for those working in established brothels. Women were still subject to exploitative debt contracts, poor working conditions, and police corruption. Some appealed to occupation authorities. In October 1946, Yoshida Sumiko wrote asking that they "make it possible for hundreds of women to go home freely to their fathers and mothers as soon as possible. We can do nothing because the employer holds the notes for our debt."[58] In Tokyo, Sakamoto Mitsuko wrote directly to General MacArthur in 1947 about proprietor Ichikawa Chūkichi's establishment, Shojikirō. "The policemen come and the owner treats them with feasts but he does not protect us women even once. With the power of the Allied forces, call on each woman and ask them to find out the evil owner's way of life."[59]

Sakamoto described her house as run in "the old manner." She likely meant a strong proprietor who used debt contracts to control his workers. In Nagoya, Tanaka Seiko also wrote to SCAP authorities to protest her working conditions. She described a situation that was in many ways typical of the prewar system, in that she incurred debt with her employer for meals that she ate at the house. Even worse, the lack of condoms at her establishment led Tanaka to contract VD, and she was forced to continue working despite her condition.[60]

For female sex workers in proprietor-type houses, tight relationships among recruiting agents, proprietors, presidents of street associations, and the police made it difficult to leave despite MacArthur's proclamation abrogating indenture contracts. Sex workers who wrote to him cannot be assumed to have been representative. But the 1955 survey conducted by the Women and Minors Bureau suggests they were not atypical, providing rare examples of sex workers telling their own stories, albeit mediated by the officials who spoke with them.[61]

One participant, "A-ko," twenty-five years old, was married and the mother of a one-year-old. Although she had graduated from Girls' Higher Normal School and was the daughter of shopkeepers, A-ko had fallen on hard times. Together with her husband she had been drawn into a ring of small-time crooks. At the time of the survey, he was serving a term in prison. Meanwhile, A-ko had become a serving maid at a hot springs resort, earning a paltry salary of 3,000 yen ($8.33) per month. A-ko, crying, insisted that "if my husband's salary had been paid, I wouldn't have done such work. When my husband is released from prison, if he doesn't understand, we will get divorced and I will go on living on my own."

Although A-ko came from a lower-middle-class background, thirty-year-old "C-ko" had lived a life of extreme poverty, so poor that she could attend school only as a nursemaid to the teacher's children. A divorcee with two children of her own, she earned a pittance as an employee of the local police station. She began to moonlight at a "special drinking place" at night. The police administration, unsurprisingly, found her part-time job problematic, so C-ko had to quit. After working at a noodle shop, she met and married a day laborer, who then went to Hokkaido for work. She reentered the sex market when, sitting near "K" station, someone solicited her. When her husband found out, he left her. For such women, facing severe hardship, sex work was the least-bad option. But it was something they could begin or end of their own volition, unlike those working off debt contracts in brothels.

When the Women and Minors Bureau first started this survey, it intended to distinguish between two types of sex workers: those who worked within red-line or blue-line districts.[62] The similarities in their social origins and the conditions in which they lived made it impossible to maintain this distinction. The practices denoted by "blue-line" appeared with great frequency in "red-line" districts, and vice versa.[63] Nevertheless, "blue-line" and "red-line" became buzzwords for journalists, writers, and film directors. "Red-line" most often evoked the former licensed quarters, while "blue-line" stood for the supposedly new bars and restaurants. The very frequency with which people persisted in their attempts to map the entertainment districts underscores the demand for some system that could represent order in a radically changed world.

If any licensed quarter might have maintained its distinctive character, it would have been the Yoshiwara, the most famous amusement quarter, glamorous, if notorious, since the beginning of the seventeenth century. After 1945, the quarter and the sex workers employed there faced unprecedented challenges: the destruction of the wartime air raids, the discontinuation of licensed sex work, and the ongoing Occupation. But the Venereal Disease Law of 1948, which required health inspections and reporting of statistics, gave proprietors and workers of the Yoshiwara the means to put forward a healthy and hygienic front in their competition with panpan. Their health union, called the New Yoshiwara Women's Health Preservation Association (Shin-Yoshiwara Joshi Hoken Kumiai), conducted weekly VD inspections. The union hierarchy wanted to show that the elite sex workers of the Yoshiwara were the healthiest in Tokyo, and thus shield them from restrictive legislation. Yet the reliability of their inspections was questionable, since sex workers were frequently examined at union headquarters, rather than at independent medical establishments. Contemporary critics viewed the unions as manipulated by proprietors.[64]

The association's newspaper, *Fujin Shinpū*, shows that the health regime was hardly perfect.[65] The newspaper showcased a range of products and services. But the most prominent spots were by far the ones addressing VD.

The major advertisers were pharmaceutical companies, many of which are today best known for name-brand food products. Morinaga, Meiji, and Sankyō all maintained that their brand of penicillin was the best. Meiji ran the most thorough campaign, and a careful reader could find its advertisements in almost every issue. Perhaps most compelling of all was Meiji's 1954 spot: a drawing of a medicine bottle labeled "Kills. Penicillin. Meiji," surrounded by five pills. Antibiotics cured everything, or so marketing implied. The early appearance of advertisements focusing on treating VD indicates that companies believed they had a good market among sex workers. The frequency and persistence of the spots suggests that they were right.

Besides the advertisements, articles in the same newspaper showed an emphasis on preventing VD within the association itself, which, after all, was officially meant to preserve health. Although some proprietors may have used the threat of VD as a scrim behind which to keep sex work legal, disease unquestionably was a business risk. For sex workers, it was a serious economic risk as well as a threat to their lives. The association sought to burnish the reputation of the Yoshiwara with its slogan "A Happy Yoshiwara Is a Healthy One!"

Accordingly, in December 1953, the newspaper featured a roundtable discussion with seven sex workers who had received "superior" medical examination results the previous month. "T-ko," "H-ko," and "K-ko" were among those who shared their preventive methods. Although T-ko used condoms, her co-worker H-ko used both condoms and the spermicide *shikuro*. K-ko was among the many who used only "cleansing." Yet, as the chair pointed out, cleansing could make things worse if proper methods were not followed. "It is important to make certain not to push the bacteria further 'inside' by trying to reach 'inside.'" The chair further instructed, "I want you to practice prevention and take medical examinations every day, and if you suspect anything, I hope you have penicillin shots immediately."[66]

Although it appeared to be an open discussion from its roundtable format, the association was in fact using prescriptive educational methods to teach effective practice for preventing VD. However, Yoshiwara sex workers did not achieve any particular success. In 1953, their diagnosed-infection case rate for gonorrhea, soft chancre—a bacterial infection that caused painful lesions—and "those in danger of infection" compared unfavorably to Shinjuku, the next most populous district, and exactly matched Tokyo's average for tested union members.[67]

Accounts in the mass media also suggest that individual sex workers might not have been so savvy about VD prevention techniques. A 1950 article in a popular magazine recounts some of the practices the reporter found circulating in the neighborhood. Sex workers, he wrote, were so afraid of failing the weekly union-sponsored tests that they first visited a private clinic in a nearby neighborhood. Yoshiwara Hospital—where infected women were quarantined—had such an awful reputation that fabulous stories circulated about folk cures and means of escape. The reporter described women who would trim their hair to get better—one was said to have been cured after cutting off all her locks. Others said urinating in a secret place in the hospital could make VD go away. Those employing this method were advised that a spot on the second floor in front of the director's office held particular potency.[68]

Hospitals were widely perceived as inadequate or even harmful. But for those forcibly interned, cost was the major concern beginning with their lost wages. By December 1948, SCAP policy was that hospitals should accept patients without reference to ability to pay but charge them for treatment. At most, the government would provide half of the payment.[69] In June 1949, Christian activist Kimiji Satō complained that women who could not pay their bills at Toyotama and Yoshiwara hospitals were not allowed to leave.[70] Later, state and prefectural authorities also paid a portion. A report on the treatment of VD in the Kure hospital revealed that in 80 percent of the cases, the cost of the treatment was split between the state and prefectural governments. In the remaining 20 percent of cases, patients paid it on their own.[71]

In attempting to stave off competition and cover the costs of doing business, proprietors and sex workers in the red-line districts thus struggled to adapt to deregulation. By conducting educational campaigns, buying drugs, and undergoing VD inspections, elite sex workers fought hard to redefine themselves as hygienic and safe. But to many observers, these responses did little to stem disorder and disorganization, and the former licensed districts came to be seen as part of a larger problem. In February 1948, one *Seikai Jiipu* reporter wrote, "These places of publicly recognized, unlicensed prostitution are an even more serious problem than that of the many streetwalkers in defeated Japan."[72]

Outside Tokyo, deregulation affected more than the red-line districts. Wherever allied servicemen were stationed, sex workers soon followed. By focusing on one particularly important base area, Sasebo, we can observe how U.S. military forces helped remake local economies, and how local leaders tried to create a new regulatory framework.

Sasebo was once a small fishing village but became an imperial naval base in 1883, largely because of its natural harbor. It would become the main staging area for U.S. and United Nations forces during the Korean War. By that point, neon lights flashed names of new businesses along Paradise Street, such as Silver Dollar and the Top Hat Bar.[73] Behind the newly built entertainment arcade stood older, rickety houses, refurnished to welcome clients into environments that would evoke America. Rooms in base districts like Sasebo's typically featured beds instead of futons, side tables, and radios arranged on shelves.[74] It was not just sex workers and proprietors who depended on this business, but also hairdressers, seamstresses, letter writers, and rickshaw pullers.

Sasebo once boasted two flourishing entertainment quarters, but both were destroyed by fires from an American air raid in May 1945. The postwar transformation began as early as New Year's Day 1946, when the *Nagasaki Shimbun* advertised the opening of the Rose Land Dance Hall. "Under great support from the occupying army," the management sought to hire two hundred applicants. "Dance and English class, free place to live, set up an appointment to discuss the details! Interview any time every day!"[75] Such advertisements indicate the extent to which such "entertainment" was initially tolerated, though it was shrouded in euphemism.

The housing market in the district surrounding the shipyards and base was soon filled with sex workers. Some women rented rooms monthly (*kashiseki*), and others found more permanent dwellings. The area was so busy and the money so good that women streamed in from rural districts. Sasebo, like other military-base towns, was struggling to reckon with what was perhaps the most important and controversial development in the commercial sex markets in the first postwar decade: the mass movement of sex workers to the vicinity of Allied military bases.[76]

The war that would rage up and down the Korean peninsula, just 110 miles from Sasebo, accelerated the trend. Approximately 15,000 to 20,000 American servicemen would be based there, with many more coming ashore from the 100 warships and freighters that were typically in port every day. Sasebo's population went from 140,000 at the end of World War II to 220,000 in 1950. Public safety records show that no fewer than 3,200 of them were *panpan* who catered to the occupying forces. Of that number, 1,000 were *yami no onna* (women without a residence), and 2,200 worked

The naval base of Sasebo boomed during the Korean War, as Japanese entrepreneurs catered to Allied servicemen. In some cases, they were accompanied by their families, but most patronized the bars and brothels on Paradise Street. Courtesy of Kokusho Kankōkai

in Japanese-style rented rooms (*kashi zashiki*).[77] SCAP offered much higher estimates, judging that as many as 10,000 sex workers were in the area.[78]

The confluence of sex workers and servicemen soon led to the spread of infection. According to one Sasebo government report from 1950, 34 percent of 2,895 verified sex workers had VD.[79] By this point, VD also affected one-quarter of servicemen in the area, according to a U.S. military survey.[80] Base commanders told city officials that until the prostitution problem was "cleaned up," the men would be kept in camp and off the streets.[81] Government authorities and private citizens quickly combined forces to respond. On the very day that base commanders declared the city off-limits to the military, a wide range of groups formed a civilian organization called the Sasebo Public Morals Purification Committee (Fūki Shukusei Iinkai), which sought to change the atmosphere through shaming offenders. The committee's three hundred executive members identified themselves by wearing armbands.[82]

Despite its "pure" name, it seems that the committee was more concerned with protecting commerce than promoting chastity. Mayor Tanaka Shōsuke explained its goals in a 1951 report to the chief of the Kyushu Coordination Liaison: "contributing to the economic development of Sasebo City" and "mak[ing] a sound recreation place of Sasebo City for the Occupation Forces."[83] The committee included representatives from the hotel association, the souvenir association, the rickshaw association, and the association for entertainment businesses, all of which would have profited from the business of sex workers if they did not actually depend on it. Maki Ken'ichi, head of the Sasebo Chamber of Commerce, and Asai Gihei, head of the Sasebo Stores Association, served as chair and vice chair.

The threat of losing all servicemen's business was enough to make the committee take rapid and efficient action. In early December, Mayor Tanaka Shōsuke signed into law an ordinance aimed at controlling prostitution. It was promulgated three weeks later after revisions ordered by occupation officials.[84] While reporting their progress to the occupation command, the committee also posted signs to encourage sex workers to act more discreetly, such as this "Appeal to all young girls!!"

To you young girls who work in Sasebo during the night! You are the people of a defeated country, but you are also the Japanese women who once had pride in "your quiet manners." STOP BEHAVING INDECENTLY in the street. Even the Americans are disgusted with you. . . . Street-girls [*yoru no onna*] in New York, London and Paris are more graceful and prudent in their manners than you are. Eliminate this night view of Sasebo which we cannot bear to look at and which can never be seen in any other part of the world, by reflecting upon your personal conduct. For the sake of the future of Sasebo! For the sake of the education of the next generation of the nation! STOP CLINGING TO FOREIGNERS ON THE STREET! For the glory of Japan! For the prosperity of Sasebo![85]

Placing equal stress on "personal conduct," "the glory of Japan," and "the prosperity of Sasebo," the Sasebo Public Moral Purification Committee made its appeal in words that were redolent of wartime rhetoric. Unlike wartime propagandists, however, Western mores were now held up as an example to emulate.

If the intention was to eliminate or even limit the sex markets in Sasebo, no evidence exists that it was effective. Even after the anti-solicitation ordinance was on the books, sex work was still very evident in the port city.[86] In 1952, journalist Kanai San'kichi visited Sasebo and asked: Is Sasebo a colony?[87] He was astonished at the way the city had come to depend on the military base: fluctuations in troop numbers in connection with the Korean War directly affected a number of businesses. From June 1950 to June 1951, rickshaw businesses increased from 20 to 850, taxis from one to seven, cabarets from three to seven, and beer halls from zero to seventeen.[88] From 1951 to 1952 (when many had shipped off to Korea), rickshaw pullers, taxi drivers, and souvenir sellers all reported less income, while the demand for beer had fallen 25 percent.[89]

Sasebo's economy rose and fell depending on the demands of American servicemen, and sex workers played a pivotal role. They kept large segments of local society employed by buying goods and services. They needed seamstresses to sew their clothes, letter writers to pen notes to servicemen, and bankers to safeguard their money. Other residents benefited indirectly. Taxi drivers and rickshaw pullers transported clients, souvenir salesmen sold trinkets to foreign men, and food and drink companies supplied proprietors. It was not, therefore, only servicemen who supported military-base economies, even if they were the catalyst.

But was everyone better off under the new economic order? Activists argued that their dependence on sex work was demoralizing, and in Sasebo as elsewhere, they focused on children. Tsuruta Heijirō, a teacher from Kasuga elementary school, wrote an essay about the economic impact of panpan on Sasebo in the 1953 volume *Kichi Nihon*, an attempt to look critically at the military bases by using children's voices.[90] The book was not an unbiased view, collected as it was by Inomata Kōzō, Kimura Kihachirō, and Shimizu Kitarō, all Socialists and peace activists. Yet these testimonies are a valuable record of children's sense of living under occupation after the San Francisco Treaty supposedly restored Japanese sovereignty. Even if they were writing to please their teachers, they articulated what their parents may have only whispered.

K (female) wrote: "What does a person from outside the city think when they see our situation? . . . It might be true that these foreigners are bringing money to Sasebo, but it doesn't mean it is good. . . . If there weren't foreigners, there would be no *yoru no onna* [women of the night] or flower-sellers and the world would be peaceful."[91] Others detailed the way prostitution blighted the city and its sense of civic pride. Chiaki Tasaki, a third-year student at Sasebo Asahi Junior High School, wrote:

It has been 7 years since the war ended and Japan has gradually taken steps to become a member of the world community. With this in mind, I go to school everyday, a proud young Japanese girl. But what about the women around me? The town is different than before—it's gotten flashy. There are people from different countries [GIs] on top of them and young women wearing garish clothes and thick makeup walking and laughing out loud. I see the women walking and it's like a dream. I truly don't want to see their disreputable houses located on my way to school. Is this punishment for losing the war? I always want to be pure and beautiful. Is this just a transient sentiment of a young girl?[92]

For the young observer, the sex workers were a manifestation of defeat and a seemingly never-ending occupation. She made explicit what for many adults was unspoken. With panpan on their streets, Japanese men, women, and children were forced to reckon with a subject many had not even considered before. As women selling sex moved into residential neighborhoods and local economies became dependent on their business, they became part of the fabric of communities. Their houses were sometimes located near schools, and biracial children were visible in the streets—streets that were now blighted with neon lights and blaring music.

It was only later, after the end of censorship, that films like Imamura Shōhei's 1961 *Pigs and Battleships* (Buta to Gunkan) could directly confront the world of American sailors, sex workers, and gangsters. They inhabit a sex-work district that cannot contain the decay, and even putrefaction, that comes from the trade, but does cover up scenes of drunken rape. The gangsters seem to care only about a scheme to raise pigs and otherwise profit from the U.S. base at Yokosuka. But by the end of the film, Japanese men are shown wallowing over the food scraps discarded by overfed servicemen.

Responding to this sense that sex work was corrupting the nation and endangering its future, journalists and activists sought to re-regulate prostitution through taxonomies, maps, moral codes, and local ordinances. Female politicians would use the burgeoning dissatisfaction to mobilize sentiment to abolish legal sex work. The first national anti-prostitution law would mark the culmination of a long process of marginalizing sex workers precisely *because* they had come to occupy such a central role in postwar society— a society that seemed to be populated by pigs and organized around battleships.

FOUR

Legislating Women

The Push for a Prostitution Prevention Law

In 1956, Socialist Fujiwara Michiko, a licensed nurse and a Christian, stood before the Upper House of the Diet and declared that debate was coming to a close on a measure that would, according to Fujiwara, "end the many centuries–long tragic history of Japanese women." After eighty-five years of struggle against prostitution, "their dearest wishes are finally about to see the light of day."[1] But unlike Fujiwara and her supporters, the state's intention was not to eradicate prostitution. Instead the Prostitution Prevention Law aimed to prevent a climate of prostitution, "in view of the fact that it harms human dignity, is against sexual morality, and disturbs virtuous social manners and customs."[2] But for those opposed to prostitution, any legislation was better than none. Japan's first national anti-prostitution law passed the Diet in 1956.

The fight to pass a national law against prostitution reveals both the potential and the disappointing reality of female politicians' power in the early postwar period. The American-written Japanese constitution granted women new freedoms, including the right to vote and hold office.[3] In April 1946, 67 percent of eligible women went to the polls, electing 39 women out of 466 members in the Lower House of the Diet.[4] Yet this power had its limits: to begin with, prostitution was one of the few issues identified by the press and by other politicians as a "women's issue," as if men had nothing to do with it. Even so, when women's coalitions put forth numerous anti-prostitution bills in the Diet, they all failed. It was only when they compromised with more conservative opponents—who had their own agendas—that they began to make headway.[5]

The road to the legal abolition of prostitution began in the late nineteenth century. A new understanding developed, influenced by contemporary European attitudes that placed prostitutes beyond the bounds of normal society. Rather than recognize how many moved in and out of the trade, Japanese activists—and their Euro-American allies—saw sex workers as fallen women who were awaiting salvation. They also began to fear VD as a moral failing and a social pathology, one that threatened the creation of a healthy nation.

Legislation could be enacted more easily on a local level than a national one. Indeed, the very same prefectures that passed postwar legislation often had long traditions of anti-prostitution activism. The prewar local abolitionist movement had its most famous success in Gunma prefecture, where Christian activists including Yuasa Jirō fought prostitution by submitting petitions to the prefectural assembly. Although abolitionists passed an ordinance abolishing the licensing of prostitution in 1889, the governor postponed its adoption, and it was not enacted until 1891.[6]

Gunma became the center for the Prostitution Abolition League, but sex work continued in the prefecture. The governor allowed the building of six new red-light areas in 1898. He was forced to leave office in 1910 only after corruption came to light. The new governor stated his opposition to licensed prostitution, but Gunma's legislation had little impact.[7] Women were not actually liberated from indentured prostitution; instead most continued to work in the sex industry or worked as licensed prostitutes (*shōgi*) in other prefectures.[8] All along, the prefecture continued to tax prostitution businesses and conduct VD inspections.[9]

Gunma activists formed the core of a national movement. If Japanese regulation of prostitution was based on European models, these abolitionists were inspired by movements in the United States and Great Britain. Many of the leaders in the postwar effort, including Kubushiro Ochimi, Ichikawa Fusae, and Katō Shizue, had spent formative years in the United States. Influenced by European and American Christian social abolitionist movements, activists viewed prostitution as immoral, though they focused on prostitutes—rather than clients—as the problem. They also criticized brothel owners as well as a government that seemed more interested in collecting taxes than ensuring the common welfare. Together they established several volunteer groups, including the Women's Christian Temperance Union (WCTU) in 1886, the National Prostitution Abolition League in 1890, and the Salvation Army in 1895.

The WCTU was particularly concerned about women who went abroad to become sex workers. Beginning in 1890, annual petitions emphasized that the international trade sullied the reputation of both Japan and Japanese womanhood. WCTU leaders worried that foreigners could not distinguish between respectable churchwomen and sex workers, and would identify Japan with prostitution. Over time, the WCTU would expand its activities beyond petitions and public meetings to include lectures on chastity at factories, stores, and schools, at the same time forming alliances with other groups and sending fact-finding missions abroad.[10]

The Salvation Army focused on freeing licensed women by criticizing brothel owners and their use of debt contracts. A later Salvation Army report admitted that not all had been sold into bondage—financial incentives had tempted some to enter the trade. But the money did not amount to much after brothel owners deducted their share. For example, an advance payment by proprietors to sex workers of 500 yen would be reduced to 300 yen, not including deductions for room and board.[11]

An American missionary, Ulysses Grant Murphy, brought a series of cases to court that challenged existing contracts that bound sex workers to proprietors.[12] In 1900, the Supreme Court (Daishin'in) ruled that contracts were not consonant with the 1898 Civil Code, and recognized the right of free cessation (*jiyū haigyō*) in the new Rules Regulating Licensed Prostitution. Although contracts binding women to proprietors were illegal, debt contracts were not. As a result of the 1900 Rules—later confirmed by a Home Ministry Ordinance in 1908—even women with debts could seek release from the profession at a police station. In practice, opposition from proprietors meant that police required "consultation," meaning that proprietors had to approve the release. In practice, women found it very difficult to leave.[13]

The Salvation Army persisted in its work on behalf of these women. Female officers visited police courts, prisons, public procurators' offices, and railway stations, while also establishing rescue homes. Salvationists also demonstrated in the licensed quarters. In 1900, a dozen entered the Yoshiwara, blowing bugles and beating drums, and preached about the shame and degradation of the licensed system. A number were wounded by rioters. When the perpetrators were arrested, one Salvationist leader refused to press charges, saying he wanted to bless them, not curse them.[14] His action paid off with impressive media coverage, and activists were encouraged to continue with these tactics. In 1923, after the Great Kantō earthquake, the Yoshiwara was nearly destroyed by fire. As far away as North America, the press reported efforts by the Purity Society (Kakusei-kai) to prevent its rebuilding.[15]

Founded in 1911, the Purity Society joined forces with the WCTU between the mid-1920s and 1935 to become the Federation for Abolishing Licensed Prostitution. In coordination with local branches, the society organized groups in forty-one prefectures, and its efforts resulted in multiple proposals in prefectural assemblies.[16] By the early 1940s, activists from the WCTU and the Purity Society had contributed to passing fifteen such bans.[17]

But although abolitionists received significant press attention, it made little difference in the lives of most sex workers. By 1930, the Salvation Army had freed a total of 7,000 women.[18] That amounted to only about 300 women a year among the more than 50,000 licensed sex workers in 1929.[19] And shelters such as the House of Light (Hikari no Ie) had little success convincing women to pursue a different line of work—for example, of 191 women who entered the home in 1930, only 56 started new careers.[20]

Changes in Home Ministry policy had a much greater impact. As Sheldon Garon has shown, they came about when a new class of reform-minded bureaucrats began to rise through the ranks. At the same time, as women became more educated and some entered professions such as teaching, social work, and journalism, it became harder for the government to ignore their pleas on behalf of the less fortunate. In 1926, a meeting of policy chiefs resolved to enforce the 1900 rules giving sex workers the right to leave proprietors.[21] The Japanese state was eager to promote its progress against prostitution to burnish a positive image abroad, especially after the League of Nations Convention on the Suppression of Trafficking in Women and Children in 1921. Japan ratified the convention in 1925 and participated in the Commission of Enquiry into Traffic in Women and Children in the East. Even so, it was not immune to criticism by the Commission for continuing to uphold a system of licensed prostitution.[22]

In 1937, Japanese representatives to the League commission proudly reported that the Home Ministry had distributed 114,000 yen to destitute women in northeastern Japan to dissuade them from becoming prostitutes.

The ministry had also funded the creation of women's hostels and clubs, encouraged associations for good morals in towns and villages, and sponsored more than 1,000 talks in Yamagata prefecture on protecting women and children. The report declared that prostitution was a "social vice" and that "authorisation of this profession is to be deprecated from both a social and a moral standpoint." It also cited the passage of bills that would have licensed prostitution.[23]

The government admitted that the place of sex work in Japanese society was complicated. Farmers felt they had little choice but to consign their daughters to debt contracts with brothel owners. Japanese society recognized their sacrifice—even the report commented on sex workers' "unselfish motive." Public opinion was more critical of parents and the social danger of brothels.[24]

The Japanese state actually did little to stop domestic trafficking, instead focusing on the international trade, especially of European women. They had been the main focus of foreign attention and inspired the first agreement among states, in 1904, to suppress "white slavery." Police were ordered to watch boats and railway stations and to question suspicious people.[25] The Japanese claimed in a 1937 League report that in the previous five years, no European women had been caught and that six suspects had been deported.[26]

At the same time, Japan—like other signatories to the convention— exempted its own colonies. By 1930, Japanese emigration to other parts of the world may have been much reduced, but there was outgoing traffic to Manchuria, Korea, and China—places where licensed prostitution flourished and where no passports were needed.[27] In 1930, Korea had 25 licensed quarters, 510 establishments, and 303 licensed prostitutes (207 of whom were Korean).[28] These statistics suggest that many more women were working as unlicensed prostitutes. In the Japanese metropole, the equivalent statistics for the end of 1929 show 541 licensed quarters, 11,154 licensed brothels, and 50,056 licensed prostitutes.[29] Although most Japanese prostitution activists did not protest the conditions in the colonies, the Salvation Army maintained a home in Darien, and activists such as Masutomi Masasuke from the YMCA sought to rescue women from Manchuria.[30]

In 1931, Purity Society members introduced a bill to abolish licensed prostitution to the Diet, only to meet ridicule from other Diet Members. Nevertheless, proprietors grew nervous that the Home Ministry might act in response to international criticism. In a show of strength, they persuaded a majority of the Lower House to cosponsor a bill that would have enshrined the Home Ministry's Rules Regulating Licensed Prostitution in law. Subsequently, activists shifted their focus to stamping out unlicensed prostitution.[31]

After 1934, the Home Ministry cracked down on students' visiting cafés and other red-light establishments. The National Prostitution Abolition League changed its name to the National Purification Federation (Kokumin Junketsu Dōmei) and made wartime-influenced arguments about eugenics and purity. In 1938, Kubushiro Ochimi, the longtime head of the WCTU, coordinated discussions among politicians, ministry officials, the police, and educators on students and cafés. Many of these activists continued their work after the war, and they would be inspired by many of the same ideas and would offer many of the same solutions.[32]

The limitations of the pre-war abolitionist movement help explain some of the problems of anti-prostitution campaigns in the postwar period. The movement focused on making sex work illegal, in that way saving women while at the same time purifying society. Legislative proposals would have punished prostitutes, which permitted proprietors to pose as their protectors. The shift to opposing unlicensed prostitution served the industry's interest in limiting competition. At no point did abolitionists succeed in mobilizing mass support. And it does not appear that they ever raised a protest about the government's comfort stations in occupied East Asia. This allowed the state to pretend to be combating the trafficking of Japanese women while creating a vast system that enslaved tens of thousands of non-Japanese.

In 1948, growing sentiment against base prostitution and panpan led the Ashida government to present the first anti-prostitution bill of the postwar era to the Second Session of the Diet. The Punishment of Prostitution and Related Activities Bill (Baishuntō Shobatsu Hōan) was drafted by the attorney general's office, then submitted for approval to General Headquarters on May 8, 1948, the usual practice during the Allied Occupation. It defined "prostitution" as sexual intercourse (seikō) for pay and would have made both clients and sex workers liable for up to two years of hard labor and a 10,000-yen fine for a first offense.[33] Sex workers were defined as female by the use of the word shōfu, the second character of which translates as "women." The bill, then, concentrated on punishment, applying the same penalty equally to the client and to the provider. It did not provide for rehabilitation, either through the court system or through welfare institutions.

The majority of female Diet members supported the bill. But a few spoke up against it, arguing that the law would be ineffective or would unfairly victimize sex workers. In May 1948, officials from the Public Health and

Welfare Section met with an unofficial delegation of Lower House politicians, including Democratic Party member Takeda Kiyo, an educator and activist for women's rights, and two future political luminaries: Nakasone Yasuhiro, later to be prime minister from 1982 to 1987, and Japan's second female cabinet minister, an educator known for always wearing Japanese dress, Kondō Tsuruyo.[34] Spokeswoman Takeda made a five-point critique of the proposed law, maintaining that it could not be enforced effectively, that rape and VD would increase, and that it would leave some women destitute. Public opinion was not ready for such a law, and if it passed, Takeda argued, prostitution would be driven underground, "spreading immorality and venereal disease all over."[35]

Diet member Mogami Hideko, elected after her husband was purged because of his wartime activities, also attacked the bill in a July 1948 article for *Nippon Fujin Shinbun*. Sex workers, maintained Mogami, worked of their own free will. The law would put 150,000 of them out of a job. It would also put girls of "well-to-do families" at risk—the same argument that led to the creation of the Recreation Amusement Association. If such an unenforceable law was passed, other laws would lose their authority. Mogami's core contention would soon become a pillar of the conservative case: society was not yet ready for such a law. "Prostitution should be eradicated," she concluded, not by the law but through the raising of consciousness.[36]

Upper House member Miyagi Tamayo represented the more common view among female legislators. She favored the bill, even while pointing to its shortcomings. Miyagi, who had a background in rehabilitation—she was the first female probation officer at Tokyo Juvenile Court—fought against prostitution during her tenure as a member of the Ryokufūkai (Green Wind Party). She visited occupation authorities in December 1948 to argue that the proposed anti-prostitution program lacked a sufficient welfare budget, and made a case that Japan was in a state of social crisis. Although it was true, she said, that some women had become prostitutes for "easy money," many others were war victims and repatriates, or mothers forced to work to feed their children. Miyagi placed emphasis on Japanese families affected by the spread of VD through sex workers.[37]

As long as prostitution was defined as a women's issue and female politicians were themselves divided, there was little prospect for passing a national law prohibiting the practice. There were too many vested interests supporting it, and Allied authorities, also divided, would not insist on such a measure. The 1948 bill failed in committee. It was not until the end of censorship in 1949 and a new surge of foreign troops with the onset of the Korean War in 1950 that Japanese discontent with base prostitution burst out into the open. A coalition then began to form that could pass national legislation.

In the meantime, local regulations against sex work started to appear in communities throughout Japan. Prefectural governments were permitted to initiate laws so long as they did not contravene the National Constitution (Chapter VIII, Article 94). Powers to enact laws relating to health and morals were specifically granted to local bodies. Until the passage of the 1956 Prostitution Prevention Law, sex work would therefore be regulated at the prefectural, city, town, or village level.[38]

In the postwar period, many of the prefectures that passed ordinances had a history of local activism. In August 1949, Gunma prefecture, for example, passed an anti-prostitution ordinance.[39] But Miyagi prefecture was the first to pass an ordinance against prostitution in 1948.[40] Located in Japan's poor northeastern region, Miyagi was widely known as an important recruiting ground for sex workers. Once the regulations were in place, the police quickly moved into action in Sendai, the regional capital. According to the popular press, eight days after the law was enacted, the Sendai police took four sex workers into custody, claiming the local regulation was the first of its kind enforced since the Meiji Restoration.[41] Niigata quickly followed suit. Soon after, the Tokyo metropolitan area held its own debate on whether Tokyo, too, should pass such a measure.

By this point, sentiment against panpan was running high in the capital. On a neighborhood level, groups of women registered their disapproval against streetwalkers. In Tokyo's Minato ward, for instance, one hundred women from the Ward Women's Organization and from the Federation of Housewives demanded to meet with a women's affairs officer from SCAP in Shiba Children's Hall in January 1949.[42] The women from Minato ward complained about knocks on their doors from sex workers demanding shelter for the night, children in the neighborhood acting as touts, and even their own children engaging in panpan play. The SCAP officer could only encourage the local organization members to go to their police stations and to the U.S. military police, since no local ordinances were yet in place.[43]

On the afternoon of March 5, 1949, the first public hearing for the Tokyo Anti-Prostitution Measure (Baishuntō Torishimari Jōrei) took place at the Metropolitan Assembly building, drawing an audience that included police commissioners as well as proprietors. The panel included such feminists as future Diet member Kamichika Ichiko, an activist infamous for stabbing anarchist Ōsugi Sakae in 1916, and author Hirabayashi Taiko.[44] Twenty-four-year-old Koizumi Hisae, a sex worker there to represent the profession's interests, argued that prostitution was not a social good, but that women were forced to sell sex out of economic need. Passing the bill would therefore be unreasonable.[45]

But Koizumi's protests found little support, and the Tokyo ordinance, the third one in Japan after the war, was enacted on May 31, 1949. Nonetheless, it failed to cover significant aspects of sexual services. Early reports pointed out that the measure lacked a provision against male sex workers, who, in one infamous incident, beat up the chief of police when he tried to lead a raid against them in Ueno Park.[46] The ordinance explicitly defined a sex worker as female, and prostitution as sexual intercourse with an unspecified partner for remuneration. Under the ordinance, the sex worker and the client were each fined 5,000 yen, while habitual offenders paid 10,000 yen.

During the Allied Occupation, U.S. officials closely tracked prefectural initiatives such as this one, submitting them to section heads for approval. Judge Alfred C. Oppler, a German refugee who became head of SCAP's Courts and Law Division, articulated Legal Section's position: local anti-prostitution legislation was inferior because these measures tended to be poorly composed. Oppler found that local ordinances were too wide in scope or defined legal terms such as *prostitution* with inexact or vague language. Furthermore, Oppler objected to the severity of penalties and their breadth—for instance, subjecting clients, and not just sex workers, to punishment.[47] His office made telephone calls and staff visits to local military officials to oppose the Tokyo ordinance. Though the Legal Section viewed itself as a protector of women's rights and democracy, Oppler's view closely resembled what conservative leaders would argue in their struggle over the 1956 Prostitution Prevention Law.

In a meeting with police authorities in 1948, the Legal Section pressed home its opposition.[48] Howard Meyers, chief of the section's Criminal Division, who oversaw the revision of the Criminal Code, stated that the Venereal Disease Law of 1948 was an adequate measure against prostitution, arguing that an anti-prostitution ordinance would drive sex workers underground. Meanwhile, Superintendent Inoue Guntarō of the Metropolitan Police Division claimed he could not take a position: the growing unpopularity of prostitution had tied his hands and the matter was now the responsibility of the Tokyo Metropolitan Council.[49] Despite Legal Section's

Servicemen were often seen fraternizing with Japanese women while alcohol flowed. This BCOF sergeant, possibly on a double date with the friend who photographed him, is on a boat sightseeing. He was attached to a regiment that would fight in Korea. Courtesy of the Australian War Memorial

opposition, the number of anti-prostitution measures continued to grow, especially after the start of the Korean War.

The impact of the war on Japan was enormous. The U.S. contribution to UN forces alone totaled more than 300,000, and most of these men passed through Japan at one point or another.[50] They came for processing at Camp Drake near Tokyo, for transshipment at Sasebo, or to take R&R in Fukuoka. The number of U.S. servicemen based in Japan also increased from 1949 to 1952, rising from 126,000 to 260,000.[51]

As more and more Allied troops moved to military bases in Japan, the number of sex workers around these bases also increased, augmenting popular dissatisfaction with prostitution. In 1951, the United States adopted a Uniform Code of Military Justice, which seemed to cover every conceivable offense except prostitution. That same year, Japanese town, city, village, and prefectural authorities took matters into their own hands, passing a total of twenty-five sets of regulations.[52] The majority were passed in areas where foreign troops were located, such as major cities and military bases. The correlation between this wave of local ordinances and the timing of large troop deployments to the Korean front is further evidence that Japanese men's and women's opposition was directed primarily at military prostitution (see Appendix).

With the influx of servicemen and sex workers, new grassroots opposition organizations also emerged, along with a series of new arguments about how prostitution endangered Japanese children—and the future of the nation more generally. These organizations included large national bodies as well as local groups and student circles. Meanwhile, intellectuals, Christian activists, and female Diet members, among others, used the power of the mass media to influence public opinion.

At first the WCTU had cooperated with Allied forces, urging increased police power and restrictions on sex workers' personal freedom. It also provided lodging to sex workers who had been rounded up by the Allied forces.[53] Although the group had declining influence within the broader abolitionist movement, its longtime leader, Kubushiro Ochimi, remained influential. Kubushiro, whose father was a minister, had spent a significant amount of time in the United States, where her experience with Japanese immigrants influenced her interest in licensed prostitution. After her return to Japan in 1923, she became active in the abolition movement as well as in the fight for suffrage.

Kubushiro served on important government committees, penned numerous articles, and contributed her views to roundtables sponsored by a variety of publications, most frequently the women's magazine *Fujin Kōron*.[54] Beginning in 1951, Kubushiro led the Council for Opposing Restoration of Licensed Prostitution, formed by the WCTU and other groups to ensure that Imperial Ordinance 9 of 1947 remained in force after the end of the Allied Occupation. The ordinance would punish those who lured women into prostitution—though not the act of prostitution itself. The council presented the Diet with a petition bearing 960,000 signatures, which helped to convince the Diet to make the Imperial Ordinance a permanent statute.[55]

After this measure became part of the Japanese legal code in 1952, Kubushiro's group was renamed the Council for Promoting Enactment of the Anti-Prostitution Law. It included many other women's associations that had formerly agitated for abolitionist legislation, including the WCTU, the Housewives Association, the League of Women's Voters, the National Federation of Regional Women's Associations, and the National PTA.[56] Its officers included Kamichika Ichiko and Uemura Tamaki as vice chairs. This institutional coalition reflected a new and powerful commitment by women's organizations to passing anti-prostitution legislation, especially when other groups such as Christian churches and the left wing of the Socialist Party joined.[57]

Uemura, a Christian activist, petitioned MacArthur's successor, General Matthew Ridgeway, to ban brothels. The letter was picked up by the *New York Times*.[58] But as the Occupation was officially coming to an end in April 1952, the WCTU and other groups focused on changing opinion in Japan itself. They wrote letters to Diet members, waged national petition campaigns, hung posters, and distributed leaflets. The keynotes in this campaign were the seemingly ubiquitous presence of the panpan and the problem of biracial children. Intellectuals, Christian activists, and Diet members helped make the case to Japanese women that anti-prostitution legislation was essential to their well-being and that of their families.

Pride in the quality and purity of the Japanese race motivated at least some advocates of anti-prostitution legislation, such as Ichikawa Fusae and Diet member Fujiwara Michiko. In 1952, Fujiwara observed in the Upper House Committee on Welfare that she had "heard that these mixed-blood children are, in many cases, sort of idiotic. I suspect one reason for the high rate of idiocy among them is their mothers, who are prostitutes, and, again, idiotic in very many cases." On the other hand, after traveling to Southeast Asia, Fujiwara reported that a "mix with Japanese blood" made the local offspring of Japanese fathers superior beings.[59]

A critical part of new proposals for national legislation was the provision that they not just ban prostitution, but rehabilitate prostitutes as well. There were already a number of women's homes, some run by activists themselves, meant to serve as models. But contemporary reports showed that many appeared to institutionalize a harsh and contemptuous attitude toward sex workers, for all the rhetoric about rehabilitation.

In 1949, a sociology professor at Senshu University submitted a devastating report to SCAP based on two years of research in Tokyo, Yokohama,

Japanese women stand forlornly in the rain as the U.S. troopship *Aiken Victory* pulls away from the dock in Kure. It was bound for Pusan and the war in Korea. Women who were widowed or abandoned by servicemen, especially those with children, would become a matter of growing public concern. Courtesy of the Australian War Memorial

Nagoya, Osaka, Hiroshima, and Kyoto. The best quarters, he found, were "severe and prison like in atmosphere, the worst hardly more than hovels." None of the programs actually provided any occupational training. Instead, women did piecework, typically spinning, sewing, embroidering, or painting china. He found that the women were hardly more than bond servants to the managers of these institutions, who reaped all the profits. The staff were untrained and looked at the work as a means to secure free room and board, providing as little as possible to the inmates while collecting exorbitant salaries for themselves.[60]

SCAP Welfare Services Advisor Marta Green found that some homes were better than others. Shiriziku, which was run by Catholic Charities in Kanagawa prefecture, was a clean but spartan home adjoining a convent. It provided women with training in making fine embroidery and lace for progressively higher wages. But the home did not accept anyone with VD or any other disability, and strictly regulated its inhabitants. They were not permitted to talk during work or meals and sat for hours in straight-backed chairs, clutching their work without armrests or adequate lighting.[61] The Salvation Army's home in Tachikawa, Shinsei-ryō, despite being located in a former factory that was in ill repair, also received a basically positive evaluation from Green.[62]

In other cases, what was supposed to be a rehabilitation home was "purely and simply a workshop."[63] Such houses lacked any vocational training or educational program, and some were filthy. In one, "hordes of flies swarmed through the entire building." Ironically, the worst of all was the institution run by the WCTU. In the kitchen, vegetables were scattered over the floor, with garbage dumped in the corner.[64] Inmates were charged an exorbitant 1,300 yen a month for living expenses. They were sent out to work in local factories, and the sale of their goods paid staff salaries. In nineteen months of operation, 55 of 181 women had run away.

As difficult as life was for sex workers, it is understandable why many would prefer the street to a rehabilitation home. Homes offered little freedom and low wages for menial labor, wages that would not support a family. Most provided no useful job training. Moreover, women who had VD might not even qualify. Yet the idea of rehabilitation homes was so appealing to activists and the public that they chose to ignore evidence of how these institutions were failing—or did not bother to find out.

Nevertheless, the promise of rehabilitation would prove crucial in solidifying a broad coalition of women and Christian Diet members behind a national anti-prostitution law. Some of them, such as Kondō Tsuruyo and Mogami Hideko, had objected to the 1948 bill because it would have left women destitute and driven prostitution underground. If the new law established consultation services and shelters, it might provide a means to reintegrate them in Japanese society. Much of the subsequent debate centered on securing adequate funding for such a system. Without it, sex workers would find themselves consigned to Dickensian workhouses.

After the failure of the 1948 bill, female Diet members pointed to local ordinances as evidence that citizens wanted national action. Miyagi Tamayo remained active, joined by independent Ichikawa Fusae. Ichikawa had been relegated to the sidelines after being purged from 1947 to 1950, but she was elected to the Upper House in 1953 and stayed in office for most of the next three decades. Socialist Kamichika Ichiko also continued to agitate against prostitution. Organized in a cross-party coalition, known as the Female Diet Members' Alliance (Shūsan Fujin Giindan), they persevered in pressing their cause at committee sessions in both chambers of the parliament and by submitting bills from the Diet floor (*giin rippō*). Using these methods, female Diet members fought against government stalling.

In 1951, Miyagi pressed the issue at an Upper House Joint Committee Session. She testified that Japanese men and women felt much more strongly about prostitution near military bases than other sorts of prostitution. "Ordinary people have no sympathy concerning base prostitution."[65] In 1953, Miyagi and other Diet members proposed the Prostitution Punishment Bill (Baishun Shobatsu Hō) at the Diet's Fifteenth Session.[66] The bill, which retained most of the ideas of the 1948 version, retained sex-specific definitions of sex workers and penalties for both parties, and also penalized the practice of giving advance money (*maegashi*)—that is, providing payments to relatives that women would have to work off in a brothel.[67] Although this bill also died in committee, it received significant press attention and spurred women's organizations to further action. By proposing bills in the Diet, legislators gained publicity for the anti-prostitution cause, outlined a new approach, and demonstrated their commitment to activist supporters.

At the Eighteenth Extraordinary Session of the Diet, in 1953, Socialist Katō Shizue and Democrat Fukagawa Tamae demanded once again that the Diet take up the issue of anti-prostitution legislation. The Japan Liberal Party government of Yoshida Shigeru, wary of taking up the controversial issue, decided to stall. Prime Minister Yoshida and Justice Minister Inukai Ken announced that the Ministries of Labor, Justice, and Welfare would cooperate in creating a bill. But rather than sponsoring a bill at the Nineteenth Session of the Diet, the government on December 18, 1953, established the Prostitution Problem Countermeasure Conference (Baishun Mondai Taisaku Kyōgikai).[68]

The popular media extensively covered the 1953 bill in newspapers and on the radio. Diet women had provided the public with inspirational reading material, publishing tracts such as *Let's Rid Japan of Prostitution*. The Women and Children's Bureau also distributed a pamphlet demanding abolition.[69] In the face of what they saw as government inaction, female Diet members continued pressing their own parliamentary measures. In the Nineteenth Session, Socialist Tsutsumi Tsuruyo, who was elected to her husband's seat after he died of tuberculosis, led a cross-party group of mostly female politicians in submitting a bill to the Upper House.[70] The early 1954 bill, nearly identical to the 1953 bill, was carried over to the Twentieth Extraordinary Session. But it was dropped when that session ended early with the resignation of the fifth Yoshida cabinet. Tsutsumi again formally proposed the bill in the Twenty-First Session, which met under the first cabinet of Hatoyama Ichirō. This time it died in committee. It would later emerge that sex-industry entrepreneurs were paying off Diet members to protect their interests. The net effect was that two years of hard committee work produced no concrete parliamentary results.

Over the summer of 1955, the popular and women's press began to uncover a series of child-related prostitution scandals that would change the terms of debate. The Matsumoto Incident first hit the headlines of the Tokyo daily *Asahi Shimbun* on May 10, 1955, just one month before Diet testimony began on yet another Prostitution Punishment Bill. The sex scandal revolved around the teahouse Saryō Matsumoto and its owners, Matsumoto Michio and his wife, Tatsue. It was located in Kagoshima, a city at the far southwestern reaches of the Japanese archipelago. Michio and Tatsue opened it with retirement money from Michio's former job at a construction company. His work contacts provided him with connections to powerful local men, among them construction-company employees, politicians, and newspaper editors. His wife found female employees—some of them high-school students—in the local red-light district (Tenmonkan) or by word of mouth. Some were on permanent salary, while others received payment for each liaison. Nine of the twenty-four workers in the establishment were under eighteen—and they wore school uniforms at work.[71]

The public prosecutor's office in Kagoshima launched an investigation into the teahouse and found Matsumoto Tatsue and the maid who laid out the establishment's futons guilty of the crime of lewd solicitation (*inkō kanyūzai*).[72] Both women received jail sentences: Matsumoto Tatsue five years, and the maid four months. However, the two women served no time, ending up with only three years of probation, while Matsumoto Michio, the head of the house, received no punishment at all. Local groups, outraged at the results, organized around the case, intending to show their dissatisfaction with a legal system that apparently permitted underage prostitution.

The events in Kagoshima exemplified Japan's inadequate prostitution laws. Imperial Ordinance 9 outlawed all acts that pressured a woman to prostitute herself. The Labor Standards Law prohibited forced labor. The Employment Security Law proscribed recruiting someone to do work injurious to public health or morals, such as prostitution. The Child Welfare Law punished anyone who made a girl under eighteen commit an obscene act. And the Venereal Disease Prevention Law prohibited the act of prostitution by a woman suffering from VD.

However, for even the most dedicated of prosecutors, standards of proof and lack of punishment provisions made it difficult to secure convictions. None of these laws specifically prohibited selling sex for money. Some municipalities or prefectures had passed local ordinances against solicitation or other sex-work practices, but such regulations could be applied only in localities where they were valid. As social critic Kanzaki Kiyoshi pointed out in a *Fujin Asahi* article, had Matsumoto Michio lived in nearby Fukuoka instead of Kagoshima, the public prosecutor might have been able to convict him.[73]

The extensive coverage of the Matsumoto Incident also allowed critics and politicians to refigure prostitution as a crime against children, rather than an offense against women. This was due in no small measure to broader social changes. In the late 1940s, the status of children under Japanese law had begun to change. Rather than a source of income or security for loans for their families, they began to receive governmental protection. Although the state focused on abuses in agriculture and fishing, the same logic could apply to minors engaged in prostitution.[74] Kanzaki himself had invoked the importance of protecting children with his book *Towns Selling Girls: A Kanzaki Report*.[75] Respectable women had already been told that panpan play endangered their children's morals. Here was a much graver threat to their families, and a reason parent-teacher associations would now join the fight for an anti-prostitution law: their children might actually become sex workers.[76]

The Matsumoto Incident also demonstrates how women's organizations were now working with female Diet members and the national media. Female students at women's organizations, the Red Cross, the Farmer's Union (Nōkyō), and the prefectural teachers' union urged the national press to pick up the Matsumoto story. Diet members Fujiwara Michiko and Ichikawa Fusae, realizing the importance of the case, traveled to Kagoshima in June to investigate and quickly rallied around outraged local women. Ichikawa became particularly incensed and reported in *Fujin Asahi* that the matter had come up at the Twentieth Meeting of the Female Diet Members' Alliance.[77] Attending were some of the most vocal pro-legislation activists, including Kamichika Ichiko, Miyagi Tamayo, Fujiwara Michiko, Socialist Akamatsu Tsuneko—a leader in the women's labor movement—and Socialist Fukuda Masako, an obstetrician-gynecologist. The end result was a resolution to promote the activities of the Prostitution Problem Countermeasure Conference within the Diet's Committee on Judicial Affairs, as well as to agitate in other committees. On June 9, 1955, Kamichika raised questions in the Diet regarding the progress of the bills. The response of Justice Minister Hanamura Shirō was unambiguous: "As soon as the Prostitution Problem Countermeasure Conference comes to a conclusion, the government will prepare a bill and submit it to the Diet. However, the problem of prostitution cannot be resolved merely by law: it requires social measures."[78] Yet the government still did not propose a bill. Female Diet members therefore decided to submit their own bill from the Diet floor.

Proponents began to press the argument that Japan could not be a member of the international community in good standing until it outlawed prostitution.[79] It was a sensitive point for the Japanese government. Japan had long sought international recognition and had been active in the League of Nations before withdrawing in 1933 over the League's challenge to Japan's occupation of Manchuria. After signing the San Francisco Peace Treaty in 1951, entry to the United Nations was an essential step on the road to readmission to the international community. Japan first applied to join the UN in 1953, but its request, subject to Security Council approval, was rejected by the Soviets.

Japan was just one of many countries denied UN membership because of Cold War competition. But women's groups—many in close contact with their counterparts abroad—argued that the country could improve its credentials by conforming to international norms.[80] Conversely, Fujita Taki, chair of the Women and Minors Bureau of the Ministry of Labor—whose father, a Nagoya judge, had rendered the judgment making advance money invalid in 1900—claimed that joining the UN would improve women's status.[81] At issue was the UN Convention for the Suppression of the Traffic in Persons and of the Exploitation of the Prostitution of Others. Adopted in 1949 and entering into force in 1951, the treaty would require Japan to criminalize prostitution.

In June 1955, Kamichika Ichiko argued before the House of Councillors Judicial Committee that most democratic nations had anti-prostitution legislation and the UN had passed a resolution prohibiting forced labor and earning money from prostitution. She argued that if Japan was to become a member of the United Nations in the near future, it had to pass anti-prostitution legislation.[82] Two days later, in the House of Representatives, she insisted once again that keeping prostitution legal would become a major obstacle in Japan's path toward gaining an honorable position in the international community and realizing the objectives of the Universal Declaration of Human Rights.[83] In a roundtable in *Fujin Kōron* a year earlier, Kamichika had referenced Eleanor Roosevelt's visit to Japan and her criticism of Japan's lack of a legal prohibition against prostitution. Activist abolitionist Itō Hidekichi agreed: in July 1955, in testimony before the Committee on Judicial Affairs of the House, he argued that if Japan joined the UN, it had a responsibility to adhere to the 1949 Convention.[84]

Time and again, Diet members such as Kamichika Ichiko and Fujiwara Michiko would drive home the same point: Japan's failure to outlaw prostitution was an international embarrassment. To that end, Kamichika suggested that Japan was under investigation.[85] In fact, in this period the UN depended on self-reporting when it surveyed sex work.[86] And in the case of Japan, it blamed Allied servicemen, suggesting that their presence had delayed social development.[87] Nevertheless, the UN's reporting helped abolitionists shame politicians.

Kamichika declared that it was embarrassing for Japan to find itself in the same category as Turkey and Costa Rica, which also allowed licensed prostitution. Japan, Kamichika argued, was far behind other Asian countries in recognizing women's rights. Other Asian representatives were astonished, she said, when she had to acknowledge that Japan still had not passed a prostitution punishment bill.[88] Fujiwara Michiko said that she was ashamed in Jakarta when someone asked her, "Do you keep silent when newspapers in the world reported that Japan has been a country of prostitution for hundreds of years?"[89]

By the summer of 1955, abolitionists were finally winning reluctant recognition from the national leadership that legislation might be necessary. Socialist Katō Shizue directly confronted Prime Minister Hatoyama Ichirō. She asked whether he agreed on the need for a law against women's prostitution and a law against making money by buying or selling people.[90] Hatoyama replied:

> Certainly I consider a system that degrades the character of women an embarrassment in a democratic state, the citizens of which ought to respect each and every member's dignity. However, we cannot get to the goal just by setting a punishment. We also have to think about welfare protection plans for prostitutes and measures to prevent women from falling into prostitution.[91]

Justice Minister Hanamura added that "Japan should get fully prepared for joining the UN."[92]

The argument that Japan had to outlaw prostitution for the sake of its international reputation had important implications. International conventions, after all, had long discriminated between women as more or less deserving of protection, above all white women who had been trafficked, as opposed to women who lived under colonial rule. And these conventions were concerned only with the legal status of sex work, ignoring whether and how these laws were enforced. Shaming the national leadership was rhetorically effective, but it also conveyed the message that the issue was one of appearance. Rather than address the reality of sex work, it helped convince them that it had to be driven underground.

The irony, of course, was that for most Japanese, sex work had become objectionable only when the Allies occupying their country had deregulated it. Both politicians and ordinary people had drawn a clear distinction between an established system in which young women worked off family debts within specified areas and a free market in which any woman could sell sex anywhere to anyone she pleased. This was especially the case when the clients were Allied servicemen who gave no sign of leaving even after the formal end of the Occupation. Finding a place in a new postwar international system would mean upholding an unequal alliance while at the same time paying lip service to new global norms.

FIVE

The High Politics of Base Pleasures

Regulating Morality for the Postwar Era

In July 1955, the Committee on Judicial Affairs called some remarkable witnesses to the Diet's hallowed chambers to once again consider whether the country should criminalize prostitution. Conservative member Sekō Kōichi, a longtime Lower House member from Wakayama, chaired the committee. He had a reputation for fighting corruption, having blown the whistle on the sale of military supplies on the black market. The others included journalists, professors, and the chair of the Prostitution Problem Countermeasure Conference, all of them supporters of the Prostitution Prevention Bill.[1] But there were also brothel owners and sex workers who opposed the law, a curiosity to observers in the Diet's balconies and reported at length on the radio and in newspapers, including the major dailies *Mainichi Shimbun* and *Asahi Shimbun*. Reporters focused on Kondō Haruko and Ikegami Yoshiko, a pair of sex workers who were identified in print by the pseudonyms A-ko and B-ko. The two women worked at the lower end of the sex industry in Tokyo, employed by a "Turkish salon" (*saron toruko*). Ikegami testified that she and her coworker had quit their former employment because conditions in the salon were too hard to tolerate. They worked long hours for bad food and could not come and go freely.[2]

But Sekō seemed more interested in what proprietors paid them. Kondō appeared unable to answer Sekō's questions, whispering, "I don't remember." It was difficult for Sekō to fathom: "Please say that more loudly," he prompted, followed by an unbelieving, "You don't remember well on the point of your salary?" It is possible that Kondō had her own reasons for not answering the question, such as nervousness or embarrassment, but the answer was not straightforward for women working off debt contracts. Proprietors customarily took 60 percent of earnings, and also deducted expenses from what remained. The little left over was then applied toward the original debt. For instance, Ikegami was paying 5,000 yen a month off her initial debt contract of 80,000 yen, and the house also collected for room, board, electricity, and the cost of sundry items such as cigarettes, tissues, and futons. Ikegami therefore replied to Sekō that, like Kondō, she had no idea what her monthly income totaled. In fact, she knew only that customers paid 3,000 yen, but she received much less.

If Sekō was keen to discover what proprietors paid sex workers, it may be because a number of his colleagues in the Diet were also in their debt. Brothel owners in Shinjuku had taken up a special collection of 50 million yen to distribute to conservative Diet members. Suzuki Akira, chairman of the National Council for the Prevention of Venereal Disease (Zenkoku Seibyō Yobō Jichikai), called the proposed legislation a "super-emergency." According to the *Asahi Shimbun*, Democratic Party members were initially reluctant to oppose the bill. But they suddenly switched sides, provoking accusations from women's associations that they had made a deal with proprietors.[3]

During the debate, Kondō and Ikegami were never asked for their opinions on whether Japan needed to outlaw prostitution or how it might affect them personally. And unlike other witnesses, neither was given any chance to make a statement. It is unclear who chose Kondō or Ikegami, or for what reasons. But some opposed their selection in *Fujin Shinpū*, the newspaper of the elite New Yoshiwara Women's Health Preservation Association (Shin Yoshiwara Joshi Hoken Kumiai). The anonymous author of "Opposing the Mistaken Information" criticized the portrayal of sex workers and what she considered to be the misunderstandings that had appeared in the popular press. For instance, *Mainichi Shimbun* and *Asahi Shimbun* journalists had referred to A-ko and B-ko as if they represented all sex workers. In fact, they were mere employees of a Turkish salon; worse, its owner was a "third-country national" (*daisankokunin*) and therefore ineligible to join the association. The article suggested that the association's members wished to send a more qualified "female employee representative who is a member of our union," presumably an eloquent and well-trained worker from an old-style Yoshiwara house.[4]

But even better-educated representatives of unionized sex workers could not bridge the gulf in understanding with well-meaning Diet members. Hamada Yaeko, for instance, was a media darling with a compelling life story. She had entered sex work following an attempt to take her own life and that of her child, and later headed a federation of unionized female employees who worked in restaurants and similar establishments in Nagasaki (Sekigashigyō Kumiai Rengōkai Jūgyōfu Kumiai).[5] Hamada told the committee about a recent visit to Nagasaki by Diet member Miyagi Tamayo. Miyagi had suggested that the women in Hamada's association create a newspaper and that they attempt to "enhance [the level of] their culture." Miyagi's suggestions—well-intentioned though they may have been—were more than a step removed from the reality of most sex workers, who were mainly concerned with just getting by. Echoing conservative arguments, Hamada told the Diet that she feared the law's results, suggesting that it might even "produce" criminals. For Hamada, who interacted closely with sex workers, a primary objective of legislation had to be improving (or at least maintaining) sex workers' economic situation.

In the Diet, Hamada testified that the bill might seem good "on top of the desk," or in theory, but that reality was harsher.[6] She objected primarily to the proposed protective facilities (*hogo shisetsu*) provided for in the bill. Since a sex worker would be separated from her family, Hamada argued that such an option was impractical or unappealing for many workers. As she put it, "It's not just the person herself [who is involved]." Whereas reformers worried that prostitution presented a poor example to children, sex workers knew that without it their own children might go hungry.

Sex workers themselves also supported such arguments, as a July 4, 1955, roundtable discussion from *Fujin Shinpū* demonstrates. In this forum, the women maintained that their primary concerns were food, work, and family. "What will become of us?" they asked. These women, and others like them, needed at the very least to provide food and shelter for themselves and their dependents, and sex work was their only viable means of employment. "It's not me myself," Ishii Risa explained. "I have a family to support, that's why. . . ." Among sex workers in Tokyo, many of whom came from impoverished parts of the country, particularly the Northeast, few wanted to return. They also worried about the reaction of the men and women they left behind, whom they considered unfriendly and cool (*tsumetai*). As Ishii put it, "If I go back to the countryside, there's no money, and then what will happen?"[7]

When given a chance to speak, sex workers insisted that what they did was indeed work, and that it was essential for their livelihoods. In prewar Japan, the norm was daughters working off their parents' debt, whereas after the war it was more common to see mothers supporting their own children. They campaigned for rights to better conditions, independence from exploitative proprietors, and fair pay. But for abolitionists, these women were not wage earners; they provided work for others—social work. Rather than deserving rights, they required rehabilitation.

Even proprietors adopted this rhetoric, showing how it could be used to protect their interests. Among the most important was Suzuki Akira, who led 16,000 other proprietors in the National Council for the Prevention of Venereal Disease. Suzuki stated that he and his colleagues provided a useful service to society, at the same time offering women employment and, when necessary, VD treatment. "There is nobody [else] to save them," he said, "not society, not a public office. They have no other way to live."[8]

Suzuki suggested that sex-industry proprietors were the victims of an unsympathetic society. Rather than exploiting sex workers, the proprietors claimed to be working on their behalf. And though it was true that the proprietor claimed 50 to 60 percent of their wages, the profits, according to Suzuki, amounted to a mere 20 percent of the total. The rest went to facilities, meals, and taxes, ignoring the fact that such expenses were often charged to sex workers. Suzuki complained that taxation was ruinous and that foreigners were taking over their business. As written, the bill offered them no restitution. For Suzuki, the proposed law reflected an insufficient grasp of the reality of the sex-work business.

The reality was that no national legislation was possible if it did not take into account the interests and preferences of the proprietors Suzuki led in the National Council. In the decade after its founding in 1946, it had worked closely with the occupation authorities and the Home Ministry. It also carried on an even older tradition—dating back to the founding of the National Federation of the Brothel Trade in 1924—of contributing to political parties and giving perks to politicians who patronized their establishments.[9] Although it is not possible to document, it is impossible to believe that this patronage by Diet members did not inform their views of whether they should put brothels out of business.

*"Picture my mother, my brother, my sister — have
to give money payday!"*

Bill Hume showed how servicemen were made to understand something
many Japanese social reformers chose to ignore: onrii, like many panpan,
sold sex to support their mothers, fathers, and siblings. Courtesy of David
Hume

But by 1955, the terms of the debate were shifting, to the point that some kind of national anti-prostitution law was becoming inevitable. Sex work, once seen as a necessary evil, or even as a sign of family sacrifice, was now thought to threaten public morals and endanger children. Under the Allied Occupation, streetwalking had increased dramatically. Panpan plied their trade in residential neighborhoods and worked near schools. Base towns became dependent on sex workers and the dollars they earned. But even traditional red-light districts began to seem depraved. In 1949, 70 percent of those polled were in favor of preserving the red-light districts. In 1953, the number had dropped to 37 percent. When another survey in 1957 asked about their impact on society, only 16 percent believed it was positive.[10]

After 1953, Japanese men were the main clients for sex workers, and they may have been even at the height of the Occupation. But U.S. servicemen remained disproportionately significant in the debate over criminalization even after their numbers declined. This was not just because of what their continued presence—and continuing patronage of Japanese sex workers—signified about Japan's place in the world. Servicemen still played an outsize role in the Japanese sex market. One reason was that although many sex workers preferred Japanese clients, they could charge foreign clients much more. In Tokyo, sex workers charged U.S. servicemen more than double what they charged Japanese (900 yen versus 400 yen). In 1953, this resulted in a monthly income of nearly 20,000 yen, versus 14,500 yen for specialists in Japanese clients.[11] Moreover, sex workers in base areas could also raise their rates when there were more servicemen in town. Fees tended to be relatively uniform in red-line districts.[12]

But even in base districts, Japanese clients often paid less for reasons that might not have occurred to their American counterparts—such as avoiding the 100- to 200-yen fee when they walked to an establishment, instead of taking a rickshaw.[13] And this meant that a Japanese clientele would employ fewer ancillary workers. This explains why so much of the sex industry still catered to servicemen. In 1953, the Women and Minors Bureau carried out an investigation of sex-work districts in Japan. When they surveyed twenty sex-work districts in eighteen prefectures with military bases, seventeen of them counted American clients, and nine catered exclusively to Americans. In 1953, another study in Tokyo found that 61 of 141 sex workers arrested catered exclusively to non-Japanese clients.[14]

Some of those Japanese men taking the place of U.S. patrons were members of the new Self-Defense Force. What began in 1950 as the National Police Reserve, renamed and expanded two years later as the National Safety

Forces, would become—in everything but name—a new army, navy, and air force. Conservative proponents believed it would make the country more independent. But Washington pressured the Yoshida government—already considered slavishly pro-American—to agree to rapid expansion, paid for with $150 million in weaponry just in the first year.[15]

In Sasebo, where the Maritime Self-Defense Force and the U.S. Navy would share a base, longtime residents joked that the signs advertising sex changed from Japanese to English and back to Japanese again.[16] In fact, in 1953, six of the twenty sex-work districts in base prefectures were already serving Japanese clients alongside British Commonwealth and American servicemen. Japanese critics—and perhaps clients, too—may have found this no less disturbing than the earlier practice of keeping them segregated. Although the racial dimension of official anti-fraternization policies had come to be resented, when it came to brothels, some may well have preferred to maintain some breathing room.[17]

By 1955, the strengthening of opposition to prostitution was unmistakable. The 1955 Prostitution Punishment Bill resembled the 1953 bill of the same name. Imposing higher penalties for offenses, it emphasized the criminality of prostitution, and penalized both the client and the sex worker. It would also punish third parties associated with prostitution: brokers, pimps, and touts could face imprisonment of up to one year or a fine of 10,000 yen. Habitual offenders risked up to three years in prison or 25,000 yen. Relatives, employers, and other people who used a special relationship to recruit a woman into sex work—along with those who did so by confusing or tricking them—were sentenced to up to five years or 35,000 yen.[18]

Although the Diet women's coalition wanted to include rehabilitation and protective measures, the proposed law would not provide sufficient funding. It did, on the other hand, meet the goal of prohibiting the act of prostitution. While the coalition and its allies stoked moral fervor, their opponents, mostly from the conservative parties, countered with legalistic arguments. Conservative parties held, for instance, that it was patently ridiculous to prohibit the act of prostitution because so many people engaged in it. If the law was enacted, a large portion of the male and female population of Japan would be unnecessarily labeled criminals. If many were actually arrested, citizens would lose respect for the law. Conservatives also claimed that the bill lacked logical consistency because it referred to prostitutes but did not include concubines (*mekake*). After all, onrii also provided sexual services outside of marriage in return for items of value.

The night before the vote, July 18, 1955, fifteen Diet members who supported the law visited the home of Prime Minister Hatoyama Ichirō to press their case. They continued arguing until 10:00 p.m. that night, but their efforts were to no avail.[19] Like the bills that preceded it, the measure was rejected nineteen votes to eleven in the Justice Committee. But this time, angry Socialists and other supporters took the bill to a plenary session of the Lower House. They were led by Kamichika Ichiko and Shiga Toshio, a staunch supporter from the Communist Party. On July 19, 1955, the day of the vote, opposing parties rushed for seats on the floor of the Diet. But the bill was rejected on straight party lines, with 190 voting against the bill and 142 voting in favor. No fewer than 135 abstained. The abstention rate infuriated the abolitionist core of the Socialist Party, which had expected party discipline: out of the 135 abstaining, 20 were Socialists.

The relatively close vote on the anti-prostitution bill in the Diet in 1955—not even half the members had voted against it—was a Pyrrhic victory for its opponents. On July 18, 1955, just before the crucial vote, *Asahi Shimbun* raised the specter of financial scandal. The newspaper speculated that the bill would be defeated because of the strength of the proprietors' organizations and the bribes they had distributed to Diet members. *Asahi Shimbun* reported angry exchanges among supporters and opponents. Sekō Kōichi—who had summoned A-ko and B-ko to testify before the Diet—said that he would not listen to women's opinions on the bill unless they had experience as prostitutes.[20] Proprietors were found not only to be bribing the conservative parties, but also disrupting female Diet members' campaigns.[21]

Diet members such as Shiina Takashi, who had spoken eloquently of the need for morality in Japan, were proven to be less than upstanding figures. After being caught taking bribes from proprietors, Shiina was imprisoned for ten months and fined 1 million yen. Eight proprietors with positions high in the national union would also be arrested, among them Suzuki Akira, who had testified so vociferously before the Diet about his profession's contributions to society. He was sentenced to one year in prison and three years on parole.[22]

Proprietors' tactics may have gone far beyond bribing allies and punishing opponents, according to an angry pamphlet published in September 1955 by the Women's Countermeasure Department, an arm of the Women and Youth Division of the Japanese Socialist Party Bureau. Although it may have come as little surprise to an observer of the sex industry that proprietors and government authorities maintained tight-woven and extensive connections, research revealing the longstanding nature of these connections was startling nevertheless. The pamphlet traced the careers of two conservative members: Hitotsumatsu Sadayoshi, a state minister for three prime ministers, and Andō Masazumi, a journalist and close ally of Hatoyama, who served as minister of home affairs in the fifth Yoshida cabinet and minister of education in the first Hatoyama cabinet. The two had continually voiced objections against anti-prostitution legislation. As it turned out, they had been attending national conferences of brothel proprietors for decades. Within the Diet itself, Suzuki Akemi, Suzuki Akira's daughter, had been hired as assistant to the research manager of the Judicial Affairs Committee of the Lower House and could therefore provide the proprietors' organization with inside information. Suzuki Akemi had become an assistant on March 13, 1953—ten days after legislators submitted the Prostitution Punishment Bill to the Lower House. Moreover, other government officials, including Kōno Chikara, the first section chief of the Supreme Court's family department, and Murata Hirō, the second chief, were accused of participating in proprietors' meetings and receiving bribes totaling more than 5 million yen.[23]

Bribery scandals had already become a perennial feature of postwar Japanese politics. But this particular one came at a delicate time, when Prime Minister Hatoyama was trying to broker the merger of the Nihon Minshutō (Japan Democratic Party)—formerly the Japan Progressive Party (Nihon Kaishintō)—and the Japan Liberal Party (Nihon Jiyūtō)—formerly the Liberal Party (Jiyūtō). Hatoyama was a member of one of Japan's great political dynasties but had only recently returned to power.[24] In 1934, after nearly two decades in the Diet, he had resigned as education minister and withdrawn from politics. Despite sitting out the war, Hatoyama was purged in May 1946 as a "militarist and ultranationalist." Some scholars have argued that Hatoyama's purge was unjust—Hatoyama, after all, had publicly denounced Hitler and Mussolini in 1936. But the key consequence was that he was unable to participate in politics until 1951, clearing the way for Yoshida—his bitter rival—to rise to power.[25]

If Hatoyama was to succeed in consolidating the two main conservative parties into one Liberal Democratic Party (Jimintō), he could create a ruling coalition that would long outlast any one prime minister—and a legacy that would outshine Yoshida. He first had to show that the two parties could work together. Both wings had previously opposed anti-prostitution legislation. But they might support a law that cost little and did not actually jeopardize the interests of proprietors. After all, they had been major political donors. It would placate activists and remove a potential source of embarrassment for Japan abroad as it continued to seek UN membership.

But if Hatoyama had politics in his blood—his father was Hatoyama Kazuo, Speaker of the Diet—he was also the son of Hatoyama Haruko, a conservative women's leader and pioneering educator. Haruko later said that she read him English-language biographies of world leaders during her pregnancy. Less than eighteen months after his birth, she returned to work teaching English at Tokyo Women's Teachers College.[26] In her 1920 book, *On the Improvement of Women's Lives*, Hatoyama stressed the importance of women's fidelity and conduct as an example to men: "Since the concept of women's sexual purity is highly respected," she wrote, "men should also be faithful to their wives. But if a husband is unfaithful, do you think his wife doesn't need to remain faithful to her husband?"[27] Her particular vision of womanly virtue may have influenced the way her son thought about prostitution.

In October 1955, after the Matsumoto Incident, July's close vote in the Diet, and the ensuing bribery allegations, Hatoyama ordered the establishment of a new body, the Prostitution Countermeasure Council (Baishun Taisaku Shingikai), to prepare more politically appealing anti-prostitution legislation.[28] When the council submitted its report in April 1956, it stressed two key points. One was that the act of prostitution itself should not be the subject of criminal procedure. Instead, it recommended punishing solicitation and procurement—in other words, the public acts that endangered public morals. Second, the report devoted an entire section to the rehabilitation of convicted sex workers. Its recommendations consisted mainly of the establishment of women's consultation offices (*fujin sōdansho*) and women's protective facilities (*fujin hogo shisetsu*).

However, the council's report did not represent the views of all its members. Like other such bodies in Japan, it included academics, vice ministers, and Diet members, including Fujiwara Michiko, Miyagi Tamayo, and Kamichika Ichiko. The female Diet members on the council found the report unacceptable because it did not declare prostitution a crime. In response, they issued their own statement:

> It is wrong to take a stance that does not impose punishment sanctions against people who are involved in prostitution, while admitting that prostitution is a social evil. The law limits itself to making an ethical declaration about prostitution, a matter outside the realm of legal jurisdiction. If we recognize prostitution as a social evil and aim to prevent and control it, it is logical to have punishment regulations, at least of a degree that can bring society to reason.[29]

This fundamental disagreement would be at the heart of the ensuing debate.

The Hatoyama government submitted the Prostitution Prevention Bill a month later. Even a quick glance demonstrated that it was not intended to abolish prostitution. Rather, the law's stated purpose was to discourage prostitution and declare it to be a "social evil." According to the bill:

> This law aims to prevent prostitution, in view of the fact that it harms human dignity, is against sexual morality, and disturbs virtuous social manners and customs. It will do so by punishing acts that encourage prostitution, and for females who by their character, conduct, or environment are inclined to prostitute themselves, provide guidance dispositions and protection and rehabilitation.[30]

The law also declares that no one shall prostitute or be the client of a prostitute, but it does not specify any penalty for violating this provision. Instead, it penalizes associated practices such as solicitation, procurement, and the concluding of a contract with a person to become a prostitute.[31] The rest of the law covered rehabilitation, establishing two kinds of facilities to care for women. The guidance dispositions mandated that, instead of issuing a criminal sentence for prostitution, the court could instruct women to be placed in a home and put under a period of "guidance" for six months (though women could be freed earlier).[32] Guidance homes were to provide moral training, vocational education, and medical treatment (a clause aimed at the treatment of VD). The protective and rehabilitation provisions did not actually require the establishment of such homes or provide funding for them. They only mandated that all prefectural governments establish women's consultation offices. These offices, to be partially funded by the prefectural governments, would inquire about women needing rehabilitation; give them temporary aid; provide them with counseling; and assist with medical, psychological, and vocational decisions.

Many female legislators viewed the punishment provisions, guidance dispositions, and protection and rehabilitation sections as woefully inadequate. The Socialist Party submitted an entirely different proposal, called the Punishment and Security Measures for Prostitution and Rehabilitation Protection Bill (Baishun Keibatsu Hoan Shobun Kōsei Hogo Hōritsuan). It closely resembled previous anti-prostitution legislation, criminalizing the act of prostitution (tanjun baishun) and recommending a substantial and well-funded rehabilitation program. Under the proposed program, convicted prostitutes would be sent to family court. While an inspector investigated, they would be put on probation under a guardian (*hogo kansatsu*) or sent to a women's rehabilitation facility (*kyōsei shobun*) unless they chose to go back through the family-court system.

By writing a bill that was, on its face, against prostitution, the government placed female Diet members between a rock and a hard place. Refusing to go along risked never having a law against prostitution. They therefore decided to withdraw the Socialist Party bill—which was more of an effort to save face than anything else—on May 12, 1956.

But female Diet members continued to attack the defects of the government's Prostitution Prevention Bill. On the first day of debate, May 17, 1956, the House of Councillors Committee on Judicial Affairs received thirty-one petitions and messages from women's regional and national groups throughout Japan. Critics doubted that without an explicit clause punishing prostitution itself, prosecutors would use the proposed legislation at all, much less use it to punish proprietors or men who had sex with minors. Pointing to the need for a more comprehensive law, Fujiwara Michiko cited the Matsumoto Incident, in which no one had actually served time or paid a fine. As an example of how ineffective the stated provisions were, she told Justice Minister Makino Ryōzō, to the assembly's great amusement, of how prosecutors would find it difficult to convict someone of prostitution:

> Let's say I was younger and a prostitute. I live in a rented house and make my living by prostitution. I don't solicit. Yet I constantly have lots of random partners coming and going. It's annoying the neighbors. But I don't solicit nor do I advertise. How exactly am I doing this? . . . There are rumors about my having constant random partners . . . but if I don't solicit, don't go out in the streets, and don't put up pictures then what is it?[33]

Makino responded to Fujiwara's point that the law was unenforceable with what became the government's standard argument: the proposal was "cultural legislation oriented toward social policy" (*shakai seisakuteki bunka rippō*). The purpose of the law was not to punish, but to create a national "social movement" (*shakai undō*). The government, then, wished to focus on making an "atmosphere" (*kokufū*) that made people realize that making money through prostitution was shameful (*hazukashii*).[34]

But even governing party members objected to the Prostitution Prevention Bill's proposals for rehabilitation and protection of females apprehended as prostitutes. The Diet women, for their part, considered the proposed system to be poorly designed, inadequately funded, and entirely insufficient. But they believed that some rehabilitation programs were necessary. Like abolitionists in other times and places, Diet members Fujiwara, Ichikawa, and Miyagi considered sex workers to be fallen women who could be rescued, which is why they had demanded an extensive budget for such programs. Consequently, should the bill lack such funding, prostitutes could not be treated and might lapse into former ways.[35]

Another point of contention concerned whether the institutions should be regulated under the jurisdiction of regional or national government. Opposition leaders worried that regionally based regulatory structures would not prove capable of controlling national proprietors' organizations. Ichikawa even argued that leaving the prostitutes to the prefectures presented serious risks to human rights. She observed that the Ministry of Welfare did not seem to care much about prostitution, and preferred the system of red-line districts as a way to prevent VD.[36] These objections fell on deaf ears, and protective institutions for prostitutes were placed under prefectural jurisdiction. Tellingly, the government's explanation was that other protective institutions, such as those intended for mentally, physically, and economically challenged populations, were also located and funded at the prefectural level.

The growing controversy surrounding military-base prostitution helped to consolidate support for the law and finally overcame conservative opposition. Kanzaki Kiyoshi had criticized military base prostitution and its impact on Japanese youth throughout the 1950s, testifying before the House of Representatives Committee on Judicial Affairs in July 1955. "The military bases have harmful effects on children," Kanzaki argued. "They destroy their humanity." Quoting a Special Education Study report from Yokosuka, Kanzaki said that in the past, many Yokosuka children had been fascinated by prostitutes because of their outfits, rich lives, and appearance. But Kanzaki noted that children were now more attracted to the prostitutes' sexual lives, which caused an increase in sexual crime.[37]

In addition to the threat to children, many Diet members were concerned that the continued presence of U.S. military personnel made the prostitution problem intractable. The formal Occupation had ended in 1952, and the Korean War wound down in 1953. That year, anti-prostitution activist Kanzaki Kiyoshi pointed out that the number of Americans in Japan had not declined since 1950, when there were 125,000 U.S. servicemen and 15,000 civilians.[38] In 1956, Asukata Ichio of the Japan Socialist Party noted that nearly 100,000 U.S. troops still remained.[39] Inomata Kōzō, a lawyer and human rights activist who would become the founder and president of the Japan branch of

Amnesty International, insisted that both the prostitute and client should be punished, including U.S. servicemen. He asked the government to explain how it would investigate and punish soldiers in military bases who paid for sex.[40]

Minister of State Hamamura Shirō replied that crimes committed by foreigners might have been overlooked and implied that Japan's Cold War alliance precluded prosecuting servicemen. But "since the tone of society is changing, we would like to take equal and strict control over prostitution, regardless of the race of the criminal." Inomata was skeptical: he related how a brothel owner had come to see him. She reported that a U.S. soldier, dissatisfied with the service he had received at her establishment, had committed arson—setting a fire that eventually burned twenty establishments. The Japanese police turned the accused soldier over to the MPs, who asked the brothel owner and her workers to take a lie detector test. "The Japanese police have the right to investigate," Inomata insisted, and "punish even cases committed by U.S. troops."[41]

It was not just the double standard that bothered lawmakers. Two days later, Shiina Takashi pointed out that the proposed law did not punish onrii, even though they too corrupted public morals. He asked, "Does the head of the social educational bureau of the Ministry of Education know the number of schools near military bases and the places where *onrii* live? Do you take any precautionary measures?"[42] Shiina warned of the danger facing schoolchildren: "Allied troops are crazy because they're of a different race and so are the women who serve them. They deliberately have their rooms wide open and the clear sight of two naked animals embracing each other enters your view even when you don't want to see it."[43]

Other Diet members worried that children who witnessed prostitution would soon become prostitutes themselves. Socialist Furuya Sadao, a lawyer and activist for tenant farmers, had requested a survey from a health clinic in Kitafuji, near a U.S. installation in Yamanashi prefecture. The survey found four prostitutes under sixteen in April 1953, twenty-one the next month, and seventeen in June. Furuya insisted that, regardless of whether the girls had acted freely or been forced into the trade, the Ministry of Education had to address the problem.[44] It was not only girls working as prostitutes that outraged Furuya. It was the elementary and junior high school students who made money as touts and errand runners, and arranged liaisons between women and U.S. troops. "They witness prostitution taking place and this becomes part of their daily play activity. Sometimes the older fifteen- or sixteen-year old boys become pimps or philopon addicts"—that

Though the Japanese media increasingly depicted sex work as a threat to children, Rokuura Mitsuo showed that many mature women entered the sex-work industry with their eyes wide open. Here, a mother in traditional attire with her baby on her back, and another breast-feeding, line up to work as *dansaa*. The sign offers them a guaranteed livelihood.

is, addicted to amphetamines. He thought this was not an isolated instance. "Considering that these things are taking place in Kitafuji—and this is just a small part of the 700 plus military installations—if we thought about it at a national scale these numbers would be tremendous."[45] But Furuya argued that prostitution could not be abolished without also establishing sexual morals. This required educating people that it was "an evil in every respect and regardless of excuses."[46]

Proponents of the bill continually framed the issue in terms of children.[47] As Fukumoto Haruo, director of the Japan Youth Conference, pointed out to the House of Councillors Judicial Affairs Committee, "The red-line district, the blue-line district, and the military bases have a great influence on young people." Fukumoto argued that even if the bill passed, current cases would not be solved all at once. The bill would instead play an important role in protecting fundamental human rights and solving problems related to prostitution.[48]

But critics pointed out that the Prostitution Prevention Bill did not specifically protect minors, an issue that had galvanized the movement. Cases like the Matsumoto Incident had demonstrated that prosecutors infrequently used legislation already on the books, and even when they did, it made little difference. Opposition leaders, particularly Fujiwara Michiko, argued that a specific provision was needed to fight child prostitution. The government pointed out that the Child Welfare Law of 1947 could be used to prosecute sex crimes involving minors—even though it applied only to those twelve and under.[49]

One of the most influential voices in the debate was that of Socialist Takada Nahoko, a teacher who became the first female director of the Japanese Teachers' Union after the war, and was now chair of the Committee on Judicial Affairs. In the plenary session of the House of Representatives, on May 9, 1956, she argued that ever since Allied troops had been stationed in Japan, "sexual morals declined and the number of prostitution cases increased dramatically."[50] Takada argued that the government should demonstrate a model of sexual morals for the nation.

> In order to improve sexual morals, I believe it is necessary that the government take the helm and lead the country by example. But there are those in this assembly who praise geisha and try to keep the teahouses the way they are. It is impossible to eradicate the social vice of prostitution without cleaning up of the environment surrounding these bases.

Takada directly addressed Hatoyama: "While I presume the prime minister, who is a Christian, has a great sense of mission in passing this bill, I would like to ask the opinion of the Education Minister."

Hatoyama himself gave the government response. He agreed that it was a "well-known fact" that the number of cases of prostitution had increased dramatically because of the confusion of social conditions, and because of the decline of sexual morals. "I don't think it's possible to abolish prostitution only by law, but I am prepared to abolish prostitution by taking various kinds of political measures."[51]

But was it possible to abolish prostitution without making the act itself illegal? Socialist Inomata Kōzō argued that without a clear definition, it would be difficult to enforce any legislation. Fujiwara Michiko and Ichikawa Fusae pointed to endemic police corruption and the long-standing links with proprietors' associations. Police officers who were supposed to protect sex workers often had close connections with brothel owners in their districts. For example, in Japan the police box found in each neighborhood played a central role in maintaining public order. But in red-line districts, it was often controlled by proprietors. When the chief of police started his job or retired, Fujiwara further noted, proprietors often held welcome parties or farewell parties in his honor. For all these reasons, she feared the law would become a "dead letter." In a pro forma response, the head of the detective section of the National Police Department, Nakayama Tōji, replied only that the department would hold internal investigations and that it would make the requisite effort.[52]

Fujiwara restated her lack of confidence in the police. In her closing remarks in the plenary session of the House of Councillors, she noted that many of the owners of prostitution businesses were actually former chiefs or high officers in the police force. She recounted a recent visit to Osaka's Amagasaki neighborhood, where she had met with proprietors and asked them how they felt about the proposed law. Fujiwara reported that proprietors had shown no apparent worry: they considered the law to be full of loopholes and had already made arrangements with the police for evading it. Others had testified regarding close relationships between the police and the brothel owners. Kanzaki Kiyoshi had testified about such a case, in which three policemen who had operated a brothel while still on the force had started other houses after they retired.[53]

On the day of Fujiwara's remarks, Hatoyama commented in his diary that the Socialists were "throwing their weight."[54] Opposition leaders further questioned the peculiar timing specified for enforcing the law. The penal dispositions would come into effect two years later than the other chapters, on April 1, 1958. The initial agreement during the council's meetings had specified January 1, 1958. Suspicious Socialists and others saw the unusual delay, and the prospect of further delays, as reason enough to question the government's sincerity.[55]

Miyagi Tamayo and other Diet members argued that the three-month delay accorded with the needs of the proprietors, who had strongly lobbied for such a change. Only two days earlier, she had received more than 1,000 postcards asking for a similar extension as well as other concessions to proprietors, such as a five-year postponement of the law's enforcement, allegedly to allow them to change their occupations.[56]

Despite their many objections, the core group of female Diet members finally decided to support the Prostitution Prevention Bill. Fujiwara spoke for them, and for their bitter disappointment.

> No one can deny the great significance of the state's intention to regulate the evil of prostitution. . . . I have to agree with the faulty law—which differs excessively from the Socialist bill—because the public opinion of the entire country is in favor of both abolishing the red-line and blue-line entrepreneurs, and regulating the evil of prostitution. Swallowing our tears, we in the Socialist Party will take the first step by both withdrawing our bill and giving up on amendments.[57]

Their fervent desire for a bill against prostitution forced compromise, and the first national Prostitution Prevention Bill passed the Diet and was issued as law No. 118 on May 24, 1956. The law went into effect on April 1, 1957. The penal provisions followed one year later.

When considered within the narrow sphere of Japanese political history, the 1956 Prostitution Prevention Law can be viewed as an institutional triumph for female legislators. While issue-based coalitions were not uncommon in the early postwar period, this law was the first in which a cross-party group of women played a significant role, thus demonstrating the potential power of a gender-based alliance.[58]

But other women, who found themselves targeted by the law, soon found that it had further narrowed their options. Prosecutors in Tokyo, who accounted for 20 percent of arrests nationwide, provided a preview when they set up a rehabilitation office in 1955. Over a thirteen-month period, two full-time officers and four part-time volunteers were responsible for counseling 3,739 women. They were supposed to help all of them enter shelters or obtain medical treatment, help them find new jobs, and cover travel expenses for women to return to their hometowns. Notwithstanding the heavy caseload, they also collected revealing data. Fully 78 percent of the women were arrested in hotels, typically in Shinjuku and Asakusa, and just 3.6 percent in red-line areas. Though the Tokyo anti-prostitution ordinance did not distinguish between licensed and unlicensed sex workers, prosecutors were clearly targeting independent operators. Of these women, 86 percent were otherwise unemployed, and more than 30 percent were supporting children. Contrary to the public hysteria over child prostitution, fewer than 2 percent were under twenty years of age. Similarly, a 1956 survey of 15,595 suspects involved in prostitution found that just 11 of them—or less than 1/10 of 1 percent—were age fourteen to sixteen. Either public concern was grossly exaggerated or under-age prostitutes were not being discovered by the police, who went after street-walkers and tended to steer clear of brothels.[59]

The law was also supposed to help sex workers transition to a different kind of life. In 1957, consultation offices opened in other major cities—in Yoko-hama in January, in Osaka in August, in Kobe in September.[60] Although the law mandated that each prefecture set up a women's consultation office, that year only eight prefectures (including the Tokyo metropolitan area) out of forty-seven had set up offices. By that point, Tokyo had forty-two consultants for 15,000 sex workers (a conservative estimate).[61] Reports soon appeared showing the rehabilitation provisions were grossly underfunded. Counselors were responsible for helping women find jobs, solve family issues, get medical examinations, and secure abortions.[62] But they spent much of their time try-ing to settle sex workers' debts, both with proprietors and with the small busi-nesses that had supplied them with clothes and cosmetics.[63] To do all this, they were paid less than 10,000 yen per month, and many went into the red after having to pay their own transportation expenses. Private organizations also contributed to the rehabilitation effort. In Tokyo, Izumi-ryō could host up to fifty women. But in 1958, only fifteen were living there.[64]

What women really needed was money. Survey after survey had shown that was the primary reason they had entered the profession. That same year, the National Serving Women or Sex Workers Association (Zenkoku Sek-kyaku Joshi Jugyōin Kumiai Renmei) calculated that replacing the average salary for a six-month transition period would require about 180,000 yen per woman.[65] This would mean a budget of some 10 billion yen, even without any overhead cost. The Ministry of Health and Welfare had requested 11 bil-lion yen for the law, but the Ministry of Finance approved only 4.5 billion, and only a small part of it ended up in the hands of former sex workers.[66]

In 1959, after the punishment provisions had been in effect for one year, consultation offices worked with nearly 8,000 women. Slightly more than 24,000 people had been taken to Public Prosecutors' Offices for violating the law. Of this number, 63 percent (15,191) were brought in for solicitation, and 18 percent—just over 4,350—for procurement. Only 4.4 percent (1,067) were prosecuted for running a house of prostitution.[67]

Although all Japanese women were supposed to benefit from the improved moral climate, it appeared to make little difference in the incidence of vio-lence against them. In fact, after a steady rise in rapes since 1949, there was a dramatic increase in 1958 to more than 8,500, a 60 percent jump over the year before. Whereas the Prostitution Prevention Law was meant to protect children, 54 percent of these rapes were committed by juveniles.[68] It is not possible to determine what, if any, relationship there was between the end of legalized prostitution and the increase in incidence of sexual violence. The least one can say is that it did not appear to have any positive effect. One group of delinquent boys even used the law as an excuse. They were arrested for gang-raping eight girls, ranging in age from thirteen to eighteen years old. The "vice president" of the group said, "I did this because I lost an outlet for my sexual desire after the Prostitution Prevention Law was enacted."[69]

Viewed within the larger social and cultural context, 1956 can be seen as a high-water mark for women's activism, demonstrating its limitations more than its achievements. What the press took to calling the sieve law (*zaruhō*)—so called because so much criminal activity slipped through—harmed the interests of its presumed beneficiaries. It brought the end of the Yoshiwara culture, which, for all its failings, nevertheless accorded a recognized place for sex workers in Japanese society. No longer protected by any sort of contract or legal guarantee, they became ever more marginalized, even while remaining essential to the process of reimagining a new Japanese nation.

SIX

The Presence of the Past

Controversies over Sex Work Since 1956

When soldiers, sailors, and airmen from several nations arrived in Japan, the people they encountered were in a state of shock. The once-mighty Japanese empire had been resoundingly defeated, and millions of colonists and troops were fleeing to safety. In a world in which the imposition of impossibly large reparations or even relegation to a pastoral state was a real possibility for defeated nations, regaining sovereignty would have seemed like a distant dream.

A farmer in Niigata, a shopkeeper in Kyoto, or a veteran in Kure—warned to expect the worst—would have found it difficult to imagine that Japan would so quickly create a two-party system, raise a new army, and be accepted into the United Nations. For a sex worker in Tokyo, on the other hand, it would have been impossible to believe that—ten years after the government recruited her to perform patriotic service in the Recreational Amusement Association—her profession would be criminalized. At the time, all this was deemed necessary for Japan to regain its place in the world, and passing the Prostitution Prevention Law might seem to be the least of it. But looking back, we can see that it was emblematic of the larger process that brought the end of the postwar era, even as it showed how a state of compromised sovereignty and social inequity could persist to the present day.

The compromises to Japanese sovereignty were written into its constitution. MacArthur himself is thought to be responsible for Article Nine, under which the Japanese renounced war and force as a way of settling disputes. But it was MacArthur who, just two weeks after the outbreak of the Korean War, ordered Prime Minister Yoshida Shigeru to create the National Police Reserve, the precursor to the Self-Defense Force (SDF).[1] The reserve included captains, majors, and lieutenant colonels of the Imperial Army.[2]

In September 1951, one year after the war started in Korea, Yoshida signed a peace treaty in San Francisco that was supposed to reward Japan with restored sovereignty. But the U.S.- Japan Security Treaty, signed the same day, gave the United States the right to move its forces across the archipelago unhindered and even to intervene to quell domestic disturbances. Though these provisions were modified by the 1960 Treaty of Mutual Cooperation and Security, a Status of Forces Agreement ensured that U.S. personnel would largely retain their extraterritorial status. Henceforth, the SDF would defend Japan, while Japan became a secure base for the United States to project military power and prosecute wars across Southeast Asia and the Middle East.

Becoming a permanent part of the U.S. overseas base system was the only way for Japan to rejoin the world community. So too was demonstrating its observance of international standards, including a global norm that required outlawing sex work. Here again, this turn of events would have been hard to believe in 1945, when Japan had just been defeated by the five powers that would make up the new U.N. Security Council. Wartime Japanese propaganda showed contempt for international opinion, and military authorities organized sexual slavery across occupied Asia. Barely a decade later, politicians were determined to join the United Nations and were embarrassed by foreign criticism of licensed sex work.

In 1945, people who had been left out of Japan's imperial project—communists and feminists, for example—might have cheered the idea that Japan would be welcomed back into the community of nations and adhere to seemingly progressive ideals. But by 1949, they were competing for power with militarists and ultranationalists. Conservatives came together in the LDP in 1956 and went on to dominate Japanese politics. It was Hatoyama and the LDP that passed a law that was ostensibly against prostitution but in fact left men in charge of sex work.

The cumulative effect of these changes was the continuity of conservatism, albeit a conservatism adapted to Cold War conditions. In postwar Japan, farmers in rural areas gained enormous subsidies, small shopkeepers were protected from competition, and veterans—once discredited as militarists—were de-purged and allowed to join the SDF. Sex workers, on the other hand, would find that this new conservative order had radical consequences. After more than 300 years of being regulated and in some cases celebrated, they were now made to represent everything wrong with postwar society. Not only was their livelihood outlawed, sex workers were directed to undergo rehabilitation as well.

Despite the Prostitution Prevention Law, commercial sex remains readily available all across Japan. Clients continue to spend large sums of money. According to one estimate, that figure is equivalent to 1 percent of GNP, or as much as Japan allocates to national defense.[3] Hundreds of thousands of women continue to work in the sex trade, some of them still catering to American servicemen.[4] Police remain in collusion with proprietors, refusing to arrest known operators. And just as opponents predicted, the Prostitution Prevention Law proved of little use to prosecutors, either because police did not care to enforce it or because of the difficulty of obtaining proof of criminal activity. In 1959, authorities made more than 20,000 arrests for violating the law. By 1975, the number had fallen to fewer than 5,000. In 2008, just 662 people were arrested.[5]

From such evidence, one might conclude that outlawing sex work had little practical consequence. However, the Prostitution Prevention Law and—still more—the impulse to define sex work as a social evil have in fact had far-reaching effects, profoundly shaping both Japan's sex industry and the lives of individual women.

To begin with, skirting the law's specific provisions led proprietors to diversify, with some offering different services, while others reduced their risks by outsourcing.[6] The first *toruko*, or "Turkish" baths, began operating in Higashi-Ginza in 1951, though their female employees would only wash customers' backs in a sauna. More toruko opened in other cities, and in 1955 some were selling sex, as shown by the embarrassed testimony of A-ko and B-ko before the Diet. Typically, an owner would collect an entry fee, and the client then would contract with a woman inside for sex. This shifted any risk of prosecution to the sex worker. In 1958, right before the law's punishment provisions were put into effect, many more proprietors began rebranding their businesses in the same fashion. The first toruko in Yoshiwara opened that year, and Tokyo's oldest red-line district had more than forty by 1965. When the Turkish embassy complained to the Japanese government, toruko changed their name again to "soaplands."[7] These and other establishments also catered to male fantasies. The female legislators who sought abolition might be shocked to see how a whole business has developed to dress women up as schoolgirls and French maids.

Proprietors also diversified the means of delivering sexual services. The law criminalized soliciting publicly, brokering prostitution, and supplying a venue for prostitution, which still leaves many ways to sell sex without risking prosecution. The daily practice of sex work has therefore mostly reflected the more easily enforceable Adult Entertainment Law. First passed in 1948 the law has evolved to accommodate changes in the industry. It recognizes and regulates many different kinds of adult entertainment businesses (*fuzoku eigyo*), including cafes, cabarets, soaplands, and adult magazine and video shops. Businesses can be issued permits if they register their name and address, along with a description of the building and its managers. Enterprises are forbidden from allowing juveniles to enter, or from operating within 200 meters of schools and libraries. Prefectural authorities can regulate business hours, and they have the authority to prevent them from locating in certain places.[8]

The police, who know where prostitution businesses operate, can use the Adult Entertainment Law to shut down adult-entertainment establishments.[9] Proprietors were able to evade its provisions by organizing outcall services. Later, the law itself was updated to regulate these practices.[10] Telephone clubs (*terakura*), which started around 1983, allowed men to call either from a club or a private location, and connected them to a woman to meet for a liaison. With the proliferation of outcall services and telephone clubs, a growing proportion of sex work was performed by amateurs.[11] In 1986, the Japanese government found that most surveyed sex workers still met clients at clubs, cabarets, and soaplands, but a quarter of them, the largest single group, now met by arrangement.[12] The 1995 Telephone Club Law requires only that these clubs register, and regulates where and how they can operate. As long as the telephone clubs are not near schools, they avoid restrictions on juveniles.[13]

In the 1990s, the popular media began to report that compensated dating (*enjo kōsai*) was increasingly common and reacted much as they had to the panpan and even earlier concerns about café waitresses. Stories proliferated in Japan's mass weeklies and also appeared on television and in newspapers. They reported that a quarter or more of high school girls were involved and featured interviews with both practitioners and their critics. In 1998, new surveys indicated that the real number was more like 10 percent of high school girls, which was still a significantly higher proportion than had engaged in sex work some fifty years earlier. Enjo kōsai is not necessarily the same as prostitution, since practitioners apparently do not always ask for money for sexual services, but many do.[14] And while the Prostitution Prevention Law has been used against it, the tiny number of prosecutions compared to the scale of the phenomenon underscores the law's irrelevance.[15]

The most dramatic example of the diversification and outsourcing of sex work in the past half-century—and another area in which the Prostitution Prevention Law has had no positive effect—is the development of sex tourism and sex trafficking. Japan itself can be regarded as the first large-scale overseas market for sex tourism, considering the hundreds of thousands of Allied soldiers who went there for R&R during the Korean War. But it was Japanese men who became known—and notorious—as the first sex tourists. This practice began after travel was liberalized in 1964, when they went on package tours to Thailand, Taiwan, and South Korea, each of which were marketed as a male paradise. The governments of these countries needed foreign exchange and investment and therefore catered to the trade. Japanese companies even sponsored "Kisaeng tours"—a traditional Korean dinner paired with erotic entertainment—for successful male employees.[16]

These trips were met by protest as early as 1973, when university students rallied against them at Kimpo airport in Korea. Women's groups, such as the Christian Women's Federation of Korea, also protested the practice, and Japanese feminists cooperated with their counterparts in Southeast Asia and Korea. In 1981, Prime Minister Suzuki Zenkō was met by large demonstrations on a visit to the ASEAN countries.[17]

The unwanted visibility given to sex tourism contributed to a shift in the 1980s: rather than Japanese men traveling to Southeast Asia for sex tourism, Southeast Asian women came to Japan to work as bar hostesses, dancers, and sex workers.[18] More came from Eastern Europe and the former Soviet republics after the collapse of communism. Outrage about this phenomenon often centered on the fate of these "Natashas," recalling early twentieth-century campaigns against "white slavery." Filipina, Thai, and Eastern European women could regularly be seen standing outside the bars of Kabuki-chō.[19]

There is tremendous controversy over the extent to which foreign women engaged in sex work know what they are getting into. Personal experience often depends on nationality. Filipina women, who generally speak English and are part of strong church-based networks, often fare better than women from Thailand, who lack these resources. And without Japanese citizenship,

Japanese fluency, or local contacts, the outlook is bleak. However, a 2002 study in Thailand revealed that sex workers were ignorant of neither the dangers they faced nor the risks of debt bondage.[20] These women at least could earn an income and remit their earnings to relatives in the home country.

Still, many who are not clear-cut victims of human trafficking work in circumstances that severely limit their choices, especially when complaining would risk deportation. Even in best-case scenarios, migrant laborers in Japan are vulnerable to the demands of proprietors because they typically are paying off the debt contracts that brought them there. In the worst cases, women are kept under surveillance and are physically and mentally abused. They can become prisoners and slaves of the proprietors.[21]

The Prostitution Prevention Law made it much harder for women to organize against these abuses and demand better working conditions. Neither can they bring a suit in court upon the denial of a payment or seek protection from criminal extortion. Police have charged very few proprietors with abusive practices.[22] Moreover, the Japanese government has made little effort to prevent human trafficking, and it does not provide aid to foreign migrants in the sex industry. Its efforts have been focused on deporting the victims, rather than prosecuting the traffickers themselves.[23]

Of course, not all this can be attributed to the Prostitution Prevention Law. Instead, Japanese examples of diversification, outsourcing, tourism, and trafficking form parts of a more global phenomenon, and the Prostitution Prevention Law is just one example of how campaigns to improve the lot of sex workers have sometimes had the opposite effect. The very different, nearly opposite responses to trafficking recalled the debate that took place in 1950s Japan. Some argued that prostitution was inherently and inevitably exploitative. They focused on the most vulnerable victims, especially children and trafficked women, and claimed to speak for them. A host of celebrities and politicians took up the cause and pursued it through foreign ministries and international organizations.[24] Others opposed the moralistic tone of the anti-trafficking campaign, emphasizing the need to address the poverty that pushed women into sex work, rather than just trying to stop them at the border. They also were critical of the impulse to criminalize sex work and in some cases argued that the profession should be recognized and regulated.[25]

Sex workers themselves insisted that rather than pity and rehabilitation, they needed workplace protections, just as they did in occupied Japan. The contemporary struggle is usually thought to have begun with the founding of the American organization COYOTE (Call Off Your Tired Ethics) by Margo St. James in 1973. Other national groups followed. The first international sex workers conference was held in Brussels in 1985, and convened once again a year later to lobby the European Union Parliament.[26]

In Japan, it took forty years for sex workers to once again organize in defense of their own interests. Even so, the Japanese movement was not nearly so developed or assertive as its contemporary counterparts in the United States, the Netherlands, and Germany.[27] Groups such as Kyoto-based SWEETLY (Sex Workers! Empower, Encourage, Trust, and Love Yourselves) largely focused on conducting research and changing attitudes through education and outreach. Similar to other unions around the world, they demanded the right to work. As activist Momocca Momocco, a founder of SWEETLY, wrote, "Sex work should be regarded as an established form of labor like any other. Any pleasure is now a commodity in society, and sexual pleasure can now be seen as a commodity. By regarding sex work as labor, we'll be able to revitalize non-business sex, to create sex without power imbalances."[28]

The most important gains came in Germany, where in 2002 the government enacted legislation that gave sex workers of German nationality a broad range of rights and benefits. These included eligibility to enter the health, unemployment, and pension insurance systems; a change in criminal law so that a person of free will and without compulsion would have the legal right to employment as a sex worker; and a change in civil law so that prostitution was no longer considered immoral (*Sittenwidrig*). Sex workers could also enforce their claims for remuneration in court. Critics questioned the law's effectiveness. Some sex workers did not register for benefits, and the law did not cover noncitizens. It nonetheless stood as pathbreaking legislation.

While other countries focused on protecting sex workers, in the 1990s Japanese politicians once again framed prostitution as a threat to children. Critics of compensated dating argued the phenomenon exploited the sexuality of juveniles regardless of whether the individuals were actually under-age or the men paid for sex. Rather than focus on the experience of the young women themselves, opponents were most concerned with how the practice threatened the nation. After all, it was said, these women would grow up to be wives and mothers. Others used the problem to criticize materialism in Japanese society, in this case high school students desiring designer bags, not unlike the panpan's consumption of stockings and cigarettes.[29]

At the same time that enjo kōsai came to public attention in Japan, child prostitution rose to prominence as an international issue. In the early 1990s, new NGOs such as End Child Prostitution in Asian Tourism began to organize and lobbied at the 1994 International Conference on Population and Development in Cairo. Because Japanese sex tourists were visible in Asia, Japan drew almost immediate attention. Child prostitution was governed by a series of local and national laws, specifically the Child Welfare Law and local obscenity regulations. Although the national age of consent was thirteen, in practice, prefectural law made it higher. Pornographers avoided the regulations by using models of eighteen or older made to look younger, for instance, by wearing school uniforms. But they also employed Southeast Asian children.[30]

The fight for a law to ban child prostitution and pornography once again led to strange alliances. Some Diet members argued that those involved in enjo kōsai were not victims since they chose to date for money. The Left opposed a bill banning the practice because they argued that it was an example of the state infringing on individual rights and that the focus should be on child prostitution.[31] LDP members, on the other hand, sold the bill as a way of ending the practice of compensated dating. They were joined by anti-prostitution activists, including groups that had pressed for the passage of the Prostitution Prevention Law.

The resulting Child Prostitution and Child Pornography Law (Jidō Kaishun Jidō Poruno Hō) was widely seen as a success for a transnational alliance of feminists, child welfare, and human rights activists. Once again they claimed to have brought Japan in line with international norms, imposing a minimum age of eighteen and targeting acts of child prostitution and pornography.[32] After its passage, the government punished pornographers. But the law's effects on child prostitution were more complex. Though the law was designed to prosecute adults, the government fined juveniles. Additionally, the law targeted enjo kōsai, but not sex tourism. It did not end child prostitution, but rather displaced it.

The tragic irony of more recent anti-prostitution campaigns, like those in the 1950s, was that criminalizing a form of commerce made real victims both less visible and more vulnerable. Only the struggle played out in a global arena, as states and international and nongovernmental organizations fought over the idea and reality of sexual exploitation. And just as in the early postwar years, the United States insisted on the end of regulated prostitution even as unregulated sex markets continued to flourish around military bases.

After 2001, and the inauguration of President George W. Bush, the United States redoubled efforts to stop trafficking and promote a global ban on prostitution. Bush signed a presidential directive against the practice and spoke at the UN. He insisted the international community fight for the "hundreds of thousands of teenage girls, and others as young as five, who fall victim to the sex trade" each year.[33] NGOs working against trafficking needed to declare opposition to legal prostitution to be eligible for U.S. government funds.

But while trafficking in women was (and is) a tragedy, activists' attempts to dramatize the need to abolish all forms of sex work led them to lose both focus and credibility.[34] When Bush addressed the General Assembly, the UN had already reduced its estimate of trafficked women worldwide from four million to one million. As a UNESCO report observed, "Trafficking of girls and women is one of several highly emotive issues which seem to overwhelm critical faculties." The authors doubted all statistics that purport to measure the problem.

> Numbers take on a life of their own, gaining acceptance through repetition, often with little inquiry into their derivations. Journalists, bowing to the pressures of editors, demand numbers, any number. Organizations feel compelled to supply them, lending false precisions and spurious authority to many reports.[35]

The problem of simply measuring sexual trafficking just in the United States indicated the much bigger challenge of mounting a global campaign to stop it. In 2000, when the State Department still estimated that there were more than 1 million female and child victims each year, of whom more than 50,000 were trafficked into the United States, Congress passed the Trafficking Victims Protection Act (TVPA),[36] which authorized international programs to prevent the practice as well as measures to help those seeking to escape. Victims and their families could obtain special visas that allowed them to remain in the United States for three years—extended to four years in 2006—and then request permanent residency. Expecting many would come forward, the law allotted 5,000 visas per year. But from 2001 to 2004, just 118 people were convicted of trafficking, and in 2004, only 520 applications were received from victims and their families. Further, fewer than half of these applicants were found to qualify. The State Department reduced its estimate of trafficking in the United States to 14,500 to 17,500 in 2004, and that figure included *all* forms of forced labor, including farm work and domestic labor, and not just sex work.[37]

In an attempt to arrive at a more exact measure of the problem, in 2005 Congress mandated a biennial report on trafficking allegations and arrests. In the first twenty-one months of operation, from January 2007 to September 2008, there were 1,229 incidents. But only 112 cases led to confirmed arrests of traffickers or successful visa applications for victims, and this at a time when activists and journalists alleged the United States was a "major importer of sex slaves" and that at least 10,000 were being smuggled in each year. The U.S. State Department estimated that 600,000 to 800,000 people were trafficked each year around the globe, 66 percent of them for prostitution. But the General Accounting Office found that this widely cited figure was the work of one person who did not document his work, and actually depended on other estimates that are now deemed unreliable.[38]

Nevertheless, the U.S. government, partnering with evangelical Christians and abolitionist feminists, persisted in a global campaign against sexual trafficking. A State Department policy placed other countries, including Japan, into three tiers (with three being the lowest) based on how aggressively they fight prostitution. In 2003, Japan was placed in Tier 2 (countries that meet "minimum standards" but whose governments need to improve). Japan then sank to "Tier 2 watch," largely because of its policy on entertainment visas for Filipinas.

The fate of these Filipina workers illustrates the unintended consequences of the anti-trafficking campaign. From the mid-1980s until 2005, most entered Japan legally on entertainer visas, typically working as bar hostesses. They usually migrated to Japan with the help of middlemen brokers, a process designed to protect them from club owners. This arrangement could also entail dependence. Women were paid part of their salary in advance, but received the balance at the end of their employment contract. U.S. State Department policy incorrectly regarded entertainer visas as a vehicle used by traffickers to bring women to Japan. It also mistakenly analyzed hostess work as a route to prostitution.[39] In 2005, Japan responded to international criticism by tightening qualifications for entertainer visas: previously a woman could qualify by obtaining a Certificate of Eligibility from the government, a process taking up to six months, but no longer.

Activists as well as the Filipino government spoke out against proposed changes, to no avail. The new requirements meant a longer "training period," which could translate into a longer period of indenture. Migrants, who were already very poor, thus incurred more debts.[40] The number of legal Filipina immigrants dropped by half.[41] But while fewer women entered on entertainer visas, more entered on other kinds of visas, or illegally.[42] Filipina hostesses as well as sex workers could still be seen in towns throughout Japan, both around bases and in Japan's rural interior. But as a result of their irregular status and the consequent sense of vulnerability they felt toward employers and customers, they found their work had become more difficult and more dangerous. Bar hostesses felt compelled to dress more revealingly and put up with the groping of bar patrons.[43] Nevertheless, the United States promoted Japan back to Tier 2 status, and the embassy lauded its "Fight Against Modern-Day Slavery."[44]

If U.S. pressure to crack down on sex work recalled the immediate postwar period, so too did Japanese fear and anger over the sexual violence of U.S. servicemen. This became a matter of international controversy only in 1995, at the same time as the media was focusing on the danger to children posed by enjo kōsai. But there was a long history of sexual violence and murders by servicemen that did not receive national news coverage in Japan. U.S. servicemen were involved in six murders between 1955 and 1974, and hostesses were the victims in four of them. They were also the victims in four out of the five murders involving servicemen in the decade that followed.[45]

It was not until a twelve-year-old schoolgirl was abducted and raped by two marines and a sailor in 1995 that national outrage erupted. The admiral who led U.S. Pacific Command, Richard C. Macke, commented at a press conference that their conduct was "absolutely stupid. . . . For the price they paid to rent the car, they could have had a girl."[46] Macke was forced to resign, but the remark revealed the real nature of U.S. policy. For decades, commanders in Okinawa not only had tolerated brothels, but had also set up a system that certified the health of sex workers.[47]

The 1995 rape incited the largest protests in Okinawa history. Despite the rich subsidies from the national government to Okinawa—and the enormous payments that went to the landowners—this is where military bases were least popular. Homeowners worried about toxic waste left behind at abandoned bases. And everyone had to endure the screams of jet engines and inebriated servicemen. But after 1995, opposition crystallized around rape cases.

What particularly outraged many Japanese was that the accused could not be interrogated. They were still protected by the Status of Forces Agreement, which seemed like a throwback to nineteenth-century extraterritorial imperialism. Accused servicemen were confined to base, and Japanese police were sometimes denied the ability to question them, which made it difficult for prosecutors to prepare a criminal case. U.S. authorities argued that

American servicemen deserved the same rights they would have in the United States. Japan's criminal justice system encouraged confession and guilty pleas and allowed imprisonment without charge for twenty-three days.[48]

In the 1995 Okinawa rape case, the Americans finally relented and turned the servicemen over to the Japanese. After confessing, the men were condemned to seven years in prison. In the case's wake, the United States and Japan revised the Status of Forces Agreement to state that in the future the United States would give "sympathetic consideration" to remanding U.S. servicemen accused of violent crimes to Japanese authorities before indictment.

However, in many cases, accused U.S. servicemen still are not surrendered to Japanese prosecutors. These crimes, especially in Okinawa, have been the subject of extensive press coverage and analysis in the Japanese media, and to some extent the American press as well. Public outcry spurred local officials to ask the national government to move bases and to hold local elections calling for the same. The issue has led to demands from Okinawans as well as other Japanese that the U.S. military presence in Japan be reduced and eventually eliminated. After yet another incident in 2008, in which a thirty-eight-year-old marine was arrested for the rape of a fourteen-year-old girl, the United States placed all servicemen and their families on twenty-four-hour curfew and reaffirmed plans to redeploy 8,000 marines to Guam.[49]

Still, in the areas around bases, some people are ambivalent or openly supportive of the U.S. presence. Men and women in the armed forces together with their families can provide huge sums for municipalities. Even in Okinawa, which still hosts thirty-eight U.S. military facilities, opponents have been unable to marshal a majority in elections where bases were the main issue. Many men and women make their livings from them—either directly through employment or rent, or indirectly through small businesses—just as they did in base towns such as Sasebo in the 1950s. Since 1978, Tokyo has also used public works money and support for the employment of base workers to assuage Okinawan opposition.[50]

For many Japanese men and women, the occupation seems never-ending. Some 47,000 U.S. servicemen and women are still stationed in Japan, along with 43,000 dependents and 5,000 Department of Defense employees. Under the 1960 Treaty of Mutual Cooperation and Security, the United States is legally responsible for Japan's defense, in return for which Japan offers military bases and a financial subsidy of $2.15 billion each year.[51] And U.S. servicemen still have a privileged status, which usually exempts them from Japanese justice. They have been charged in some 200,000 incidents between 1952 and 2005, with 10 percent—or an average of about one incident every day—involving something more than a traffic ticket or accident.[52] Even when the encounters are more positive, the relationships can seem unequal. When older Japanese see their daughters, nieces, and grandchildren date U.S. servicemen, many recall the Occupation.

Of course, the early postwar years were a very different time. It is often forgotten that the Occupation was international and multiracial. Japanese women had relationships and in some cases offspring with men from many countries. Now it is the sex workers who come from all over the world— from Thailand, the Philippines, Russia—whereas the servicemen all come from the United States. That is one reason that, even if it is still sometimes advertised with neon lights, sex work seems invisible unless and until Japanese schoolgirls are at risk.

Sex work no longer plays the catalytic role in the Japanese economy that it did during the early postwar years. At a time when Japanese industry was ravaged and the nation had little more to sell than souvenirs, the dollars and black-market goods sex workers earned helped to sustain their countrymen and jump-start the recovery. Japan has now become so rich that the government can afford to subsidize U.S. bases and buy off opposition. But if it does so, and still shields servicemen from prosecution, it is because Tokyo remains utterly dependent on a global political and economic system that is policed by the United States. This underlying and unresolved tension explains why core issues of territorial sovereignty and citizenship can still turn on rape cases and anti-prostitution campaigns.

Conclusion
Beyond Victimhood

For 300 years, sex work in Japan was highly regulated and even ritualized. All of that changed in 1945, when Japanese men and women, struggling for survival, suddenly had to make their own rules. One reason the panpan phenomenon was so disturbing was that it appeared to mean that any woman—even an educated, middle-class mother or daughter—could find a place in the sex industry. More disturbing still was that so many other people stood by, or even profited from the trade. In the areas surrounding military bases, moneylenders, letter writers, taxi drivers, rickshaw pullers, barkeeps, and black marketers all took their cut. Some policemen also owned brothels, and many politicians were patrons. Major corporations such as Morinaga, Meiji, and Sankyō found it profitable to market penicillin to sex workers. Early in the Occupation, the Japanese government itself had established brothels for servicemen, reimporting a practice once reserved for Japan's overseas empire. It seemed that everyone and everything—perhaps even Japan itself—was up for grabs.

And yet, when a national debate began over sex work, it was treated as a women's issue. It was not obvious why it should have been, nor was it inevitable. After all, some sex workers were men, and so were almost all the clients. Even if the issue was a moral one, men were compromised through sex work no less than women. No one was more culpable than those military and government officials who organized forced sexual labor through comfort stations during the Pacific War, and those who established brothels as a "bulwark" to protect middle-class Japanese women against rape by Allied servicemen. Though women may have had the most to lose, especially in an occupied territory, rape in wartime was also intended to punish husbands, brothers, and fathers. Occupation officials, for their part, were mainly concerned with protecting their own troops against infection, even though Allied servicemen came to Japan with appallingly high rates of syphilis and gonorrhea, and played a major role in starting the postwar epidemic.

Instead of investigating this very recent history and insisting that all of Japanese society—as well as occupation authorities—shared responsibility for preventing rape, protecting sex workers, and stemming the spread of disease, reformers and activists focused on the purported danger of the panpan to public morals. Female legislators' self-identification with the issue enabled them to assert their place in Japanese politics. These women claimed to speak for all mothers and made themselves protectors of children. Rather than acting in solidarity with sex workers, they treated them as victims and incompetents who had to be saved from themselves. This maternalist strategy made it impossible to organize or even imagine a different kind of movement. But a coalition based on the rights of sex workers might have been far more effective in fighting exploitative proprietors and reducing the incidence of VD.

After the Liberal Democratic Party found a way to seize leadership of the anti-prostitution movement and put sex workers back in the shadows by passing the Prostitution Prevention Law, the issue largely vanished from Japan's political agenda. LDP politicians managed to criminalize sex workers while protecting the interests of the brothel owners who paid them off. Ironically, a law that was ostensibly dedicated to defending public morals showed the moral corruption at the heart of Japan's power structure. It would be three decades before another cross-party coalition of women could pass any significant legislation, and forty years before sex work was once again on the national agenda. So in helping to push sex workers to the margins, female legislators themselves became more marginal in Japanese politics.

Much more was at stake in the fight over sex work than the fate of sex workers themselves, and more even than the fortunes of particular politicians and activists. This is another reason sex workers were not allowed to have much say, and female politicians were not permitted to decide the matter.

Instead, broader segments of Japanese society made sex workers into powerful symbols and ultimately turned them into scapegoats. Their symbolic importance was evident in the first days of the Occupation. Japanese governmental authorities and media had warned that women and children were at risk of rape. Those who consented to sex with servicemen within the Recreational Amusement Association system were meant to be sacrificial victims. Although some servicemen did force themselves on Japanese women, sexual violence never approached the level predicted before the Occupation began. Instead, Japanese were astounded at the rapid development of a market for sexual services that catered to servicemen. Whether there were actually more women selling sex than before cannot be known with certainty. But it is clear that sex workers during the Occupation came from more varied backgrounds and worked in novel ways. Sex was sold outside the formerly licensed districts and, above all, the clients were far more conspicuous. Journalists and social critics began to portray sex workers not as sacrificial victims—not for their families, or for their country—but as symbols of national shame.

Sociologists have developed the concept of moral panic to explain such episodes. They typically occur when, as in occupied Japan, societies are under severe strain. Social workers, activists, and experts seek to renegotiate moral boundaries, in this case presenting the panpan as a threat to the nation and its children. The media played a key role in stoking anxieties, at the same time stereotyping sex workers as young women who would sell themselves for cigarettes and stockings. Because the panpan were the girls next door or neighborhood wives, behavior that was previously accepted and—in the case of the RAA—even supported by the government came to be labeled as irredeemably deviant.[1]

But this particular moral panic entailed renegotiating normative boundaries not just within one society, but in terms of how Japanese men and women would relate to the rest of the world. They recoiled at the realization that streetwalkers had become intermediaries between Japanese society and the occupation forces who controlled their collective fate. Those women who engaged in long-term relationships and, still more, those who emigrated to the United States or Australia were emissaries of Japan at a time when—because of censorship and diplomatic isolation—Japan could not easily speak for itself. That helps explain why eventually all the women who worked for the Occupation, and not just sex workers, began to be stigmatized and ostracized.

Long before the government acted, people found ways to push women who associated with the Occupation beyond the pale of Japanese society. Rather than recognize that many of them were struggling to support their families, anti-prostitution activists treated them as a dangerous example for children. To the extent they were acknowledged as mothers, it was as mothers of *konketsuji*, who even sympathetic observers thought should never have been born. Even though many women engaged in relationships with servicemen and bore them children, it was sex workers—deemed mentally deficient—who were said to have created this threat to the eugenic quality of the nation.

Occupation officials themselves were witting or unwitting participants in stigmatizing women who associated with servicemen. Allied officials treated all Japanese women they encountered, even clerks and secretaries, as potential VD carriers. Commanding officers made it a practice to break up long-term relationships by transferring servicemen. Officials participated in marginalizing sex workers because they too needed a scapegoat, above all for the high rates of VD among occupation forces. Over the longer run, they also worried that interracial unions and biracial children would disrupt the clear distinction between the occupiers and the occupied upon which their authority rested.

Officials from several empires had faced some of the same challenges when they ruled other Asian societies. This book has argued that these commonalities make it useful to compare the Allied Occupation of Japan to imperial dominion. Occupation authorities gave themselves powers at least as great as those of empires in the same era. Of course, like the British Commonwealth and the French Union, occupation authorities exercised this power in the name of purportedly universalist principles. Ideals of democracy, liberty, and equality were meant to apply to women as well as men. But in fact, and from the very beginning, racial and gender discrimination structured every aspect of life.

A host of issues, from regulating prostitution to prosecuting sexual violence, reflected these inequalities, both within the ranks and between the occupiers and the Japanese. Military officials worked with their Japanese collaborators to create segregated brothels for white and black servicemen. Panpan themselves learned that it was to their advantage to specialize according to the client's race. And when Japanese women reported sexual violence, both U.S. and Commonwealth officials were far more likely to prosecute and punish non-white servicemen. Efforts to separate Japanese and foreigners were extensive and systematic, to the point that Tokyo began to resemble the Jim Crow South of the United States.

Of course, it was impossible for occupiers to completely segregate different races, no more than could imperial authorities in such places as the Dutch East Indies, French Indochina, or India under British rule. In fact, the longer the Occupation continued, the harder it became. For Allied officials—and for the Japanese themselves—biracial offspring of unions with Japanese women challenged notions of race and citizenship, at the core of national identity. Japanese laws defined citizenship according to the father's bloodline, while U.S. and Australian racial exclusion laws prevented non-whites from immigrating (in the case of Australia, this even included Americans of Asian descent). But again and again, U.S. officials were forced to make exceptions to immigration law to allow servicemen to bring their Japanese brides home—at least 5,500 by 1954. Even Australia lifted its blanket exclusion in 1952. Marriages between white men and Asian women had been rare in both of these countries. With the arrival of thousands of Japanese brides after 1945, they became increasingly common. This is another example of how empire came home—in this case, quite literally—and how even unequal relationships can create two-way flows of influence.

Another reason the power of the Occupation was never absolute was that occupation officials were themselves divided. They could never agree on a consistent policy toward sex work or VD, and it was not difficult to take advantage of these divisions. This was most clearly the case with the sex workers themselves, who learned to play on the symbolism they were supposed to embody, whether as submissive "geisha girls" or subversive panpan. What seemed like unequal or even exploitative relationships were often more complex. As we have seen, these relationships ranged across a spectrum and included situations in which women could pick and choose clients, enter into long-term relationships, or end partnerships on their own terms. Some women faced more difficult choices, especially the many who worked to pay off debt contracts to proprietors. But contrary to what many expected—including Japanese government officials—women who had servicemen for clients tended to be better off. They were less indebted and more highly paid than their counterparts who worked in former regulated districts.

It has been argued that there can be no empire without collaborators.[2] In Japan, sex workers were not the only ones who could find profit and opportunity during the Occupation. Base towns boomed when soldiers and sailors were in port, and local officials made it their business to ensure they could find what they were seeking. The reaction that all this provoked, in turn, provided opportunities for journalists, activists, politicians, and—above all—more established proprietors. In the end, the proprietors came out on top: they negotiated a law that put streetwalkers out of business and solidified their control over the industry.

But if the power of the Occupation was never absolute or unidirectional, neither did it suddenly come to an end in 1952. The Prostitution Prevention Law not only safeguarded the interests of male proprietors, it permitted sex work to continue in base areas and exempted clients from the risk of prosecution. The law's advocates wanted Japanese law to conform to international norms against prostitution, but these norms had been defined by countries that had long exempted their own empires from these strictures. Though the United States would become a champion of the fight against sex trafficking, in the twenty-first century it still tolerated sex work around overseas bases and sought to protect its own soldiers from prosecution for sexual violence. Thus, while the State Department would fight trafficking, and thus ensure that sex workers stay put, the Defense Department moves their clients from base to base all across the world.

Many intellectuals in Japan consider opposition to U.S. bases a moral obligation. For most, it is part of a larger critique of militarism. When they recall the postwar years, they focus on violence, humiliation, and dehumanizing medical treatment as intrinsic to the Occupation. They see the experience of women who served Allied soldiers as part of a longer history of victimization—including the military comfort women under *Japanese* occupation.

Sex work and sexual violence could be interrelated, if only in the minds of American and Japanese policy makers who assumed that paid sex was a substitute for rape. But this book has emphasized the vital importance of discovering how sex workers themselves experienced different regulatory regimes, and whether simply prohibiting prostitution actually improved their lot. In the case of Japan under the Occupation, sex workers still had choices. In fact, while the nation lay prostrate, they were uniquely empowered, with control over their fortunes, their families, and their fates.

When critics of the Allied Occupation compare sex workers to sexual slaves, it has the unintended effect of supporting a nationalist agenda that depends on portraying Japan as a victim. In fact, the memory of the pan-pan may well have changed the way Japanese men and women understand the experience of occupation, to the point that they have found it all too easy to believe that military comfort women voluntarily sold sex to Japanese servicemen in occupied China.

Investigating what happened in occupied Japan not only helps us understand how men and women remember or misremember the past, but also provides lessons that can and should inform contemporary debates about the future of sex work around the world. It shows how women could be worse off when authorities tried to stop prostitution, since they were subject to indiscriminate roundups and compulsory quarantine. Sex workers themselves were at the mercy of proprietors and corrupt policemen. Where they could operate in the open, and outside the confines of the older system of regulated prostitution, they tended to have fewer debts and to make more money, and could more easily support families or switch to another line of work.

Any attempt to improve the lives of sex workers must therefore be based not merely on moral principle, but on a critical analysis of the practical and symbolic politics of such measures. Since sex markets can be transnational in nature and are a point of both tension and negotiation in international relations, this analysis must follow these links and connections wherever they lead.

Recent decades have seen many societies struggle with the perception—and reality—of lost sovereignty, leaving individuals vulnerable to global forces beyond their control or comprehension. In that way, the experience of the Japanese under international occupation can be seen as foreshadowing these larger trends. It can also help explain why, when globalization appeared to accelerate in the 1990s, the plight of trafficked women and children came to seem emblematic of its dark side. A sense of compromised sovereignty can lead a society to focus on its most vulnerable members, and those who "think globally" think first of women and children who are bought and sold across international borders. Unfortunately, the history of Japan under occupation also shows that it is all too easy to treat the most vulnerable people as symbols. But it is precisely when individuals are most at risk that it is most important that their voices be heard. As long as international relations continue to be negotiated with and through women's bodies, these women will instead be forced to serve other people's agendas.

Reference Matter

Appendix

National legislative intiatives, 1948–1956

Year introduced	Diet session introduced	English name	Japanese name	Introduced by
1948	2nd	Prostitution Punishment Bill	Baishuntō Shobatsu Hōan	Government [Japan Liberal Party]
1953	15th [19th] [21st]	Prostitution Punishment Bill	Baishuntō Shobatsu Hōan	Key Diet Sponsors Itō [Tsutsumi Tsuruyo]
1955	22nd	Prostitution Punishment Bill	Baishuntō Shobatsu Hōan	Key Diet Sponsors [Kamichika Ichiko]
1956	24th	Punishment and Security Measures for Prostitution and Rehabilitation Protection Legislative Bill	Baishun Keibatsu Hoan Shobun Kōsei Hogo Hōritsuan	Diet Members [Socialist Party]
1956	24th	Prostitution Prevention Bill	Baishun Bōshi Hōan	Government [Liberal Democratic Party]

SOURCES: *Baishun Taisaku Shingikai ed., Baishun taisaku no genkyō*; Fujime, "Higashi Ajia reisen to jendā."

Local anti-prostitution regulations, 1948–1955

Miyagi prefecture	7/10/1948	Fuji Yoshida City	9/4/1951
Niigata prefecture	11/1/1948	Nishinomiya City	9/29/1951
Tokyo metropolitan area	5/31/1949	Gifu City	10/18/1951
Beppu City	8/20/1949	Wajiro Village (Fukuoka)	10/23/1951
Gunma prefecture	8/23/1949	Hakodate City	10/26/1951
Nakano Town (Yamanashi)	6/27/1950	Yaizu City	11/23/1951
Hiroshima prefecture	8/14/1950	Otaru City	12/1/1951
Yamato Town (Kanagawa)	9/10/1950	Kumamoto City	12/8/1951
Asaka Town (Saitama)	9/11/1950	Fukuoka prefecture	1/10/1952
Ōmiya City	10/25/1950	Amagasaki City	2/12/1952
Zentsuji Town (Kagawa)	11/1/1950*	Himeji City	4/1/1952
Osaka City	12/1/1950	Kyoto City	5/31/1952
Yokohama City	12/4/1950	Yamanishi prefecture	6/13/1952
Sasebo City	12/8/1950	Kakogawa City	7/8/1952
Kōfu City	12/15/1950	Kamakura City	8/1/1952
Hashioka Town (Kagawa)	1/1/1951	Saga prefecture	8/29/1952
Saitama prefecture	1/19/1951	Hachinohe City	9/1/1952
Toyonaka City	1/25/1951	Ichikawa City	11/25/1952
Ashiya City	2/6/1951	Okayama City	8/4/1953*
Nara City	2/14/1951	Moriguchi City	9/24/1953
Sapporo City	2/18/1951	Yao City	10/1/1953
Kawanishi City	2/28/1951	Gifu prefecture	10/3/1953
Tochigi prefecture	3/20/1951	Shizuoka prefecture	10/13/1953
Yokosuka City	4/1/1951	Fussa Town (Tokyo)	11/5/1953
Kobe City	5/28/1951	Omisawa Town (Aomori)	11/15/1953
Iwakuni City	6/3/1951	Sunakawa Town (Tokyo)	12/21/1953
Chitose Town (Hokkaido)	6/21/1951	Ikeda City	2/15/1954
Karuizawa Town (Nagano)	7/1/1951	Chigasaki City	3/28/1954
Ito City	7/4/1951*	Kawasaki City	4/1/1954
Kokura City	7/16/1951	Hōfu City	6/1/1954
Tsukumi City	8/31/1951	Moriyama City	11/25/1955
Shimizu City	9/2/1951*		

SOURCES: Baishun Taisaku Shingikai, *Baishun taisaku no genkyō*; Fujime, "Higashi Ajia reisen to jendā."
*Listed in Fujime, but not in initial Ministry of Labor data.

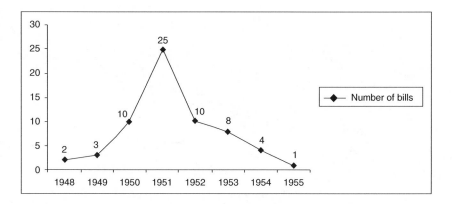

Local regulations by year, 1948–1955

Notes

Abbreviations

ATL   Alexander Turnbull Library, Wellington, New Zealand
AWM   Australian War Memorial, Canberra, Australia
GWP   Gordon W. Prange Collection, University of Maryland, College Park
LNA   League of Nations Archive, Geneva, Switzerland
NAA   National Archives of Australia
NANZ   National Archives of New Zealand, Wellington
NDL   National Diet Library, Tokyo
SLNSW   State Library of New South Wales, Australia
USNA   U.S. National Archives, College Park, Maryland

INTRODUCTION

1. "Ikite iru kottōhin," *Sandee Mainichi*, March 30, 1949, 36.

2. A useful overview can be found in Bernstein, *Temporarily Yours*, 6.

3. For some particularly important examples, see Ellis, *Studies in the Psychology of Sex*, Vol. 2, and Freud, "The Most Prevalent Form of Degradation in Erotic Life." For the transmission of sexology in Japan, see Frühstück, *Colonizing Sex*.

4. See, for example, Vance, *Pleasure and Danger*; and Duggan and Hunter, *Sex Wars*. Some critics argued that women's subordination to men was underpinned by sexuality, for example, Barry, *Female Sexual Slavery*, and MacKinnon, *Feminism Unmodified*.

5. Leigh, "Inventing Sex Work," 225; and Kempadoo and Doezema, *Global Sex Workers*, 3.

6. Commercial sex workers tend to focus on the importance of "decriminalization." Such a system stands in opposition to "legalization," meaning a state system of regulation and control. Scholars supportive of decriminalization include Pheterson, *Vindication of the Rights of Whores*; Bell, *Reading, Writing, and Rewriting the Prostitute Body*; and Rubin, "Thinking Sex," 267–319. On the sex workers' movement, see Jenness's book on the history of the sex workers' union COYOTE, *Making It Work*; also Nagle, *Whores and Other Feminists*.

7. McClintock, "Sex Workers and Sex Work: Introduction"; Pheterson, *Prostitution Prism*; Davidson, *Prostitution, Power, and Freedom*; Scambler and Scambler, *Rethinking Prostitution*; Weitzer, *Sex for Sale*.

8. For an exhaustive summary of historical thinking until 1999, see Timothy J. Gilfoyle's review article, "Prostitutes in History." Some pathbreaking historical monographs include White, *Comforts of Home*; Guy, *Sex and Danger in Buenos Aires*; and Hershatter, *Dangerous Pleasures*.

9. On sex work as labor, see White, *Comforts of Home*, 11–13; Walkowitz, *Prostitution and Victorian Society*, 31; Stansell, *City of Women*, 172.

10. For other examples of client-oriented research, see Allison, *Nightwork*; Bernstein, "The Meaning of the Purchase"; and Mackey, *Pursuing Johns*.

11. Johnson, *Sorrows of Empire*; and Bacevich, *American Empire*.

12. On the contrast between early U.S. and Japanese accounts, see Dower, "Occupied Japan as History," 485–86, 501–4.

13. Dower, *Empire and Aftermath*; and Takemae, *Inside GHQ*.

14. For an important example, see Ward and Sakamoto, *Democratizing Japan*.

15. Dower's work helped to inspire these new directions, especially *War Without Mercy* and *Embracing Defeat*. On race, see, for example, Koshiro, *Trans-Pacific Racisms and the U.S. Occupation of Japan*; and on gender see Shibusawa, *America's Geisha Ally*, and Koikari, *Pedagogy of Democracy*.

16. On the potential for a broader view, see Vera Mackie's review of *Pedagogy of Democracy* in *American Historical Review* 115, no. 2 (2010): 522–23, as well as Gerster, *Travels in Atomic Sunshine*.

17. Tanaka, *Japan's Comfort Women*.

18. Fujime, "Japanese Feminism and Commercialized Sex"; Hirai, "Nihon senryō o 'sei' de minaosu"; Tanaka, *Japan's Comfort Women*.

19. Spongberg, *Feminizing Venereal Disease*, 3–5.

20. On Germany, which has been relatively well examined by historians, see especially Biddiscombe, "Dangerous Liaisons"; Goedde, *GIs and Germans*; Höhn, *GIs and Frauleins*; and Willoughby, *Remaking the Conquering Heroes*. On Korea, see Moon, *Sex Among Allies*.

21. Benvenisti, *International Law of Occupation*, 1.

22. The Allied powers insisted on "unconditional surrender" in Japan—and in Germany—using the logic of the legal notion of *debellatio*. Should a country be in debellatio, its national institutions would have collapsed, and its territory would not be occupied—thus, the Hague Regulations would be inapplicable. But while debellatio may have existed in Germany, most observers would have found Japan—with its functioning government—still intact. Benevisti, *International Law of Occupation*, 91–92.

23. Doyle, *Empires*, 30.

24. Stoler, "Carnal Knowledge and Imperial Power," 57.

25. Packard, *Protest in Tokyo*, 8. The status of U.S. bases is the subject of continual negotiation. These bases currently extend over some 77,000 acres.

26. For a good introduction to the complexity of sex work in the early modern era, see Stanley, "Pinning Down the Floating World." Works on elite sex workers in this earlier period include Stein, *Japans Kurtisanen*; Ishii, *Edo no yūjo, Edo jidai manpitsu*, 2; Takikawa, *Yūjo no rekishi, Nihon rekishi shinsho*; Seigle, *Yoshiwara*. On the non-elite workers, see Sone, "Baijo"; Sone, "Prostitution and Public Authority in Early Modern Japan," 169–85; Sone, "Conceptions of Geisha," 213–33. In studying sex work in Japan, it is impossible to ignore nonscholarly histories, memoirs, and pictorial works usually placed under the rubric of "manners and customs" (*fūzoku*). These works and others are listed in the bibliography.

27. For a tabular presentation of this hierarchy and its equivalents in Shimabara, see Stein, *Japans Kurtisanen*, 362.

28. Sone describes women selling sexual services outside the city walls in "Prostitution and Public Authority in Early Modern Japan," 175. Watanabe's anecdotal report of his twentieth-century archival visit to seaside towns demonstrates the extent to which sex work existed outside cities in the Edo period. See Watanabe, *Edo yūri seisuiki*.

29. Stanley, "Pinning Down the Floating World," 95–96, 220, 232.

30. Fujime, *Sei no rekishigaku*; Garon, *Molding Japanese Minds*, 88–114.

31. Fujime, *Sei no rekishigaku*, 89–90, and "The Licensed Prostitution System and the Prostitution Abolition Movement in Modern Japan"; Davis, "Bodies, Numbers, and Empires."

32. Saveliev, "Rescuing the Prisoners of the Maria Luz," 75–81; Ramseyer, "Indentured Prostitution in Imperial Japan," 97–98.

33. Ramseyer, "Indentured Prostitution in Imperial Japan," 98.

34. Sanders, "Prostitution in Postwar Japan," 34.

35. Ibid., 2.

36. Garon, *Molding Japanese Minds*, esp. 98–99; Yoshimi Kaneko, *Baishō no shakaishi*, 107–19; Takemura, *Haishō undō*.

37. Fujime, "The Licensed Prostitution System," 142.

38. Akamatsu, *Yobai no minzokugaku*, 10.

39. Fujime, "The Licensed Prostitution System," 152.

40. Mihalopulos, "Finding Work Through Sex," 8.

41. Mihalopulos, "Ousting the Prostitute, Retelling the Story of the Karayuki-san," 181.

42. Mihalopulos, "Finding Work Through Sex," 320, 329.

43. Warren, *Ah Ku and Karayuki-san*, 164.

44. Mihalopulos, "Finding Work Through Sex," 334–35.

45. Song, "Japanese Colonial Rule and State-Managed Prostitution."

46. Fujime, *Sei no rekishigaku*, 148; Song, "Japanese Colonial Rule," 172–74.

47. Tipton, "Pink Collar Work," http://wwwsshe.murdoch.edu.au/intersections/issue7/tipton.html (accessed August 8, 2009).

48. Silverberg, *Erotic Grotesque Nonsense*, 73–107.

49. Garon, *Molding Japanese Minds*, 106–10; Fujime, *Sei no rekishigaku*, 288.

50. Yoshiaki, *Comfort Women*; see also Soh, *Comfort Women*.

CHAPTER ONE

1. Sergeant Clyde E. Edwards, "Japanese Open Tokyo 'USO,' Featuring Beer, Hostesses," *Stars and Stripes*, September 8, 1945, Pacific Edition, 3. For more details on the history of *Stars and Stripes*, see Cornebise, *Ranks and Columns*.

2. Five yen was equal to 26 cents in 1945, and $3.15 in 2010 dollars; www.mea suringworth.com/calculators/uscompare/result.php. In 1945, the lowest-ranking enlisted man in the army or navy earned $60 per month when deployed abroad. A first sergeant with three years of service earned $173 per month overseas. Officers' pay started at $175 per month, with a 10 percent bonus for foreign deployment. All servicemen could also be entitled to an allowance for food and lodging when these were not provided to them.

3. Takemae, *Inside GHQ*.

4. The 1955 calculation is based on the figure of 500,000 female sex workers used by the mass media and politicians in the Diet. Nihon Tōkei Kyōkai, *Nihon chōki tōkei sōran*, 1:80.

5. Political scientist Cynthia Enloe was one of the first scholars to analyze the historical patterns of commercial sex that occur between militaries and local communities, especially around military bases, in *Does Khaki Become You?* and *Bananas, Beaches and Bases*. Other useful works on military prostitution in Asia include Moon, *Sex Among Allies*; Sturdevant and Stoltzfus, *Let the Good Times Roll*; and Truong, *Sex, Money and Morality*.

6. Penicillin was distributed to the military for the treatment of VD in 1944. In 1945, prices fell from $20 per vial to under a dollar, and in 1949, 650 billion units were produced. Brandt shows that such dramatic progress was due to the "exigencies of war" and that U.S. authorities credited penicillin with preventing a major VD epidemic; Brandt, *No Magic Bullet*, 161, 170.

7. Levine, "Rereading the 1890s," 590.

8. Brandt, *No Magic Bullet*, 97, 115.

9. Briggs, *Reproducing Empire*, 30–32. On Hawaii, see Bailey and Farber, "Hotel Street," 54–77.

10. Sandos, "Prostitution and Drugs," 621–45.

11. Tanaka, *Japan's Comfort Women*, 89; Roberts, "The Price of Discretion," 1002–3.

12. Pivar, *Purity and Hygiene*, 204, 210. For an example of de facto regulation, see Best, *Controlling Vice*.

13. Brandt, *No Magic Bullet*, 162, 166. The May Act, intended to be temporary but extended in 1948, made it a federal offense to engage in prostitution or to solicit for the purpose of prostitution within a "reasonable distance" of any military base. Public Law 772, 80th Cong., June 25, 1948, Section 1384, Title 18, U.S. Codes, Crimes, and Criminal Procedures.

14. Fujime, *Sei no rekishigaku*, 89–90; also see Frühstück, *Colonizing Sex*, and Davis, "Bodies, Numbers, and Empires."

15. Frühstück, *Colonizing Sex*, 17, 40.

16. Ibid., 75.

17. Sanders, "Prostitution in Postwar Japan," 135; Soh, *Comfort Women*, 107–42; Yoshimi, *Comfort Women*, 43–51.

18. Dower, *Embracing Defeat*, 124.

19. Kobayashi and Murase, *Minna wa shiranai kokka baishun meirei*, 10–11.

20. For more on the RAA, see Yamada, *Senryōgun ianfu*.

21. The initial figure was 50 million yen but ultimately totaled about 33 million yen because loans stopped on January 10, 1946. Kobayashi and Murase, *Minna wa shiranai kokka baishun meirei*, 10–11.

22. Hirai, "R.A.A. to 'akasen' Atami ni okeru tenkai," 82–88.

23. See, for example, Hirai, "Nihon senryō o 'sei' de minaosu," 108; Tanaka, *Japan's Comfort Women*.

24. Kobayashi and Murase, *Minna wa shiranai kokka baishun meirei*, 12.

25. Hirai, "R.A.A. to 'akasen' Atami ni okeru tenkai," 82.

26. Molasky, *American Occupation of Japan and Okinawa*, 109.

27. Hirai, "R.A.A. to 'akasen' Atami ni okeru tenkai," 94; Molasky, *American Occupation of Japan*, 107.

28. Kobayashi and Murase, *Minna wa shiranai kokka baishun meirei*, 18.

29. Hirai, "R.A.A. to 'akasen' Atami ni okeru tenkai," 82.

30. Sergeant Dick Koster, "Tokyo G.I.s Lead Kimona-Clad Girls in Jitterbug at Nip 'U.S.O.,'" *Stars and Stripes*, September 18, 1945, Pacific Edition, 4.

31. Sergeant Robert Cornwall, "Garden Spot in Rubble Proves Oasis for Tokyo G.I.s," *Stars and Stripes*, November 6, 1945, Pacific Edition, 4.

32. Hirai, "R.A.A. to 'akasen' Atami ni okeru tenkai," 83, 90–91.

33. Hirata uses the figure of 70,000 citing Inoue, *Senryō ianjo*, "hon senryō o 'sei' de minaosu."

34. Kobayashi and Murase, *Minna wa shiranai kokka baishun meirei*, 1992.

35. Isamu Nieda, M.D., "Summary Report of Venereal Disease Control Activities in Japan October 1945–December 1949," circa December 1949, NDL, 1374C, Reel 775024, RG 331, SCAP PHW Section/Division Administrative Branch Subject File 1945–53, Summary Report of Venereal Disease Control Activities in Japan, October 1945–December 1949 to Results of Nutrition Survey, Japan, Box 9440.

36. "Proposed Directive, Law to Prohibit Prostitution and Its Allied Activities," n.d., USNA, RG 331, SCAP, Public Safety Division, Folder Prostitution and Sex Vices, Assistant Chief of Staff G2 (Intelligence), Decimal File 1946–50 (.005C).

37. Oscar M. Elkins, "Examination of Prostitutes by Japanese Physicians," October 5, 1946, USNA, RG 331, SCAP, Public Health and Welfare Division, Preventive Medicine Division, Abolition of Licensed Prostitution, No. 1 (1945–1948), No. 2 (1949–1950).

38. Oscar M. Elkins, "Venereal Disease Control in the Tokyo and Yokohama Area," October 11, 1946, NDL 1374C, Reel 775024, RG 331, SCAP PHW, Venereal Disease Control, No. 1, September 1945–December 1946, Box 9370.

39. Ibid.

40. "Summary of Initial Venereal Disease Control Reports," March 28, 1947, NDL 1374C, Reel 775024, RG 331, SCAP PHW, Venereal Disease Contact Tracing, No. 1 (1948), No. 2 (1949–1951), November 1945–July 1951, Box 9370.

41. Note that the number of cases is not the same as the number of people infected, since the same person can be counted as two cases if not cured after the first examination, and one person can also have multiple cases if infected multiple times. Cecil S. Mollohan, "Comparative Rates of Venereal Disease," July 14, 1949, NDL 1374C, Reel 775024, RG 331, SCAP PHW, Venereal Disease Control, No. 3, December 1948–November 1950, Box 9370. On Yoshiwara, see James H. Gordon, "Conference with Dr. H. Yosano and Dr. Fukai," October 3, 1945, NDL 1374C, Reel 775024, RG 331, SCAP PHW, Venereal Disease Control, No. 3, December 1948–November 1950, Box 9370.

42. "Digest of Letter," Hara Endo to General Douglas MacArthur, January 8, 1947, NDL 1374C, Reel 775024, RG 331, SCAP PHW, Venereal Disease, Control No. 2 (1947–1948).

43. Crawford Sams, untitled memorandum, December 26, 1946, USNA, RG 331, SCAP, Public Health and Welfare Section, Preventive Medicine Division, Abolition of Licensed Prostitution, No. 1 (1945–1948), No. 2 (1949–1950).

44. "Suppression of Prostitution in Japan," USNA, RG 331, SCAP Public Health and Welfare Section, Preventative Medicine Division, Abolition of Licensed Prostitution, No. 1 (1945–1948), No. 2 (1949–1950).

45. See Sams, *Medic*, 106–7. Figures from Takemae, *Inside GHQ*, 29.

46. "Shūsen chokugo no kushin," *Asahi Shimbun*, August 15, 1955, 12, as quoted in Fish, "The Heiress and the Love Children," 43–44.

47. Nalty, *Strength for the Fight*, 258; Koshiro, *Trans-Pacific Racisms and the U.S. Occupation of Japan*, 56.

48. Hirai, "R.A.A. to 'akasen' Atami ni okeru tenkai," 82–88.

49. James H. Gordon, "Conference with Major Philip Weisbach, MC, CO, 15th Med Squadron, 1st Cavalry Division," September 30, 1945, NDL 1374C, Reel 775024.

50. "Sailors and Sex: Prostitution Flourishes in Japan," *Newsweek*, November 12, 1945.

51. K. B. Wolfe to Commanding General U.S. Air Force, "Removal of Prostitutes near Fifth Air Force Installations," November 3, 1945, NDL 1374C, Reel 775024, GHQ SCAP PHW, 726.1 reference only, Box 477.

52. "Neck in Private or Face Stockade: Public Affection Between Soldiers, Jap Women Out," *Stars and Stripes*, March 23, 1946, Pacific Edition, 1.

53. "Subject—Public Display of Affection," April 3, 1946, NAA, Canberra, A 5954/69/890/1.

54. "The Navy Provides Social Protection for Servicemen in Japan," 82–89; "Sailors and Sex: Prostitution Flourishes in Japan," *Newsweek,* November 12, 1945.

55. James Forrestal to Clyde Doyle, December 7, 1945, quoted in "The Navy Provides Social Protection," 86–87.

56. Altschuler, "U.S. War Department Venereal Disease Control Program"; Mast, "Venereal Disease Control in the U.S. Navy."

57. R. J. Porter, "On Prostitution," *Stars and Stripes*, December 14, 1945, Pacific Edition, 2.

58. "The Navy Provides Social Protection for Servicemen in Japan."

59. "V.D. Rate Shows Sharp Rise Among Army Men," *Stars and Stripes*, December 3, 1945, Pacific Edition, 3; Corporal M. K. McClellan, "Japan's V.D. Rate Is World's Highest, Says Noted Medic," *Stars and Stripes*, September 29, 1945, Pacific Edition, 8. The "noted medic" was a private physician, not a public health official, and he did not bother to cite statistics or otherwise support his claim.

60. "The Harvest," *Time*, August 27, 1945.

61. "Conference Re Prostitution," December 17, 1945, USNA, RG 338, Records of U.S. Army Operational, Tactical, and Support Organizations, X Corps, Provost Marshal Section, Investigative and Related Records, 1943–36 [*sic*] Investigations, June–September 1945 to Unit History 216th Military Company 1943–5, Entry A-1 588, Box 405.

62. Ibid., December 15, 1945.

63. "Chart of State of Affairs Since the Close of Prostitute Quarters," December 15, 1945, USNA, RG 338, Records of U.S. Army Operational, Tactical, and Support Organizations, X Corps, Provost Marshal Section, Investigative and Related Records, 1943–36 [*sic*] Investigations, June–September 1945 to Unit History 216th Military Company 1943–5, Entry A-1 588, Box 405.

64. SCAPIN 642, January 21, 1946, USNA, RG 331, SCAP, Public Health and Welfare Section, Preventive Medicine Division.

65. Although policy banned troops' access, in practice troops may have continued to visit these establishments. According to Hirai, in Atami, RAA establishments continued to accept troops after the imposition of the off-limits policy. Hirai, "R.A.A. to 'akasen' Atami ni okeru tenkai," 90–91.

66. Fujino, *Sei no kokka kanri*, 176.

67. "Information of General Application Pertaining to Memorandum Number SCAPIN-643 PHW, General Headquarters, Supreme Commander for the Allied Powers, Subject: Abolition of Licensed Prostitution in Japan," August 1946, USNA, RG 331, SCAP, Assistant Chief of Staff, G-2, Public Safety Division, Decimal File, 1946–50, 000.5 A-010, Box 263.

68. H. H. Wilke to Commanding General U.S. Army Forces, Pacific, February 21, 1946, NDL 1374C, Reel 775024, RG 331 SCAP, Box 477.

69. Koshiro, *Trans-Pacific Racisms and the U.S.*, 61–62; on Germany, see Goedde, *GIs and Germans*; Höhn, *GIs and Fräuleins*; Kleinschmidt, *"Do Not Fraternize."*

70. Sams, untitled memorandum, December 26, 1946.

71. Roberts, "The Price of Discretion," 1007–8.

72. "V.D. Control in Army Air Force Personnel," November 20, 1946, USNA, RG 331, SCAP, Public Health and Welfare Section, Preventive Medicine Division, Abolition of Licensed Prostitution, No. 1 (1945–1948), No. 2 (1949–1950).

73. "V.D. Rate Shows Sharp Rise Among Army Men."

74. Sams, untitled memorandum, December 26, 1946.

75. Mollohan, "Comparative Rates of Venereal Disease."

76. Watt, *When Empire Comes Home*, 112–13.

77. "Number of Cases and Death Rates of Reportable Diseases in Each Prefecture," 1949, 1950, 1951, 1952, 1953, provided to the author by Dr. Kimura Mikio of the Kokuritsu Kansenshō Kenkyūjo. In a 1953 government report, it was found that Fukuoka had more sex workers than any other prefecture, including 2,637 panpan who catered to foreign clients, cited in Rōdōshō Fujin Shōnen Kyoku, *Baishun ni kansuru shiryō kaiteiban*, 1955.

78. Koikari, "Rethinking Gender and Power in the US Occupation of Japan, 1945–1952," 313–35; Koikari, *Pedagogy of Democracy*, 170–77.

79. Brandt, *No Magic Bullet*, 167.

80. Meyer, *Creating GI Jane*, 106–7.

81. McNinch, "Recent Advances in Medicine and Surgery."

82. See Bresnahan, "Dangers in Paradise," 42.

83. Ibid.

84. Commander Naval Activities Japan, "Control of Venereal Disease," August 2, 1946, NDL 1374C, Reel 775024, RG 331, SCAP Public Health and Welfare Section.

85. "Recreation Facilities in Okayama," November 17, 1945, RG 338, Records of U.S. Army Operational, Tactical, and Support Organizations, X Corps, Provost Marshal Section, Investigative and Related Records, 1943–36 [*sic*] Investigations, June–September 1945 to Unit History 216th Military Company 1943–5, Entry S-1 588, Box 405.

86. "V.D. Control in Army Air Force Personnel."

87. Meyer, *Creating GI Jane*, 107.

88. "Venereal Disease Examination," circa 1947, AWM, 114/417/1/27, Pt. 2.

89. For an authoritative description of the diagnosis and treatment of these diseases, see Sheila A. Lukehart, "Chapter 162. Syphilis," Sanjay Ram and Peter A. Rice, "Chapter 137. Gonococcal Infections," and Walter E. Stamm, "Chapter 169. Chlamydial Infections," all in Fauci et al., *Harrison's Principles of Internal Medicine*.

90. Roberts, "The Price of Discretion," 1012.

91. Brandt, *No Magic Bullet*, 170.

92. Medical Department, U.S. Army, *Preventative Medicine in World War II*, Vol. 5, *Communicable Diseases* (Washington, DC, 1960), 281.

93. "Suppression of Prostitution," February 28, 1947, USNA, RG 331, SCAP, Public Health and Welfare Section, Preventive Medicine Division, Abolition of Licensed Prostitution, No. 1 (1945–1948), No. 2 (1949–1950).

94. "Check Sheet," March 11, 1947, USNA, RG 331, SCAP, Public Health and Welfare Section, Preventive Medicine Division, Abolition of Licensed Prostitution, No. 1 (1945–1948), No. 2 (1949–1950).

95. "Check Sheet," October 6, 1950, USNA, RG 331, SCAP, Public Health and Welfare Section, Preventive Medicine Division, Folder 37.

96. Faubion Bowers, "The Late Great MacArthur, Warts and All," 168; see also Sanders, "Prostitution in Postwar Japan," 113.

97. Davies, *Occupation of Japan*, 176; "Australia Distressed by Geisha," February 23, 1946, *Sydney Morning Herald*; "Cablegram," June 8, 1946, NAA, A 5954/69/890/1; "Personal Instruction from Lt. Gen. John Northcott Commander-in-Chief, BCOF, to all ranks of BCOF Concerning Fraternization," March 2, 1946, NAA, A 5954/69/890/1.

98. "Cablegram," June 8, 1946.

99. Grey, *Australian Brass*, 140, 148.

100. "Should Australian Soldiers Dance with Jap Taxi-Girls?" *Sydney Morning Herald*, March 23, 1946, SLNSW, Sydney, Australia, Mitchell Collection, MLMSS 1431/45.

101. "Our Men in Japan Can't Help Fraternising," *Telegraph*, March 4, 1946, SLNSW, MLMSS 1431/45.

102. Brian C. H. Moss, "Diaries," March 28, 1946, ATL, Manuscript Collection, Folder 7. Also see Davies, *Occupation of Japan*, 238.

103. "BCOF Fraternization Policy," October 18, 1949, NAA, Melbourne, MP 85/1/1018.

104. "Fraternization," October 3, 1946, NANZ, Box 27 87/11/16, Pt. 1.

105. Ibid.

106. Wood, *Forgotten Force*, 99.

107. Barrett, *We Were There*, 361.

108. John, *Uneasy Lies the Head that Wears a Crown*, 87.

109. "Venereal Diseases-BCOF (Japan)," circa 1949, AWM 114 267/6/17.

110. S. R. Burston, "Report on Visit to BCOF," October 1946, AWM 114/130/1/45; "Anti-V.D. Committee Meeting," January 6, 1948, AWM 114/417/1/27; "Notes on C-in-C Conference at British Com Base," June 1, 1946," NANZ, WA-J 70/3.

111. "Visit of Minister to Japan," March 24, 1947, NAA, Melbourne, MP 217/1/21; Burston, "Report on Visit to BCOF," October 1946, AWM 114/130/1/45.

112. "Survey of V.D. Problem, Ito," February 4, 1949, AWM 114/417/1/27, No. 4.

113. "With the Opening of Our Own Radio Station—WLKW—for All Troops in this Area, *Rice Wafer* Suggests that Information of this Nature Would Be of Great Value," *Rice Wafer*, n.d., NANZ, WA-J 19 1.

114. "Condoms/P.A.C. Treatments," October 7, 1947, NANZ, WA-J 69.

115. "Control of V.D.," May 30, 1947, AWM 114/417/1/27, No. 4.

116. "Minutes of a Conference of the Anti-V.D. Advisory Committee Held at HQ BCOF 12/48 at 1400 Hrs," December 1948, AWM 114/417/1/27.

117. "Conference Re Prostitution," December 17, 1945.

118. "Report by Major General J. C. Haydon, DGO, OBE (COSK) and Air Commodore O. J. Mackinolty, O.B.E., R.A.A.F. on their visit to Japan 18th September to 18th October 1946," October 28, 1946, AWM 114/130/2/17.

119. "Visit of Minister to Japan," December 24, 1946, NAA Melbourne, MP 217/1/21.

120. "Patients Discharged 6 NZGH," February 26, 1948, NANZ, WA-J69; "Monthly Venereal Disease Report of the Eighth Army for the Four-Week Period Ending 28 January 1949," February 28, 1949, AWM 114/417/1/27, No. 4.

121. "Venereal Disease BCOF," December 19, 1946, AWM 114/267/6/17.

122. Davies, *Occupation of Japan*, 244.

123. Burston, "Report on Visit to BCOF," October 1946.

124. "Venereal Disease Contact Questionnaire," June 26, 1946, AWM 114/267/6/17.

125. Koikari, *Pedagogy of Democracy*, 170–77; Ideoka Manabu, "Karikomi to seibyōin—sengo Kanagawa no seiseisaku," in *Senryō to sei*, 124–28.

126. "Criminal Report #2," July 18, 1946, NANZ, WA-J 69 a13.

127. "Round-up of Prostitutes" and "Information Report from Miss Renko Takekawa," USNA, RG 331, SCAP, Civil Information and Education Section, Information Division, Policy and Program Branch, Women's Affairs Activities, 1945–50, Prostitution Folder, Box 5250. For more on this episode, see Koikari, *Pedagogy of Democracy*, 171–72, and Hopper, *New Woman of Japan*, 199–203.

128. "Protest of a Virgin to the Round-up of Street Girls" USNA, RG 331, SCAP, Civil Information and Education Section, Information Division, Policy and Program Branch, Women's Affairs Activities, 1945–50, Prostitution Folder, Box 5250.

129. For a critical analysis of U.S.-Japanese cooperation in protecting women's rights, and especially the limits to this cooperation, see Koikari, *Pedagogy of Democracy*, 170–74.

130. John D. Glismann to Colonel Devine, "Operation of Kyoto City Vice-Squads," February 17, 1948, NDL 1635A, Reel 775024, RG 331, SCAP PHW, Venereal Disease Control—Staff Visits, No. 1 (1945–1948), No. 2 (1949–1950), October 1945–August 1950, Box 9336.

131. John D. Glismann, "Care and Treatment of Girls Apprehended by Vice Squad," February 12, 1948, NDL 1635A, Reel 775024, RG 331, SCAP PHW, Venereal Disease Control—Staff Visits, No. 1 (1945–1948), No. 2 (1949–1950), October 1945–August 1950, Box 9336.

132. Nieda, "Summary Report," December 1949.

133. Washington to CINCAFPAC, "Incoming Message, Restricted," December 22, 1945, NDL 1374C, Reel 775024, RG 331, SCAP PHW, Summary Report of Venereal Disease Control Activities in Japan, October 1945–December 1949, Box 9440.

134. Crawford Sams, "Summary of Venereal Disease Control Activities in the Civilian Population of Japan, September 1945 to February 1946," March 9, 1946, NDL 1374C, Reel 775024, RG 331, SCAP PHW, Summary Report of Venereal Disease Control Activities in Japan, October 1945–December 1949, Box 9440.

135. William M. Kitrell to Commanding General Eighth Army, "Penicillin in Sulfa Resistant Venereal Disease Cases in Civilians," April 4, 1946, NDL 1374C, Reel 775024, RG 331, SCAP PHW, Summary Report of Venereal Disease Control Activities in Japan, October 1945–December 1949, Box 9440.

136. J. W. Mann to Commanding General Eighth Army, April 4, 1946, NDL 1374C, Reel 775024, RG 331 SCAP PHW, Summary Report of Venereal Disease Control Activities in Japan, October 1945–December 1949, Box 9440.

137. "Anti-V.D. Campaign," June 30, 1947, AWM 114/417/1/27.

138. "Venereal Disease," October 27, 1947, NANZ, WA-J 69.

139. "V.D. Examination, Japanese Women," January 9, 1947, NANZ, WA-J Z032 24/5 518.

140. "V.D. Control, Minute Paper," July 7, 1947, AWM 114/417/1/27, No. 4.

141. B. S. Wetzel to President V.D. Council GHQ Far East Command, "Venereal Disease Control," November 5, 1947, NDL 1635A, Reel 775024, RG 331, SCAP PHW, Abolition of Licensed Prostitution, 1945–46–47–48.

142. "British Commonwealth Occupation Force, Deputy Director of Medical Services, Medical Technical Instruction No. 12 of 1948, Venereal Disease," May 13, 1948, AWM 114/267/6/17.

143. "V.D. Control—Military," May 1, 1947, AWM 114/422/7/8.

144. "V.D. Control, Minute Paper," July 7, 1947, AWM 114/417/1/27, No. 4.

145. "Provost Report," December 1947, NANZ, WA-J 3 a 467.2.

146. "V.D. Control," July 24, 1947, AWM 114/417/1/27, No. 4.

147. "Extracts from Report of 12 May 1948 to the Minister of the Army by Major-General C. E. M. Lloyd and Mr. Massey Stanley on a Study of Some Problems Affecting the British Commonwealth Force in Japan in April–May 1948," July 27, 1948, NAA, A5954 1886/2.

148. Davies, *Occupation of Japan*, 241.

149. "V.D. Rate in Japan: Discussion by Cabinet," June 1, 1948, *Sydney Morning Herald*.

150. Home Ministry Ordinance No. 16 held that someone who practiced unregulated prostitution (or who procured or solicited it) would be committed to penal servitude, Morrison, "Teen Prostitution in Japan," 464–65.

151. Eric Feldman, *Ritual of Rights in Japan*, 64.

152. "Control of Venereal Disease," May 6, 1946, AWM 114/267/6/17.

153. "Police Control on Public Morals Violations," October 6, 1946, USNA, RG 331, SCAP, Assistant Chief of Staff, G-2, Public Safety Division, Decimal File, 1946–50, 000.5 A-010, Box 263.

154. "Detention of Japanese Girls in Sapporo," August 23, 1948, Public Safety Division, Decimal File, 1946–50, 000.5 A-010, Box 263.

155. "Communications from Japanese NRP," November 16, 1948, USNA, RG 331, SCAP, Assistant Chief of Staff, G-2, Public Safety Division, Decimal File, 1946–50, 000.5 A-010, Box 263.

156. "Control of Venereal Disease, Prefecture of Hiroshima," February 8, 1949, 1120–21, AWM 114/417/1/27, No. 4.

157. "Extract from Change No. 7 to S.C.A.P. Occupation Instruction No. 5," July 26, 1949, NAA, A 5954/69/890/1.

158. "Minute by the Defence Committee at Meeting Held on Thursday 6 October 1949," October 6, 1946, NAA A 5954/69/890/1.

159. "Australians in Japan," September 30, 1949, NAA, A 5954/69/890/1.

160. "Venereal Diseases—BCOF (Japan)," circa 1949, AWM 114 267/6/17.

161. Mollohan, "Comparative Rates of Venereal Disease."

162. Nieda, "Summary Report," December 1949.

163. Isamu Nieda, M.D., "Staff Visit by Dr. I. Nieda PH&W and R. Naka-hara, Ministry of Welfare," October 15, 1948, NDL 1374C, Reel 775024, RG 331, SCAP PHW, Venereal Disease Control—Staff Visits, No. 1 (1945–1948), No. 2 (1949–1950), October 1945–August 1950, Box 9336; Isamu Nieda, M.D., "Staff Visit by Dr. I. Nieda and Dr. R. Nakahara, Ministry of Welfare," June 24, 1948, NDL 1374C, Reel 775024, RG 331, SCAP PHW, Venereal Disease Control—Staff Visits, No. 1 (1945–1948), No. 2 (1949–1950), October 1945–August 1950, Box 9336.

164. Kimiji Sato to SCAP, June 11, 1949, NDL 1374C, Reel 775024, RG 331, SCAP PHW, Venereal Disease Control—Staff Visits, No. 1 (1945–1948), No. 2 (1949–1950), October 1945–August 1950, Box 9336.

CHAPTER TWO

1. Yamada, *Nihon kokusaku ianfu*, 9.

2. *Chian jōsei*, No. 8 (August 22, 1945) and No. 30 (August 31, 1945) in *Chian jōsei kempei shireibu*, August–September 1945, NDL, Japanese Army and Navy Archives, Reel 229, T1555/fo2498-02511; Yamada, *Nihon kokusaku ianfu*, 10–11; Tanaka, *Japan's Comfort Women*, 113.

3. *Chian jōsei*, No. 8 (August 22, 1945) and No. 30 (August 31, 1945); Tanaka, *Japan's Comfort Women*, 113.

4. "Kikisugita joshi sokai: Kanagawa-ken de kairan-ban kara konran maneku," *Asahi Shimbun*, August 19, 1945; Tanaka, *Japan's Comfort Women*, 113.

5. *Chian jōsei*, No. 10 (August 23, 1945); Tanaka, *Japan's Comfort Women*, 113.

6. "Rengōgun hondo shinchū zengo no kokoro e," and "Hikaeyo fujoshi no hitori aruki: fushidara na fukusō wa Tsutsushima," in *Yomiuri Hōchi*, August 23, 1945; Tanaka, *Japan's Comfort Women*, 115.

7. Petty, "Yap and Tinian," 55–71.

8. Dower, *War Without Mercy*, 45.

9. Angst, "Gendered Nationalism," 100–101, and Angst, "The Sacrifice of a Schoolgirl," 243–66.

10. Dower, *Embracing Defeat*, 124.

11. "Rengō-gun shinchū go ni okeru jiko hassei chōsa-sho," NDL, MOJ 6, Japanese Police Intelligence Reports (Naimushō, Keiho-kyoku, 1910–1945), Reel 2; Tanaka, *Japan's Comfort Women*, 116–17.

12. "Rengō-gun shinchū go ni okeru jiko hassei chōsa-sho."

13. Kanagawa-ken Keistasushi Hensan Iinkai, *Kanagawa-ken Keisatsu-shi*, 2:378; Tanaka, *Japan's Comfort Women*, 117. Tanaka writes that in Yokohama alone, 119 rape cases were reported in September 1945 (Tanaka, *Japan's Comfort Women*, 118). But this figure, which actually covers the period from the time of landing until the

end of October 1945, is based on the recollection of a typist who worked in a liaison office. The aforementioned reports in contemporary archives are more credible. Fujiwara Akira, *Shōwa 20–nen, 1945–nen*, 219.

14. "Documents on Japanese Police Activities," NDL, MOJ 38 (Naimushō Keiho-kyoku, 1912–1946), Reel 13, frame number 383043; Tanaka, *Japan's Comfort Women*, 113.

15. "Tokkō Report No. 7056, October 2, 1945," NDL, MOJ 8, "Japanese Government Documents and Censored Publications," Reel 4, "Police Intelligence Reports" NDL, MOJ 38, "Documents on Japanese Police Activities," NDL, MOJ 38 (Naimushō Keiho-kyoku, 1912–1946), Reel 13, frame number 383111; "Documents on Japanese Police Activities," NDL, MOJ 38 (Naimushō Keiho-kyoku, 1912–1946), Reel 13, frame number 383122; Tanaka, *Japan's Comfort Women*, 118–23.

16. Clifton, *Time of Fallen Blossoms*, 167–71.

17. "Provost Weekly Resume of Serious Incidents in BCOF Area During Week Ending 1200 Hrs. 27 Mar. 47," April 3, 1947, NANZ, WA-J 70/4.

18. "Provost Weekly Resume of Serious Incidents for Week Ending 8 May 1947," May 8, 1947, NANZ, WA-J 70/3, 4.

19. "Tokkō Report No. 7056, 2 October 1945," NDL, MOJ 8, "Japanese Government Documents and Censored Publications," Reel 4, "Police Intelligence Reports"; Tanaka, *Japan's Comfort Women*, 118–23.

20. General Headquarters U.S. Army Pacific, Adjutant General Office, Radio and Cable Center, "Incoming Message: Japanese Government Radio C.L.O.–18 Cont'd: 11 Cases Against Women," USNA, GHQ/SCAP Records, Box 408, Sheet No. AG(a)-00022-00023; see also Tanaka, *Japan's Comfort Women*, 120.

21. Brownmiller, *Against Our Will*.

22. Dworkin and MacKinnon, *Pornography and Civil Rights*. See also Dworkin on sexuality and pornography: *Intercourse* and *Pornography*.

23. Bos, "Feminists Interpreting the Politics of Wartime Rape," 999.

24. Lilly, *Taken by Force*, 20–21; Bos, "Feminists Interpreting the Politics of Wartime Rape," 999.

25. On Nanjing, which has been the subject of historical debate and revisionism, see Yoshida, *The Making of the "Rape of Nanking."* On Berlin, see Naimark, *Russians in Germany*, 69–140, and Grossman, "A Question of Silence," 33–52. On more recent cases, see Allen, *Rape Warfare*, and Sharlach, "Rape as Genocide," 89–102.

26. On impregnating women, see Allen, *Rape Warfare*, and Card, "Rape as a Weapon of War." On ethnically cleansed women, see Fisher, "Occupation of the Womb," and Olujic, "Embodiment of Terror." On abortions, see Nikolic-Ristanovic, *Women, Violence and War*.

27. Olujic, "Embodiment of Terror."

28. See, for example, Takemae, *Inside GHQ*, 53–54, and Bourke, *Rape*, 357.

29. Susan Brownmiller, foreword to Tanaka, *Japan's Comfort Women*, xvi.

30. Tanaka, *Japan's Comfort Women*, 116.

31. Kanagawa-ken, *Kanagawa-ken keisatsu-shi*, 2:378.

32. Duus, *Haisha no okurimono*, 76–86, and Fujime, "The Licensed Prostitution System and the Prostitution Abolition Movement in Modern Japan." Statistics can be found in Japanese national government documents such as *Chian jōsei* (Conditions of Public Peace and Order), published by the Kempeitai headquarters; secret reports by the governor of Kanagawa, Fujiwara Takao, to the minister of home affairs, Yamazaki Iwao; reports by the Police and Security Bureau of the Ministry of Home Affairs, including reports from the Special Intelligence Police (Tokkō); and letters and radio messages from the Central Liaison Office (CLO) to GHQ. These reports are limited to the early weeks of the Occupation. Prefectural records can be found in police histories. SCAP and BCOF records contain broad crime statistics in monthly and weekly provost reports, as well as a range of descriptive accounts. Japanese newspapers initially reported crimes by servicemen, but after the press code forbidding negative coverage of Allied troops was enacted September 19, such reports disappeared. For example, statistics appeared in the September 8 issue of the *Mainichi Shimbun* (Kanagawa Edition); Takemae, *Inside GHQ*, 67. It was not until 1953 that articles on rape reappeared in the media. English-language newspapers, such as the *New York Times*, also reported on crime, including rape, during the Occupation. Such observers as Japanese journalist Kanzaki Kiyoshi, American reporter Mark Gayn, and Australian officer Allan S. Clifton wrote contemporary accounts.

33. Roger Brown first reported this error on H-Japan on October 12, 2004. Brown, "U.S. Occupation and Rapes," October 12, 2004, http://h-net.msu.edu (accessed September 8, 2011). Tanaka used a table from a book by Yamada Meiko (itself containing an error) that misread Masayo Duus's 1979 book on the RAA. Duus gives a total of 1,326 crimes from August 30 to September 10. Duus, *Haisha no okurimono*, 76–86. Yamada, *Senryōgun ianfu*, 34–36. In response to Brown, on October 20, 2004, Tanaka explained to readers that "statistical data was not my main concern" and urged readers to examine his new book. Tanaka, "Re H-Japan (E): U.S. Occupation and Rape," October 20, 2004 (http://h-net.msu.edu). Incorrect data from his *Hidden Horrors* has nevertheless been reproduced—see, for instance, Takemae, *Inside GHQ*, 67.

34. Duus, *Haisha no okurimono*. In the case of *Japan's Comfort Women*, original figures from the Hiroshima Prefectural Police Report can be found in Hiroshima-ken, *Shinpen Hiroshima-ken keisatsushi*, 888–89. Tanaka, *Japan's Comfort Women*, 126.

35. Tanaka, *Japan's Comfort Women*, 117–18.

36. "The B.C.O.F. Commandments," n.d., NANZ, WA-J Z081 67/26.

37. "Minutes of Anti-V.D. Conference Held at HQ BCOF (rear) on the 7 June 1948 at 1100 Hrs," AWM, AWM 114/267/6/17.

38. "Minutes of Conference Held at Eta Jima on 3 Apr at 1400 hrs," April 3, 1948, AWM 114/417/1/27.

39. "Security Bulletin: 10/46–7/47," October 1946, AWM 114/423/11/25.

40. Lilly, *Taken by Force*, 118.

41. For a good summary of the research, see Bourke, *Rape*, 372–86.

42. Kimiji Sato to SCAP, June 11, 1949, NDL, 1374C, Reel 775024, RG 331, SCAP PHW, Venereal Disease Control—Staff Visits, No. 1 (1945–1948), No. 2 (1949–1950), October 1945–August 1950, Box 9336.

43. "Rape: Number of Offences Reported or Complaints Received," March 8, 1950, and "Statistics in re Rape," March 11, 1950, USNA, RG 554, Records of General HQ, Far East Command, SCAP, and UN Command, Adjutant General's Section, Operations Division, General Correspondence 1949, 291.2, Box 115.

44. "Statistics in re Rape," March 11, 1950.

45. Brownmiller, *Against Our Will*, 175–76.

46. Lilly, *Taken by Force*, 13, 155, 160.

47. Takemae, *Inside GHQ*, xxix.

48. Nalty, *Strength for the Fight*, 258. For a review of the literature on blacks in the army criminal justice system, see Verdugo, "Crimes and Punishment."

49. See, for example, "Provost Weekly Resume of Serious Incidents in BCOF Area During Week Ending 1200 Hrs. 9 Jan 47," and "Provost Weekly Resume of Serious Incidents in BCOF Area During Week Ending 1200 Hrs. 8 Dec 1948," NANZ, WA-J 70 q34; "Minutes of Administrative Conference held at HQ BCOF on 9 May at 0900 hrs," April 12, 1947, NANZ, WA-J 70/4.

50. Lilly, *Taken by Force*, 11, 169, 182.

51. "Statistics in re Rape," March 14, 1950, and "Rape: Number of Offences Reported or Complaints Received," March 8, 1950.

52. *Hanzai Tōkeisho*, 22–25. Though John Dower does not venture to guess how many rapes may have occurred, he concludes that the incidence was low relative to the number of U.S. troops; *Embracing Defeat*, 130.

53. John LoCicero and Jo LoCicero, interview with author, New York, April 24, 2002.

54. "Letter of Transmittal for Court-Martial Charges," May 10, 1950; "Advice to the Commanding General," June 14, 1950; Letter from Virgil B. Hearon, Asst. Adj. General, to Commanding Officer 32nd Infantry, APO 7, Unit 3, June 19, 1950, USNA, RG 554, Records of General HQ, Far East Command, SCAP, and UN Command, Adjutant General's Section, Operations Division, General Correspondence 1949, 291.2, Box 115.

55. This definition is adapted from Månsson, "The Man in Sexual Commerce," 7.

56. Sheldon, *Honorable Conquerors*, 107.

57. Leonard Forman, "Gaikokujin to Nihon musume," *Kaizō*, November 1951, 97.

58. "Minutes of Anti-V.D. Conference Held at HQ BCOF (rear) on 9 August 1948 at 1400 Hrs," August 1948, AWM 114/417/1/27.

59. "Only Fake Geishas Entertain GIs in Tokyo; Police Reveal Old Houses Are Still Closed," *New York Times*, November 28, 1945, 5.

60. Hume, *Babysan*.

61. For one half-Japanese woman who achieved particular power, see Blussé, *Bitter Bonds*.

62. Ōya, "Batafurai bitaishi."

63. "Onrii ni aijō kansatsu," *Sandee Mainichi*, August 2, 1953, 78–79.

64. Mitsuko Yasui, Affadavit, September 19, 1950, USNA, RG 331, SCAP, Government Section, Central Files Branch, Miscellaneous Subject File, 1945–52.

65. Yuko Tanaka, Statement, September 17, 1950, USNA, RG 331, SCAP, Government Section, Central Files Branch, Miscellaneous Subject File, 1945–52. Kitamura Yasuko, Statement, September 17, 1950, USNA, RG 331, SCAP, Government Section, Central Files Branch, Miscellaneous Subject File, 1945–52.

66. "Charge Sheet, " July 6, 1949; "Sentence," July 15, 1949; "Certificate of Diagnosis for Michiko Takeda," July 16, 1949; "Criminal Investigation Report," July 3, 1949; "Venereal Disease Contact Report," June 21, 1949; "Venereal Disease Contact Report," June 26, 1949; "Medical Report," June 23, 1949; "Statement of Pedro J. Montano," June 25, 1945; "Statement of Grady L. Freeman," June 26, 1949; "Statement of Michiko Takeda," June 25, 1949, all in USNA RG 338, Records of U.S. Army Operational, Tactical, and Support Organizations (World War II and thereafter), I Corps, Provost Marshal Section, Provost Court Case Records, 1946–50, Case 257-64, Entry A1 414, Box 519.

67. "Statement of Michiko Takeda," June 25, 1949; "Venereal Disease Contact Report," June 21, 1949.

68. "Provost Court Case No. 262," July 20, 1949; "Charges Against Miss Nakano," July 11, 1949; "Charge Sheet," July 5, 1949; "Sentence," July 20, 1949; "Sentence," July 15, 1949; "Result of Examination," June 13, 1949; "General Investigative Report," June 29, 1949; "Venereal Disease Contact Report," June 22, 1949; "Result of Examination," June 13, 1949; "Statement of George C. Edwards," June 27, 1949; "Statement of Sumiko Nakano," June 25, 1949; "Venereal Disease Contact Report," June 28, 1949; "Statement of George C. Edwards," June 24, 1949, all in USNA, RG 338, Records of U.S. Army Operational, Tactical, and Support Organizations (World War II and thereafter), I Corps, Provost Marshal Section, Provost Court Case Records, 1946–50, Case 257-64, Entry A1 414, Box 519.

69. "Trial of Venereal Disease Carrier," July 6, 1949; "Fujiwara Misako, Japanese Female Reported as a Prostitute," July 5, 1949, "Court Report as Translated," July 5, 1949; "Fujiwara Misako, Japanese Female Convicted by a Civil Court for Carrying on Prostitution While Infected with V.D.," June 3, 1949, AWM 114/417/1/27 No. 4.

70. Though marriage was permitted for those in the Women's Army Corp, they were subject to being discharged if they became pregnant; Morden, *Women's Army Corp, 1945–1978*, 81, 138–40.

71. "Shinto Weddings: Japanese Women, Australian Soldiers," *Evening Post*, March 30, 1948, NANZ, 87/11/16, Pt. 1, Box 27.

72. Graham, "The Adoption of Children from Japan by Individual Families, 1952–1955."

73. "AMF Component Instruction 62: Entry of Japanese Women into Australia," April 3, 1948, AWM 114/475/2/1; "Message," from ARMINDIA to Defence Melbourne, May 11, 1946, NAA, A 5954/69/890/1.

74. "Application to Marry: 606587 WO Carnegie Adj.," January 18, 1948, NANZ, WA-J Z007 3/74.

75. JCOSA Minute No. 246: "Policy Regarding Marriage BCOF," June 6, 1946, NAA, A 5954/69/890/1.

76. "British Commonwealth Occupation Force Administrative Instruction 39: Marriages in Japan," August 28, 1946, AWM 114/475/2/1.

77. "British Commonwealth Occupation Force Administrative Instruction 36," September 28, 1946.

78. Bates, *Japan and the British Commonwealth Occupation Force, 1946–52*, 119.

79. "Strict Ruling in Japan on Marriage," *Sydney Morning Herald*, March 16, 1948.

80. "Japanese Wives: Ban on Entry to Australia," *Sydney Morning Herald*, March 12, 1948.

81. Ibid.

82. "Weaver Taken off Liner Japan Bound," *Sydney Morning Herald*, November 14, 1951; "Japanese MP Wants to Adopt Weaver," *Sydney Morning Herald*, January 29, 1952; "Weaver (8th Time Out) Won't Be Back," *Sydney Morning Herald*, May 11, 1952; "Weaver Breaks out of Japanese Gaol," *Sydney Morning Herald*, June 9, 1952; "Weaver Seeks Fare Home," *Sydney Morning Herald*, July 10, 1952; "Weaver to Stay out of Japan," *Sydney Morning Herald*, August 17, 1952.

83. Letter to Jacob Javits from K. B. Bush, Brigadier General, Adjutant General, November 28, 1949, USNA, RG 554, Records of General HQ, Far East Command, SCAP, and UN Command, Adjutant General's Section, Operations Division, General Correspondence 1949, 291.2, Box 115.

84. Graham, "The Adoption of Children from Japan."

85. Ngai, *Impossible Subjects*, 237–38, and Koshiro, *Trans-Pacific Racisms and the U.S. Occupation of Japan*, 147–48.

86. "Gov't Eases Ban on Entry of Japanese Wives," *Sydney Morning Herald*, March 30, 1952.

87. Editorial, *Sydney Morning Herald*, March 31, 1952.

88. Tamura, *Michi's Memories*, 11–12, 53.

89. Brandt, "'There Was No East or West/When Their Lips Met . . .'"

90. *Sayonara* has provided fertile material for scholars of Asian and American history and film, especially its implications as an interracial love story in the 1950s. The film differed significantly from the novel version (itself originally serialized in *McCall's*). For an excellent analysis, see Suh, "'Movie in My Mind,'" and see also Marchetti, "Contradiction and Viewing Pleasure," and Marchetti, *Romance and the "Yellow Peril,"* 125–57.

91. Shibusawa, *America's Geisha Ally*, 48–50.

92. For use of the tactic of reassignment in Germany, see Höhn, *GIs and Frauleins*, 106.

93. Robertson, "Blood—in All of Its Senses—as a Cultural Resource," 7.

94. Murphy-Shigematsu, "Multiethnic Lives and Monoethnic Myths," 208–15.

95. "Police Predict 14,000 G.I. Babies by June," *Stars and Stripes*, March 10, 1946, Pacific Edition.

96. Kanō, " 'Konketsuji' mondai to tan'itsu minzoku shinwa," 219.

97. "Shinto Weddings: Japanese Women, Australian Soldiers," *Evening Post*, March 30, 1948, NANZ, Box 27 87/11/16, Pt. 1.

98. Fish, "The Heiress and the Love Children," 195–97.

99. Darrell Berrigan, "Japan's Occupation Babies," *Saturday Evening Post*, June 19, 1948, 24–25, 117–18.

100. Ibid.; Kanō, " 'Konketsuji' mondai to tan'itsu minzoku shinwa," 215.

101. Watt, *When Empire Comes Home*, 112–13.

102. Norgren, *Abortion Before Birth Control*, 38–44. For Taniguchi quote, see Proceedings of the House of Councilors, Session 3, Committee on Health and Welfare, No. 22, November 11, 1948. http://kokkai.ndl.go.jp/SENTAKU/sangiin/003/0790/main.html (accessed on September 2, 2009).

103. Fish, "The Heiress and the Love Children," 198.

104. See Okuizumi Eizaburō, ed., *Senryōgun ken'etsu zasshi mokuroku: kaidai* (Tokyo: Yūshōdō Shoten, 1982), 10–14, cited in Rubin, 85. Rubin discusses literary deletions and notes that while mentions of fraternization were open, terminology was opaque. For more on literary censorship, see Rubin, "From Wholesomeness to Decadence." For a different view of the nature of censorship, see Etō, "Senryōgun no ken'etsu to sengo Nihon."

105. Norgren, *Abortion Before Birth Control*, 80–81.

106. Chung, *Struggle for National Survival*, 173.

107. For example, see Ichikawa Fusae, " 'Dokuritsu' Nihon no fujin mondai: panpan to konketsuji mondai no kaiketsu o," *Tōyō Keizai Shimpō Bessatsu*, May 1952, 51–55.

108. Fish, "The Heiress and the Love Children," 54.

109. Koshiro, *Trans-Pacific Racisms*, 164.

110. Kanō, " 'Konketsuji' mondai to tan'itsu minzoku shinwa," 224.

111. Ibid., 223.

112. Robertson, "Blood—in All of Its Senses—as a Cultural Resource."

113. Kanō, " 'Konketsuji' mondai to tan'itsu minzoku shinwa," 225.

114. Fish, "Mixed-Blood Japanese," 46.

115. Fish, "The Heiress and the Love Children," 49.

116. Koshiro, *Trans-Pacific Racisms*, 162.

117. Stoler, "Sexual Affronts and Racial Frontiers," 198.

118. Kanō, " 'Konketsuji' mondai to tan'itsu minzoku shinwa," 219.

119. Koshiro, *Trans-Pacific Racisms*, 1999.

120. Robert A. Fish has documented Sawada Miki's efforts to establish orphanages to care for interracial children in postwar Japan in "The Heiress and the Love Children." See also Koshiro, *Trans-Pacific Racisms*, on miscegenation, 159–200.

121. Kanō, " 'Konketsuji' mondai to tan'itsu minzoku shinwa," 232–33.

122. Ibid., 235–36, 238.

123. "Don't Say Mixed-Blood," *Mainichi Shimbun*, March 25, 1953.

124. Kanzaki Kiyoshi, "Kyōfu kara no jiyū o: gaikokuhei no seiteki hanzai no bōshi," *Fujin Kōron*, September 1953, 128–33.

125. For a more extensive discussion of the implications of "panpan play" on Japanese society, see Dower, *Embracing Defeat*, 108–10.

126. Rōdōshō Fujin Shōnen Kyoku, *Fūki ni tsuite no yoron*, 29.

127. Ibid., 30.

128. Ichikawa, "'Dokuritsu' Nihon no fujin mondai: panpan to konketsuji mondai no kaiketsu o." Ichikawa's other articles include "Watashi no kokkai dayori: baishun tō shobatsu hōan no yukue," *Fujin Asahi*, October 1953, 88–91, and "Matsumoto jiken to shūsan fujin giindan: baishun kinshihō no jitsugen wa dō shite konnan ka?" *Fujin Asahi*, July 1955, 48. Kamichika Ichiko, a Socialist Diet member, was also prolific, publishing on prostitution-related issues in several other journals. Like any politician, her arguments differ to some extent according to the audience she addressed. Some selections include "Baiin wa nakunaranu ka," *Josei Kaizō*, November 1948, 34–35; "Baishun wa fujinkai no gan de aru," *Keisatsu Jihō*, April 1953, 18–20; and "Watashitachi wa makenai," *Kingu*, October 1955, 278–81.

129. Koshiro, *Trans-Pacific Racisms*, 161, 199.

130. Fish, "The Heiress and the Love Children," 2002.

131. "Hiroshima Orphans: BCOF Men Defended," *Sydney Morning Herald*, April 26, 1948.

132. Uemura Tamaki, "Baishō no inai sekai o," *Fujin Kōron*, April 1953, 44.

CHAPTER THREE

1. Such surveys began in 1949, when the National Public Opinion Research Institute of the Japanese government conducted a survey of attitudes toward prostitution. See the institute's *Japanese People Look at Prostitution*. Later surveys conducted by the Women and Minors Bureau of the Ministry of Labor include Rōdōshō Fujin Shōnen Kyoku's *Fūki ni tsuite no yoron* and *Sengo arata ni hassei shita shūsho chiiki ni okeru baishun no jitsujō ni tsuite*. A wide range of literary accounts, some recently translated into English, paint a similar picture. See Molasky, *American Occupation of Japan and Okinawa*.

2. Fujime, *Higashi Ajia reisen to jendaa*, 41–43, and Fujino, *Sei no kokka kanri*, 195–97.

3. Garon, *Molding Japanese Minds*, 94.

4. The 1955 estimate compares the figure of 500,000 female sex workers widely used by the mass media and politicians in the Diet with Japanese population statistics from Nihon Tōkei Kyōkai, *Nihon chōki tōkei sōran*, 1:80.

5. Tsubota, *Senchū sengo no josei*, 29.

6. "Publications Analysis," February 2, 1946, USNA, RG 331, SCAP, Civil Information and Education Section, Media Analysis Division, 4.

7. S./L. D. R. F. C. Bibby, to Assistant Provost Marshal, December 12, 1950, AWM 114/417/1/27 No. 4.

8. "Procuring Servicemen for Prostitutes and Prostitution in Iwakuni," December 6, 1950, AWM 114/417/1/27 No. 4.

9. Lindesay Parrott, "The Geisha Girl, G.I. Version," *New York Times Magazine*, November 25, 1945.

10. By 1949, the authoritative *Gendai yōgo no kiso chishiki*, a dictionary of current usage, reported: "It was a fashionable word in the postwar, the returned sailors used it since during the war"; *Gendai yōgo no kiso chishiki*, 139. Early etymological accounts may be found in the contemporary popular press by authors such as Kanzaki Kiyoshi, for instance in the pages of the magazine *Zadan* in 1949. Historians of Japan have also discussed the word's origins. See Dower, *Embracing Defeat*, 132; Garon, *Molding Japanese Minds*, 197; Pflugfelder, *Cartographies of Desire*, 330.

11. Biddiscombe, "Dangerous Liaisons," 617.

12. For a particularly striking image, see Dower, *War Without Mercy*, 191.

13. "Jap Sailor Strikes GI's Date in Tokyo," *Stars and Stripes*, November 8, 1945, Pacific Edition.

14. "Monthly Occupation Intelligence Summary No. 11—From Month of February 1947," March 8, 1947, AWM 114/130/2.

15. "Monthly Occupation Intelligence Summary No. 10—From Month of January 1947," February 8, 1947, AWM 114/130/1.

16. National Public Opinion Research Institute, *Japanese People Look at Prostitution*, 2.

17. U.S. Strategic Bombing Survey, *Summary Report (Pacific War)*, 17.

18. Y. Yamamoto, Briefer, "News Matter or Table of Contents," "Shūshoku ga ari shitugyō gohyakuman," *Fujin Asahi*, March 1946, GWP.

19. "Shūshoku ga ari shitugyō gohyakuman" (censored comments), *Fujin Asahi*, March 1946, GWP.

20. In 1948, Ōtani Susumu estimated a population of 1,500 to 2,000, depending on seasonal conditions. Ōtani, *Ikite iru*.

21. Kanzaki Kiyoshi, "Ori no nai dōbutsuen," *Josei Kaizō*, April 1949, 65–67.

22. Ōtani, *Ikite iru*, 73.

23. Kanzaki , "Ori no nai dōbutsuen." Rooms in Japan are measured in terms of the number of tatami mats, which usually measure about 1 foot by 5.3 feet.

24. Silverberg, *Erotic Grotesque Nonsense*, 98–102.

25. Ōtani, *Ikite iru*, 70.

26. Ibid., 91.

27. Minami Hiroshi et al., "Panpan no sekai," *Kaizō*, December 1949, 74.

28. Rōdōshō Fujin Shōnen Kyoku, *Sengo arata ni hassei shita shūsho chiiki ni okeru baishun no jitsujō ni tsuite*; see also Garon, *Molding Japanese Minds*, 94–95.

29. "Report on the Enforcement of Prostitute and etc. Control Ordinance," July 19, 1950, USNA, RG 331, SCAP, Assistant Chief of Staff, G-2, Public Safety Division, Police Branch, Subject File, 1945–52, Pistols to Prostitution, Box 334.

30. Sanders, "Prostitution in Postwar Japan," 43.

31. Nihon Tōkei Kyōkai, *Nihon chōki tōkei sōran*, 1:156, 439.

32. Rōdōshō Fujin Shōnen Kyoku, *Sengo arata ni hassei shita shūsho chiiki ni okeru baishun no jitsujō ni tsuite*, 9; Nihon Tōkei Kyōkai, *Nihon chōki tōkei sōran*, 4:256–57, 272.

33. Rōdōshō Fujin Shōnen Kyoku, *Sengo arata ni hassei shita shūsho chiiki ni okeru baishun no jitsujō ni tsuite*, 66.

34. Hirata and Morita, *Gaishō to kodomotachi*, 20.

35. National Public Opinion Research Institute, *Japanese People Look at Prostitution*, 2–3.

36. Ibid., 5.

37. "Petition," May 17, 1949, AWM 114/143/10/10.

38. "Request that Owners of Houses of Ill-Repute be Ostracized from Society," February 1, 1949, USNA, RG 331, SCAP, Preventive Medicine Division, Abolition of Licensed Prostitution, No. 1 (1945–1948), No. 2 (1949–1950). For yet another petition focusing on the effects on children, see "Petition," circa November 1950, AWM 114/417/1/27 No. 4.

39. "Petition," November 20, 1950, AWM 114/417/1/27 No. 4.

40. Ibid.

41. "Special Class of Women Calling Our Attention," November 22, 1950, *Chugoku Shimbun*, AWM 114/417/1/27 No. 4.

42. "Tōkyoku no me o moguru gyōsha," *Shūkan Yomiuri*, November 28, 1953, 10–11.

43. Loans accompanying indentured contracts remained legal until 1955, when the Japanese Supreme Court officially ruled them void in the case *Fujita v. Okazaki*. Rōdōshō Fujin Shōnen Kyoku, *Sengo arata ni hassei shita shūsho chiiki ni okeru baishun no jitsujō ni tsuite*.

44. U.S. Strategic Bombing Survey, "The Effects of Bombing on Health and Medical Services in Japan, Medical Division," 224.

45. Molasky, *American Occupation of Japan and Okinawa*, 108; Kobayashi and Murase, *Minna wa shiranai kokka baishun meirei*, 96–97; Sanders, "Prostitution in Postwar Japan," 145.

46. Rōdōshō Fujin Shōnen Kyoku, *Sengo arata ni hassei shita shūsho chiiki ni okeru baishun no jitsujō ni tsuite*, 11. Ono Tsuenori claims the practice may have begun as early as 1876, when police began using red lines on maps to denote areas with adult entertainment (*fūzoku eigyō chitai*). Ono Tsunenori, *Angura Shōwashi: sesoura no ura no hijihatsukokai* (Minami Shuppanbu: Hatsubai, Shuei Shōbo, 1981), note 11, as cited in Nagai, *Fūzoku eigyō torishimari*, 238.

47. For more on Suzuki, see his testimony before the Proceedings of the House of Representatives, Session 22, Judicial Affairs Committee No. 32 (July 7, 1955). In

the 1955 survey conducted by the Women and Minors Bureau, it was found that just 20 percent of brothels in base areas belonged to trade associations, compared with 70 percent of those in metropolitan areas; Rōdōshō Fujin Shōnen Kyoku, *Sengo arata ni hassei shita shūsho chiiki ni okeru baishun no jitsujō ni tsuite*, 5.

48. Kanzaki, "Shinjuku no baishun chitai," in *Musume o uru machi*, 131–33.

49. Imokawa Sakuko, to Civil Information and Education Section, January 8, 1951, USNA, RG 554, Records of General HQ, Far East Command, SCAP, and UN Command, Adjutant General's Section, Operations Division, General Correspondence 1951, 250.1, Box 317.

50. See, for example, Takahashi Ichiro and Hori Tadatsugu, "Re Action against Violation of VD Prevention Law and Tokyo-to Prostitution Control Ordinance," August 15, 1949, USNA, RG 331, SCAP, Assistant Chief of Staff, G-2, Public Safety Division, Police Branch, Subject File, 1945–52, Pistols to Prostitution, Box 334; Chief, Crime Prevention Division, Metropolitan Police Division, "Control over Prostitutes," September 19, 1949, USNA, RG 331, SCAP, Assistant Chief of Staff, G-2, Public Safety Division, Police Branch, Subject File, 1945–52, Pistols to Prostitution, Box 334.

51. "VD and Prostitution Control Under Japanese Law," September 19, 1949, USNA, RG 331, SCAP Assistant Chief of Staff, G-2, Public Safety Division, Police Branch, Subject File, 1945–52, Pistols to Prostitution, Box 334.

52. "Use of Military Police to Assist Japanese Police in Enforcement of Tokyo Prostitution Control Ordinance," October 6, 1949, USNA, RG 331, SCAP, Assistant Chief of Staff, G-2, Public Safety Division, Decimal File, 1946–50, 000.5 A-010, Box 263.

53. "Disorders in and Around Camp Drake Increasing, Due to Insufficient Number of Military Police and Japanese Police and Over Abundance of Prostitutes, Solicitors, and Gangsters," August 24, 1950, USNA, RG 331, SCAP, Assistant Chief of Staff, G-2, Public Safety Division, Police Branch, Subject File, 1945–52, Pistols to Prostitution, Box 334.

54. Ibid.

55. "Report on the Enforcement of Prostitute and etc. Control Ordinance," July 19, 1950, USNA, RG 331, SCAP, Assistant Chief of Staff, G-2, Public Safety Division, Police Branch, Subject File, 1945–52, Pistols to Prostitution, Box 334.

56. Ibid.

57. "What a Swan Would Be," May 15, 1949, USNA, RG 331, SCAP, Assistant Chief of Staff, G-2, Public Safety Division, Police Branch, Subject File, 1945–52, Pistols to Prostitution, Box 334.

58. Yoshida Sumiko, maidservant, Nagoya, to Colonel Allen, October 15, 1946, translated by SCAP, USNA, RG 331, SCAP, Civil Information and Education Section, Information Division, Policy and Program Branch, Women's Affairs Activities, 1945–50, Prostitution Folder.

59. Sakamoto Mitsuko to General Douglas MacArthur, February 7, 1947, USNA, RG 331, SCAP, Public Health and Welfare Section, Preventive Medicine Division, Abolition of Licensed Prostitution, No. 1 (1945–1948), No. 2 (1949–1950).

60. Tanaka Seiko to General Headquarters, Received May 26, 1950, Translation Digest, USNA, Public Health and Welfare Section, Preventive Medicine Division, RG 331, SCAP, Subject File Abolition of Licensed Prostitution, No. 1 (1945–1948), No. 2 (1949–1950).

61. Rōdōshō Fujin Shōnen Kyoku, *Sengo arata ni hassei shita shūsho chiiki ni okeru baishun no jitsujō ni tsuite*. The interviewers used the roman letters "A," "B," and "C," to identify the women. To these letters they appended the suffix "ko," a common female name ending in Japanese. Therefore, the women are identified in the case studies—and this article—only as "A-ko," "B-ko," and "C-ko."

62. Rōdōshō Fujin Shōnen Kyoku, *Sengo arata ni hassei shita shūsho chiiki ni okeru baishun no jitsujō ni tsuite*, 4.

63. Clever journalists took these appellations a step further, calling districts with illegal brothels white-line (*paisen*) districts (the white denoted the space above the black dots marking these brothels). See, for instance, Morimura Akira, "Henbō suru jinniku ichiba," *Saikei* (bessatsu shūkan), December 25, 1957.

64. Shiga-Fujime, "The Prostitutes' Union and the Impact of the 1956 Anti-Prostitution Law in Japan," 3–27.

65. The newspaper contained materials of interest for elite sex workers, including poetry, film reviews, and news on the latest developments in the law. See Shiga-Fujime, "The Prostitutes' Union and the Impact of the 1956 Anti-Prostitution Law in Japan," and Rowley, "Prostitutes Against the Prostitution Prevention Act of 1956," 39–55.

66. "Dō shitara seibyō wa yobō dekiru ka," *Fujin Shinpū*, December 1, 1953, 2.

67. "Shidō kenshin no tōkei o miru," *Fujin Shinpū*, October 1, 1953, 2.

68. "Yoshiwara," *Ooru Yomimono*, October 1950, 90–91.

69. "Prevention and Control of Venereal Disease," December 19, 1947, AWM, 114/267/6/17.

70. Letter from Kimiji Sato, June 11, 1949, NDL 1374C, 775024, GHQ SCAP, PHW, Venereal Disease Control—Staff Visits, No. 1 (1945–1948), No. 2 (1949–1950), October 1945–August 1950, Box 9336.

71. "Treatment of V.D. at Japanese hospital, Kure," August 3, 1949, AWM 114/417/1/27 No. 4.

72. "Extract from Publications Analysis #221," November 9, 1948, Military Intelligence Section, General Staff Allied Translator and Interpreter Division, C. V. Starr East Asian Library, Columbia University, New York.

73. Honda, *Furusato no omoide shashinshū*, 132–33.

74. Rōdōshō Fujin Shōnen Kyoku, *Sengo arata ni hassei shita shūsho chiiki ni okeru baishun no jitsujō ni tsuite*, 1955, 22.

75. "Dansaa 200 mei ōbōshū," *Nagasaki Shimbun*, January 1, 1946.

76. This trend paralleled prostitution in the United States, which flourished near military bases. In 1949, the American Social Hygiene Association found in a survey of 213 communities that most with "unsatisfactory prostitution problems" were close to army camps, air force installations, or naval bases. "State of the Union Regarding Commercialized Prostitution," 148.

77. Haiki kōaniinchō happyō dai 14, in Sasebo Joseishi no Kai, *Sasebo no Joseishi*, 3:47.

78. John W. Rouk, "Venereal Disease Control," November 24, 1950, USNA, RG 331, SCAP, Public Health and Welfare Section, Preventive Medicine Division.

79. Sasebo hokensho 1950 in Sasebo Joseishi no Kai, *Sasebo no Joseishi*, 3:47.

80. McNinch, "Recent Advances in Medicine and Surgery."

81. "By-Law Against Solicitation Passed in Sasebo," December 15, 1950, USNA, RG 331, SCAP, Public Health and Welfare Section, Preventive Medicine Division.

82. Masasuke [Shōsuke] Nakata to Chief of Kyushu Liaison and Coordination Office, January 22, 1951, USNA, RG 331, SCAP, Public Health and Welfare Section, Preventive Medicine Division, Prostitution and VD Control Folder.

83. Tanaka Shōsuke,"Memorandum from Mayor's Office of Sasebo," January 5, 1951, USNA, RG 331, SCAP, Public Health and Welfare Section, Preventive Medicine Division, Prostitution and VD Control Folder.

84. "Memorandum from Mayor's Office of Sasebo," January 5, 1951, USNA, RG 331, SCAP, Public Health and Welfare Section, Preventive Medicine Division.

85. "An Appeal to All Young Girls" (*wakai josei no minasan ni onegai*), by Sasebo Morals Purification Committee, December 1, 1950, USNA, SCAP, RG 331, Public Health and Welfare Section, Preventive Medicine Division, Prostitution and VD Control Folder.

86. In 1953, the *Sandee Mainichi* reported that the City of Sasebo was giving licenses to sex workers who engaged in an ongoing relationship with a serviceman (onrii). Decades later, Uchida Fumio, purveyor of a shop that wrote and translated letters for sex workers by the dockside, recorded ongoing sex-work practices in his 1989 memoir. "Onrii ni aijō kansatsu," *Sandee Mainichi*, August 2, 1953, 78–79; Uchida, *Paradaisu dōri no onna tachi*.

87. Kanai San'kichi, "Onna ni yashinawareru Nihon—sono shukuzu wa Sasebo," *Tōyō Keizai Shimpō Bessatsu*, July 1952.

88. Sasebo Chamber of Commerce, June 1951, as found in Inomata et al., *Kichi Nihon*, 197.

89. Kanai, "Onna ni yashinawareru Nihon."

90. Inomata et al., *Kichi Nihon*.

91. Ibid., 200.

92. Hirata and Morita, *Gaishō to kodomotachi*, 31.

CHAPTER FOUR

1. Proceedings of the House of Councillors, Session 24, Plenary Session No. 51 (May 21, 1956), 9–10.

2. "Baishun Bōshi Hō," in Baishun Taisaku Shingikai, *Baishun taisaku no genkyō*, 29.

3. Nishi Kiyoko puts these institutional and political reforms in the context of other SCAP policies that affected women, such as education and work rights. Nishi, *Senryōka no Nihon fujin seisaku*, 17–25.

4. Mackie, *Feminism in Modern Japan*, 123.

5. Beginning with political scientist Susan Pharr, scholars who have written on women in the Occupation have emphasized their achievements, describing how American women helped liberate their Japanese counterparts. See Susan J. Pharr, "The Politics of Women's Rights," in Ward and Sakamoto, *Democratizing Japan*, 221–52. Others who have shared the same focus on cooperation among middle- and upper-class women include Helen Hopper, who wrote a political biography of Katō Shizue, and Sally Hastings and Ogai Tokuko, who published articles on Diet members: Hopper, *A New Woman of Japan*; Hastings, "Women Legislators in the Postwar Diet," 271–300; Ogai, "The Stars of Democracy." Memoirs by former occupation officials have contributed to this positive view, notably Gordon, *Only Woman in the Room*, and Johnson, *Wave-Rings in the Water*.

6. Fujime, "The Licensed Prostitution System."

7. Ibid., 149–50.

8. Dern, "'For God, Home, and Country,'" 146–47; Fujime, "The Licensed Prostitution System," 150.

9. Fujime, "The Licensed Prostitution System," 152.

10. Mihalopoulos, "Mediating the Good Life," 24–28, 30–31; Garon, *Molding Japanese Minds*, 98–114; Fujime, *Sei no rekishigaku*, 87–116.

11. "The Salvation Army and the Abolition of Licensed Prostitution," 1931, LNA, Geneva, Switzerland, s173 bis, Printed Matter Concerning Prostitution in (Burma), India, Indo-china, Straits Settlements, Dutch East Indies and Japan.

12. Murphy, *Social Evil in Japan and Allied Subjects*.

13. "The Salvation Army and the Abolition of Licensed Prostitution," 12.

14. Ibid., 7.

15. "Japanese Open War on Licensed Vice," December 23, 1928, *Philadelphia Public Ledger*, LNA, Geneva, Switzerland, s181, Press Clippings.

16. Yang, "The Movement for Abolishing Licensed Prostitution."

17. Nihon Kirisutokyō Fujin Kyōfukai, *Nihon Kirisutokyō Fujin Kyōfukai hyakunen-shi*, 605–13, 1038.

18. League of Nations, Commission of Enquiry into Traffic in Women and Children in the East, *Report to the Council* (Document number 1932.IV.8, Geneva, 1932), 107.

19. Ibid., 120.

20. "The Salvation Army and the Abolition of Licensed Prostitution," 21.

21. Ibid., 20; Garon, *Molding Japanese Minds*, 104.

22. League of Nations, *Report to the Council*, and Garon, *Molding Japanese Minds*, 105.

23. Garon, *Molding Japanese Minds*, 105; League of Nations, *Report to the Council*, 94.

24. League of Nations, *Report to the Council*, 73, 104, 107.

25. Ibid., 114.

26. Ibid., 106.

27. Ibid., 114.

28. Ibid., 102.

29. Ibid., 120.

30. "The Salvation Army and the Abolition of Licensed Prostitution," 16.

31. Garon, *Molding Japanese Minds*, 105–6.

32. Ibid., 107–10.

33. In 2011, legislation that penalizes clients rather than sex workers for purchasing sexual services remains rare. One example is Sweden's 1999 Act Prohibiting the Purchase of Sexual Services, which penalizes the purchaser of sexual services with a fine or up to six months of imprisonment.

34. In 1962, Ikeda Hayato appointed Kondō minister of science and technology during his second cabinet. She was the last female minister appointed until 1984.

35. "Discussion of Proposed Anti-Prostitution Legislation with Diet Members," May 28, 1948, USNA, RG 331, SCAP, Public Health and Welfare Section, Preventive Medicine Division, Abolition of Licensed Prostitution, No. 1 (1945–1948), No. 2 (1949–1950).

36. Mogami Eiko [Hideko], "On Prostitution Law," *Nihon Fujin Shinbun*, July 5, 1948, USNA, RG 331, SCAP, Civil Information and Education Section, Information Division, Policy and Program Branch, Women's Affairs Activities, 1945–50, Prostitution folder.

37. Miyagi Tamayo, untitled statement, December 14, 1948, USNA, RG 331, SCAP, Civil Information and Education Section, Information Division, Policy and Program Branch, Women's Affairs Activities, 1945–50, Prostitution folder.

38. These local regulations addressed such issues as public morals, solicitation, and prostitution. The Ministry of Labor and the Bureau of Women and Minors counted some fifty-nine local regulations. Fujime and Fujino, who both included regulations enacted at the village level, counted sixty-three and sixty-two, respectively. Fujime, "Higashi Ajia reisen to jendā," 41–43; Fujino, *Sei no kokka kanri*, 195–97.

39. Yoshimi, *Baishō no shakaishi*, 54.

40. The Regulations Controlling Prostitution (Baiintō Torishimari Jōrei) were passed on July 6, 1948, and enacted four days later. According to the Miyagi ordinance, "'Prostitution' in the regulations shall mean sexual intercourse with any indefinite party receiving the gain for the act or under the prearrangement of receiving it." It punished both sex worker and client with a fine of 5,000 yen each, and a habitual offender with 10,000 yen.

41. "Anti-Prostitution Law in Action," *Jiji Press*, July 18, 1948, 1, SCAP translation, USNA, RG 331, SCAP, Legal and Law Division, Decimal File 1945–51, Folder 012.1a, "Punishment of Prostitution."

42. "Stamping out of Street Girls," *Tokyo Shimbun*, January 16, 1949; "Miss Smith Encouraged Women's Association to Root out Prostitution," *Nippon Fujin Shimbun*, January 21, 1949, translated by SCAP, USNA, RG 331, SCAP, Civil Information and Education Section, Information Division, Policy and Program Branch, Women's Affairs Activities, 1945–50, Prostitution folder.

43. "Miss Smith Encouraged Women's Association to Root out Prostitution."

44. "Hantai no koe mo deru," *Asahi Shimbun*, March 5, 1949, 6.

45. "Press Translation," *Asahi Shimbun*, March 6, 1949.

46. "Anti-Prostitution Hearing to Be Held," n.d., Jiji Press, SCAP translation, USNA, RG 331, SCAP, Legal and Law Division, Decimal File 1945–51, Folder 012.1a "Punishment of Prostitution."

47. Isamu Nieda, "Memorandum for the Record," December 31, 1948, USNA, RG 331, SCAP, Public Health and Welfare Section, Administrative Division, Public File 1945–51, "Prostitution Bill."

48. "Notes of meeting between Inoue Guntaro, Metropolitan Police Board, Police Superintendent, Public Peace Section, Sanitary Division Chief, and SCAP Authorities," n.d., USNA, RG 331, SCAP, Legal and Law Division, Decimal File 1945–51, Folder 012.1a, "Punishment of Prostitution."

49. "Memorandum," October 22, 1948, USNA, RG 331, Supreme Command Allied Forces, Legal and Law Division, Decimal File 1945–51, Folder 012.1a, "Punishment of Prostitution."

50. Table A-1, in *Historical Dictionary of the Korean War*, ed. James I. Matray (New York: Greenwood Press, 1991), 552.

51. Takemae, *Inside GHQ*, 126.

52. For a complete breakdown, see Appendix, Table 2.

53. Fujime, "The Licensed Prostitution System," 40–41; Nihon Kirisutokyō Fujin Kyōfukai, *Nihon Kirisutokyō Fujin Kyōfukai hyakunen-shi*, 702–3.

54. The indefatigable Kubushiro devoted her entire life to the struggle to abolish prostitution, revealed by the title of her autobiography, which translates as "A Single-Minded Devotion to Abolishing Prostitution." See Kubushiro, *Haishō hitosuji*.

55. Garon, *Molding Japanese Minds*, 199.

56. Ibid., 199.

57. Fujime, "The Licensed Prostitution System," 9.

58. "G.I. Brothel Ban Is Asked," *New York Times*, April 21, 1952, 12. A version of what became a letter-writing campaign to Ridgeway's wife was reprinted in the Japanese women's magazine *Fujin Kōron*, complete with pictures of Uemura and Ridgeway's wife. "Panpan ni atarashii michi o hiraku tame ni wa," *Fujin Kōron*, May 1952, 36–40.

59. For Ichikawa Fusae's views on mixed-race children, see "'Dokuritsu' Nihon no fujin mondai: panpan to konketsuji mondai no kaiketsu o," *Tōyō Keizai Shimpō Bessatsu*, May 1952, 51–55; Fujiwara quoted in Koshiro, *Trans-Pacific Racisms*, 177–78.

60. Marta Green, "Conference with Prof. Watanabe on Rehabilitation of Prostitutes," September 14, 1949, NDL, 1374C, Reel 775024, RG 331, SCAP PHW, Venereal Disease Control—Staff Visits, No. 1 (1945–1948), No. 2 (1949–1950), October 1945–August 1950, Box 9336.

61. Marta Green, "Field Trip to Kanagawa Prefecture by Ms. Green WD/PHW," September 28, 1949, NDL, 1374C, Reel 775024, RG 331, SCAP PHW, Venereal Disease Control—Staff Visits, No. 1 (1945–1948), No. 2 (1949–1950), October 1945–August 1950, Box 9336.

62. Marta Green, "Inspection Visit to Shinsei Ryo Rehabilitation Home for Prostitutes—Tachikawa," September 28, 1949, NDL, 1374C, Reel 775024, RG 331, SCAP PHW, Venereal Disease Control—Staff Visits, No. 1 (1945–1948), No. 2 (1949–1950), October 1945–August 1950, Box 9336.

63. Green, "Field Trip to Kanagawa Prefecture."

64. Green, "Inspection of Jai Ryo Rehabilitation Home for Prostitutes," September 22, 1949, NDL, 1374C, Reel 775024, RG 331, SCAP PHW, Venereal Disease Control—Staff Visits, No. 1 (1945–1948), No. 2 (1949–1950), October 1945–August 1950, Box 9336.

65. Proceedings of the House of Councillors, Session 11, Judicial Affairs Committee and Educational Affairs Committee Joint Investigative Session, No. 1 (September 4, 1951), 6.

66. "Baishun Shobatsu Hō" in Baishun Taisaku Shingikai, *Baishun taisaku no genkyō*, 355.

67. The bill's definitions of prostitution closely resembled those of the 1948 Prostitution Punishment Bill. It defined prostitution as "sexual intercourse with an unspecified person for compensation, or the promise thereof, by a woman." It penalized both the provider and the client for prostitution. In an appended section, the proposed legislation stated its reasons for making the act of prostitution illegal: most important, defending women's human rights and advocating the "protection of public morals." In so doing, the bill would contribute to "maintaining a perfect social order." "Baishun Shobatsu Hō," in *Baishun taisaku no genkyō*, 356–57.

68. For more information on the work of the Prostitution Problem Countermeasure Conference (Baishun Mondai Taisaku Kyōgikai), see Fujino, *Sei no kokka kanri*, especially 224–25, 231–33.

69. Shūsan Fujin Giin Dan, Baishun Shobatsu Hō Sokushin Iinka, *Nihon kara baishun o nakushimashō*; Rōdōshō Fujin Shōnen Kyoku, *Baishun o nakusu tame ni*.

70. Though female supporters were in the majority, men also sponsored it. Support for abolitionism came from across the political spectrum. From the Japanese Socialist Party's right-wing came Tsutsumi Tsuruyo, Tokano Satoko, Yamaguchi Shizue, and Issei Sei'ichi; from its left-wing came Kamichika Ichiko, Hagimoto Takeko, Fukuda Masako, and Inomata Kōzō. The Socialists were joined by Takahashi Teiichi and Yamashita Harue from the Japan Progressive Party and, from the Japan Liberal Party, Ōishi Yoshie, Yamamoto Masaichi, and Nakayama Masa, the vice minister of health and welfare.

71. Kanzaki, *Musume o uru machi*.

72. The state charged them with violating the Criminal Welfare Law, Article 182.

73. Kanzaki Kiyoshi, "Joshi kōkōsei no Matsumoto jiken," *Fujin Asahi*, July 1, 1955, 44.

74. For more on the debate over children, see Sanders, "Prostitution in Postwar Japan," 81–82, 128–34.

75. Kanzaki, *Musume o uru machi*.

76. Sanders, "Prostitution in Postwar Japan," 101.

77. Ichikawa Fusae, "Matsumoto jiken to shūsan fujin giindan," *Fujin Asahi*, July 1, 1955, 48.

78. Baishun Taisaku Shingikai, *Baishun taisaku no genkyō*, 207.

79. Fujino, *Sei no kokka kanri*, 185, 219, 222, 230; Fujime, "Japanese Feminism and Commercialized Sex."

80. Pan, *United Nations in Japan's Foreign and Security Policymaking, 1945–1992*, chapter 8.

81. *Japan and the United Nations: Report of a Study Group Set up by the Japanese Association of International Law* (New York: Manhattan Publishing Company, 1958), 231.

82. Proceedings of the House of Councillors, Session 22, Committee on Judicial Affairs, No. 7 (June 21, 1955), 8. http://kokkai.ndl.go.jp/SENTAKU/sangiin/022/0488/02206210488007c.html. Accessed on August 8, 2009.

83. Proceedings of the House of Representatives, Session 22, Committee on Judicial Affairs, No. 26 (June 23, 1955), 2. http://kokkai.ndl.go.jp/SENTAKU/syugiin/022/0488/02206230488026c.html. Accessed on August 8, 2009.

84. Proceedings of the House of Representatives, Session 22, Committee on Judicial Affairs, No. 32 (July 7, 1955), 15. http://kokkai.ndl.go.jp/SENTAKU/syugiin/022/0488/02207070488032a.html. Accessed on August 8, 2009.

85. Kamichika Ichiko, Proceedings of the House of Representatives Session 22, Committee on Judicial Affairs and Social Labor, No. 1 (July 13, 1955), 3. http://kokkai.ndl.go.jp/SENTAKU/syugiin/022/0496/02207130496001c.html. Accessed on August 8, 2009; Fujiwara Michiko, Proceedings of the House of Councillors, Session 22, Committee on Judicial Affairs, No. 18 (July 19, 1955), 4. http://kokkai.ndl.go.jp/SENTAKU/sangiin/022/0488/02207190488018c.html. Accessed on August 8, 2009.

86. For example, see United Nations, *International Review of Criminal Policy* 13 (October 1958).

87. Ibid., 46–49.

88. Proceedings of the House of Representatives, Session 22, Committee on Judicial Affairs, No. 31 (July 6, 1955), 5. http://kokkai.ndl.go.jp/SENTAKU/syugiin/022/0488/02207060488031a.html. Accessed on August 8, 2009.

89. Proceedings of the House of Councillors, Session 22, Committee on Judicial Affairs, No. 18 (July 19, 1955), 27. Accessed on August 8, 2009.

90. Proceedings of the House of Councillors, Session 22, Plenary Session No. 40 (July 25, 1955), 2. http://kokkai.ndl.go.jp/SENTAKU/sangiin/022/0512/02207250512040c.html. Accessed on August 8, 2009.

91. Ibid., 2.

92. Ibid., 4.

CHAPTER FIVE

1. Other witnesses included anti-prostitution activist Itō Hideyoshi, University of Tokyo medical professor Ichikawa Atsuji, Prostitution Problem Countermeasure Council Chair Yamataka Shigeri, social critic and anti-prostitution activist Kanzaki Kiyoshi, Hamada Yaeko—head of Nagasaki Prefecture Federation of Unionized Female Employees in Establishments (Sekigashigyō kumiairengōkai jūgyōfu)—and Shigeki Shōsaku, who was a member of the National Food and Drink Industry Workers' Federation Committee (Zenkoku Ryōri Inshoku Gyōsha Rengōkai Iinkai).

2. Proceedings of the House of Representatives, Session 22, Judicial Affairs Committee no. 32 (July 7, 1955), 2.

3. "'Gosengoku-man-en no shikin zenkoku no gyōsha kara atsumeru," *Asahi Shimbun*, July 18, 1955.

4. "Ayamareru hōdō o tsuku," *Fujin Shinpū*, July 15, 1955, 4.

5. Proceedings of the House of Representatives, Session 22, Judicial Affairs Committee, no. 32 (July 7, 1955), 3.

6. Ibid.

7. "Yowai mono ijime no shobatsu hōan," *Fujin Shinpū*, July 15, 1955, 2.

8. Proceedings of the House of Representatives, Session 22, Judicial Affairs Committee no. 32 (July 7, 1955), 4.

9. Garon, *Molding Japanese Minds*, 105.

10. Note that the 1949 survey was conducted in eastern Japan, whereas the 1953 survey covered the whole country; Rōdōshō Fujin Shōnen Kyoku, *Fūki ni tsuite no yoron*. For the 1957 survey, see Sanders, "Prostitution in Postwar Japan," 153.

11. Rōdōshō Fujin Shōnen Kyoku, *Baishunfu narabi ni sono aitegata ni tsuite no chōsa*, 21–22.

12. Rōdōshō Fujin Shōnen Kyoku, *Sengo arata ni hassei shita shūsho chiiki ni okeru baishun no jitsujō ni tsuite*, 37–40.

13. Kanzaki, "Shinjuku no baishun chitai," in *Musume o uru machi*, 172.

14. Rōdōshō Fujin Shōnen Kyoku, *Baishunfu narabi ni sono aitekata ni tsuite no chōsa*, 19–21.

15. Dower, *Empire and Aftermath*, 428–70.

16. Interview with Morimoto Kumiko, Sasebo, Japan, June 20, 2002; Sanders, "Prostitution in Postwar Japan," 150.

17. Rōdōshō Fujin Shōnen Kyoku, *Sengo arata ni hassei shita shūsho chiiki ni okeru baishun no jitsujō ni tsuite*, 21. On segregation and "breathing room," see the insightful analysis of Koshiro, *Trans-Pacific Racisms*, 62.

18. Katsuo, *Jitsumu chūshin*, 53.

19. Hatoyama Ichirō, *Kaoru nikki*, 161.

20. "'Gosengoku-man-en no shikin zenkoku no gyōsha kara atsumeru," *Asahi Shimbun*, July 18, 1955.

21. Yokoyama, "Emergence of Anti-Prostitution Law in Japan," 215.

22. Shiina's imprisonment was officially for another case of bribery that had also implicated Manabe and Tarusawa. Suzuki Akira was arrested on October 12, 1957, on suspicion of bribery, and released two months later. "Baishun oshoku no sōsa owaru—Tokyo chiken kisō wa hachinin dake—zō, shūwai," *Asahi Shimbun*, January 21, 1958.

23. Nihon Shakaitō Seinen Fujin Kyoku Fujin Taisakubu, *Baishun o naku-sanakereba ikenai*, 12.

24. He was also father of Hatoyama Iichirō, a foreign minister, as well as grandfather of Hatoyama Kunio, minister of internal affairs in the Asō cabinet, and Hatoyama Yukio, prime minister from September 2009 to June 2010.

25. Itoh, *Hatoyama Dynasty*, chapter 4.

26. Ibid., 49.

27. Hatoyama Haruko, *Fujin seikatsu no kaizen*, 266.

28. The original advisory body, the Prostitution Countermeasure Council, had finally completed its report and submitted it on September 2, 1955. Although it made no conclusive recommendations, it served as the basis for the socialist bill put forth in the Twenty-Fourth Session of the Diet. Baishun Taisaku Shingikai, *Baishun taisaku no genkyō*, 4.

29. The other female signatories were Mitsumaki Akiko, Fukuda Katsu, Na-kayama Katsu, Tanabe Shigeko, and Ōhama Eiko. Yoshida Ken'ichi also signed the report. "Baishun kōi o shobatsu shinai tōshin ni wa hantai de aru," in Baishun Taisaku Shingikai, *Baishun taisaku no genkyō*, 285–86.

30. "Baishun Bōshi Hō," in Baishun Taisaku Shingikai, *Baishun taisaku no genkyō*, 29.

31. The Prostitution Prevention Law's first section is intended to be gender-neutral. "In this law, 'prostitution' means sexual intercourse with an unspecified other party for compensation or the promise of compensation." Its gender-neutral status, unlike other prostitution legislation previously before the Diet, derives from the Osaka Supreme Court Fifth Criminal Department's 1952 ruling on Amagasaki City's local regulations. These regulations were judged unconstitutional because they punished only female sex workers, an asymmetry with Article Fourteen of the constitution, which guarantees men and women equality. Nonetheless, it should be noted that the more important provisions of the law are sex-specific. The Protective and Rehabilitation Provisions, for example, are limited to females. More-over, the law governs only the act of male-female sexual intercourse.

32. Holly Sanders has argued that these guidance dispositions marked the "first instance of the state placing adults under protective custody to modify their behavior." Sex workers hated them. Sanders, "Prostitution in Postwar Japan," 204.

33. Proceedings of the House of Councillors, Session 24, Judicial Affairs Committee, no. 20 (May 17, 1956), 7. http://kokkai.ndl.go.jp/SENTAKU/sangiin/024/0488/02405170488020c.html. Accessed on August 10, 2009.

34. Proceedings of the House of Councillors, Session 24, Judicial Affairs Committee, no. 20 (May 17, 1956), 8.

35. Abolitionists in other countries very early advocated rehabilitation for prostitutes. On the earlier history of social hygiene movements, see, for example, Pivar, *Purity and Hygiene*; Henriot, *Prostitution and Sexuality in Shanghai*; and Bliss, *Compromised Positions*.

36. Proceedings of the House of Councillors, Session 24, Judicial Affairs Committee, no. 21 (May 18, 1956), 6. http://kokkai.ndl.go.jp/SENTAKU/sangiin/024/0488/02405180488021c.html. Accessed on August 10, 2009.

37. Proceedings of the House of Representatives, Session 22, Judicial Affairs Committee, no. 32 (July 7, 1955), 20–22.

38. Kanzaki Kiyoshi, in Inomata Kōzō et al., *Kichi Nihon*, 341.

39. Proceedings of the House of Councillors, Session 24, Plenary Session, no. 53 (May 23, 1956), 1. http://kokkai.ndl.go.jp. Accessed on April 7, 2010.

40. Proceedings of the House of Representatives, Session 22, Judicial Affairs Committee, no. 33 (July 9, 1955), 1. http://kokkai.ndl.go.jp/SENTAKU/syugiin/022/0488/02207090488033a.html. Accessed on August 10, 2009.

41. Ibid., 1–2.

42. Proceedings of the House of Representatives, Session 22, Judicial Affairs Committee, no. 34 (July 11, 1955), 5. http://kokkai.ndl.go.jp/SENTAKU/syugiin/022/0488/02207110488034c.html. Accessed on August 10, 2009.

43. Ibid., 6.

44. Proceedings of the House of Representatives, Session 22, Judicial Affairs Committee, no. 33 (July 9, 1955), 4.

45. Ibid., 5.

46. Ibid., 5.

47. For more on this theme, see Kovner, "Prostitution in Postwar Japan," chapter 3; and Sanders, "Prostitution in Postwar Japan," chapter 2.

48. Proceedings of the House of Councillors, Session 22, Judicial Affairs Committee, no. 18 (July 19, 1955), 18–19. http://kokkai.ndl.go.jp/SENTAKU/sangiin/022/0488/02207190488018c.html. Accessed on August 10, 2009.

49. It was not until 1999 that the Diet passed the Child Prostitution and Child Pornography Law, which superseded the previous legislation. The new law applies to persons under eighteen and specifies that sexual acts and pornography involving them are illegal. The 1999 law is also notable for its contrast with the 1956 Prostitution Prevention Law over the definition of sexual acts, including any act that "satisfies sexual curiosity" or "touches genital organs." It also covers the rights of minors between the ages of thirteen and eighteen, previously outside the realm of the law.

50. Proceedings of the House of Councillors, Session 24, Plenary Session, no. 45 (May 9, 1956), 21–24. http://kokkai.ndl.go.jp/SENTAKU/sangiin/024/0512/02405090512045c.html. Accessed on August 10, 2009.

51. Ibid., 24.

52. Proceedings of the House of Representatives, Session 24, Plenary Committee, no. 33 (May 11, 1956), 9. http://kokkai.ndl.go.jp/SENTAKU/syugiin/024/0488/02405110488033c.html. Accessed on August 10, 2009.

53. Proceedings of the House of Representatives, Session 22, Committee on Judicial Affairs, no. 32 (July 7, 1955), 20.

54. Hatoyama Ichirō, *Kaoru nikki*, 256.

55. See, for instance, the comments of Miyagi Tamayo and Fujiwara Michiko in Proceedings of the House of Councillors Judicial Affairs Committee, no. 21 (May 18, 1956), 11.

56. Ibid., 10.

57. Proceedings of the House of Councillors, Session 24, Plenary Session, no. 51 (May 21, 1956), 9–10.

58. Mochizuki, "Managing and Influencing the Japanese Legislative Process," 398–406. Joyce Gelb has made the point that using cross-party groups of women to initiate legislation is unusual in the Japanese system; however, because she begins her analysis with the 1985 Equal Employment Opportunity Law, she writes that it "appears to be a new trend." Although such legislative work by women's groups is rare, probably because of the historically small number of female Diet members, the Prostitution Prevention Law can certainly be seen as an example of such cross-party activism. Gelb, *Gender Policies in Japan and the United States*, 7.

59. Ministry of Justice, "Materials Concerning Prostitution and Its Control in Japan," 21, 26–31.

60. Ministry of Justice, "The Administration of the Anti-Prostitution Law in Japan," 9–11.

61. *Shūkan Tokyo*, April 16, 1957. On the estimated number of sex workers, see Fujita, "Prostitution Prevention Law," 493.

62. "Watashi-tachi mo ningen rashiku ikitai," *Sandee Mainichi*, September 20, 1958.

63. Sanders, "Prostitution in Postwar Japan," 193–97.

64. "Betesuda no namida," *Nihon*, July 1958.

65. "Zaru hō ni nusumareta akasen chitai," *Shūkan Tokyo*, April 16, 1957.

66. "The Administration of the Anti-Prostitution Law in Japan," 9–11.

67. Ibid., 6–8, 10.

68. Fujiki, "Recent Trends of Juvenile Crime in Japan," 220.

69. "Shōjo no teki 'ishonami kai' no 19 mei," *Shūkan Shincho*, April 20, 1959.

CHAPTER SIX

1. MacArthur to Yoshida, July 8, 1950. www.ndl.go.jp/modern/e/img_r/M010/M010-001r.html.

2. Dower, *Empire and Aftermath*, 377–400.

3. This estimate, which has been widely cited, originates from the Coalition Against Trafficking in Women. www.catwinternational.org/factbook/index.php. Accessed on August 24, 2009. Economist Takashi Kadokura has compiled a more conservative figure of 0.23 percent of nominal GDP, which in 1999 was equivalent to 1.2 trillion yen. Kadokura, "Chapter 4. Total Value of Boryokudan Activities and the Enjo Kosai Market," 74.

4. One of five Japanese working in hostess bars is a resident Korean. Chung, "Performing Sex, Selling Heart," 25.

5. See "Gurafu 1: Baishun Boshi Hō Ihan Kenkyo Kensū," www.gender.go.jp/danjo-kaigi/boryoku/siryo/bo13-1_2.pdf; and table 1-31, "Baishun Boshi Hō Ihan no Kenkyo Jōkyō no Suii," on the National Police Agency's website, www.npa.go.jp/hakusyo. Accessed on September 2, 2009.

6. Morrison, "Teen Prostitution in Japan," 492.

7. Koyano, *Nihon baishunshi*, 181–83.

8. Morrison, "Teen Prostitution in Japan," 484–87.

9. Ibid., 493; West, "Japanese Love Hotels."

10. West, *Lovesick Japan*, 148–149.

11. Leheny, *Think Global, Fear Local*, 68.

12. Ibid., 69.

13. Morrison, "Teen Prostitution in Japan," 489.

14. Leheny, *Think Global, Fear Local*, 70–73.

15. West, *Lovesick Japan*, 156–157.

16. Muroi and Sasaki, "Tourism and Prostitution in Japan," 170, 179, 183–84.

17. Ibid., 183–84. In the context of increased sex tourism to Korea by Japanese men, and a 1973 appeal by Korean Christian women at a conference of Japanese and Korean churches in Seoul, well-known feminists such as Matsui Yayori even began to push for the use of a different term for prostitution—*baibaishun*. The word, with the characters for "buy" added to those for "sell" and "spring" (*baishun*), emphasizes the role that clients play in the sex work industry; Yunomae, "Baibaishun," 643–64.

18. Muroi and Sasaki, "Tourism and Prostitution in Japan," 187. From the late 1970s until the late 1990s, the number of hostess bars expanded, and by the mid-1980s, most hostesses were Filipina. See Chung, "Performing Sex, Selling Heart"; and Mock, "Mother or Mama," 177–91. For a nuanced ethnography of Filipina hostesses in rural Japan, see Faier, *Intimate Encounters*.

19. For a balanced introduction to the issues of human trafficking in Japan, particularly concerning Thai women, see Dinan, *Owed Justice*. On Filipina migrants in Japan, see Parreñas, *Force of Domesticity*; and Faier, *Intimate Encounters*.

20. Marshall and Thatun, "Miles Away," 49.

21. Dinan, *Owed Justice*.

22. Dinan, *Owed Justice*, 147–84; Naikakufu Danjo Kyōdō Sankaku Kyoku, *Baibaishun kankei jihan kenkyo kensu tō gurafu*.

23. Some women's centers have stepped in to fill the gap: two examples are HELP, funded partially by the WCTU and partially by government funds, and CHARM, registered as an NGO.

24. Raymond and Hughes, "Sex Trafficking of Women in the United States: Links Between International and Domestic Sex Industries"; Raymond and Hughes, "Sex Trafficking of Women in the United States: International and Domestic Trends."

25. Agustín, *Sex at the Margins*; Jo Doezema, "Forced to Choose: Beyond the Voluntary v. Forced Prostitution Dichotomy," in Kempadoo and Doezema, *Global Sex Workers*, 34–50; Chapkis, "Trafficking, Migration, and the Law."

26. The sex workers' union movement has been studied and well documented by feminist scholars working together with sex workers. See, for example, Kempadoo and Doezama, *Global Sex Workers*. Sex-worker unions also maintain websites. See, for example, the Dutch organization De Rode Draad, www.rodedraad.nl, and COYOTE, www.walnet.org/csis/groups/coyote.html, or more generally, www.bayswan.org/penet.html. These sites also provide links to sex-worker unions in other countries around the world.

27. Japan's nascent sex workers' movement is still in the process of self-definition and keeps a very low profile, in contrast to the efforts of COYOTE or De Rode Draad. For instance, as of 1998, the union SWEETLY was still researching how the sex industry in Japan and Asia differed from those of Europe and the West, rather than pushing for decriminalization legislation. Momocca Momocco, "Japanese Sex Workers: Encourage, Empower, Trust, and Love Yourselves," in Kempadoo and Doezama, *Global Sex Workers*, 181. Another example is SWASH (Sex Workers and Sexual Health), created in Kyoto in 1999. See Kaname, "Sex Workers' Movement in Japan," 234–37.

28. Momocco, "Japanese Sex Workers," 180.

29. Leheny, *Think Global, Fear Local*, 75.

30. Ibid., 90.

31. Ibid., 106.

32. Gelb, *Gender Policies in Japan and the United States*, 74.

33. George W. Bush Address to the UN General Assembly, September 23, 2003. www.un.org. Accessed January 16, 2011. Weitzer, "The Social Construction of Sex Trafficking."

34. Agustin, *Sex at the Margins*; Lindstrom, "Regional Sex Trafficking in the Balkans"; Long, "Trafficking in Women and Children as a Security Challenge in Southeast Europe."

35. UNESCO Bangkok Trafficking and HIV/AIDS Project. www.unescobkk. Accessed August 19, 2009.

36. *Trafficking of Women and Children in the International Sex Trade*, 75.

37. Weitzer, "The Social Construction of Sex Trafficking," 462; U.S. Department of Justice, "Characteristics of Suspected Human Trafficking Incidents, 2007–08," www.ojp.usdoj.gov. Accessed on September 2, 2009. See also Shafer, "Sex Slaves, Revisited"; U.S. Department of State, "Victims of Trafficking and

Violence Protection Act of 2001, Trafficking in Persons Report," July 2001; U.S. Department of State, "Victims of Trafficking and Violence Protection Act of 2001, Trafficking in Persons Report," June 2002; U.S. Department of State, "Trafficking in Persons Report," U.S. Department of State, June 2003, "Trafficking in Persons Report," June 2004; U.S. Department of State, "Trafficking in Persons Report," June 2005, all accessible through www.state.gov.

38. "Human Trafficking: Better Data, Strategy, and Reporting Needed to Enhance U.S. Antitrafficking Efforts Abroad." www.gao.gov/new.items/d06825.pdf. Accessed June 13, 2011. See also UNESCO Bangkok Trafficking and HIV/AIDS Project.

39. Parreñas, *Force of Domesticity*, 154–58.

40. Ibid., 160.

41. Patricia Marcelo, "Recruiters: Japan's Migration Law Forcing Entertainers to Go Illegal," *Sun-Star Manila*, March 30, 2006. www.sunstar.com. Accessed on September 2, 2009.

42. Parreñas, *Force of Domesticity*, 160.

43. Faiber, *Intimate Encounters*, 44, 215.

44. Scott Hansen, "Japan's Fight Against Modern-Day Slavery (Part 1)," Embassy of the United States, Tokyo, http://tokyo.usembassy.gov. Accessed on June 23, 2009.

45. Fujime, "Japanese Feminism and Commercialized Sex," 45.

46. "Admiral Has to Quit Over His Comments on Okinawa Rape," *New York Times*, November 18, 1995.

47. Fujime, "Japanese Feminism and Commercialized Sex," 46.

48. Johnson, "Three Rapes."

49. Justin McCurry, "Rice Says Sorry for US Troop Behaviour on Okinawa as Crimes Shake Alliance with Japan," *The Guardian*, February 28, 2008.

50. See, for example, Cooley, *Base Politics*, 150–51; Keyso, *Women of Okinawa*.

51. This number was to be reduced 1.5 percent to 24.9 billion yen for 2009 and 2010. www.mofa.go.jp/announce/announce/2007/12/1176614_840.html.

52. Proceedings of House of Representatives Session 162, Foreign Affairs Committee, no. 11, July 1, 2005. http://kokkai.ndl.go.jp/SENTAKU/syugiin/162/0005/main.html. Accessed on September 2, 2009.

CONCLUSION

1. British sociologist Stanley Cohen first used the concept of moral panic to analyze the reaction to working-class youth culture in Great Britain in the mid-1960s, *Folk Devils and Moral Panics: The Creation of the Mods and Rockers* (New York: St. Martin's Press, 1972). Other sociologists have since used the same approach to explain the regulation of sexual behavior. See, for instance, Bernstein, *Temporarily Yours*.

2. Robinson, "Non-European Foundations of European Imperialism," 128–51.

Bibliography

This study employs a range of published and unpublished materials from multiple countries. These include local newspapers, magazines, government surveys, and parliamentary debates. Articles that occupation officials censored can now be found in the Gordon W. Prange Collection in College Park, Maryland. The Allies also collected letters from sex workers, police reports, and local posters against prostitution, though they are now scattered from Washington to Canberra to Wellington. National archives in the United States, Australia, New Zealand, and Japan also helped me to reconstruct official policy. The League of Nations Archives in Geneva contained records of Japanese participation in international debates on sex work in the 1920s and 1930s, as well as Salvation Army records. The stories of particular communities came to light in the archives and libraries of Sasebo, Kure, and Yokosuka. A selection of documents and images can be found at www.sarahkovner.com.

Western-Language Sources

Agustin, Laura. *Sex at the Margins: Migration, Labour Markets and the Rescue Industry.* London: Zed Books, 2007.

Allen, Beverly. *Rape Warfare: The Hidden Genocide in Bosnia-Herzegovina and Croatia.* Minneapolis: University of Minnesota Press, 1996.

Allison, Anne. *Nightwork: Sexuality, Pleasure, and Corporate Masculinity in a Tokyo Hostess Club.* Chicago: University of Chicago Press, 1994.

Altschuler, Major Louis. "U.S. War Department Venereal Disease Control Program." *Journal of Social Hygiene* 33, no. 6 (1947): 259–72.

Angst, Linda. "Gendered Nationalism: The Himeyuri Story and Okinawan Identity in Postwar Japan." *PoLAR: Political and Legal Anthropology Review* 20, no. 1 (1997): 100–113.

———. "The Sacrifice of a Schoolgirl: The 1995 Rape Case, Discourses of Power, and Women's Lives in Okinawa." *Critical Asian Studies* 33, no. 2 (2001): 243–66.

Bacevich, Andrew J. *American Empire: The Realities and Consequences of U.S. Diplomacy.* Cambridge, MA: Harvard University Press, 2004.

Bailey, Beth and David Farber. "Hotel Street: Prostitution and the Politics of War." *Radical History Review* 52 (Winter 1997): 54–77.

Barrett, John. *We Were There: Australian Soldiers of World War II Tell Their Stories.* Ringwood, Australia: Viking, 1987.

Barry, Kathleen. *Female Sexual Slavery.* New York: New York University Press, 1979.

Bates, Peter. *Japan and the British Commonwealth Occupation Force, 1946–52.* London: Brassey's, 1994.

Bell, Gail Shannon. *Reading, Writing, and Rewriting the Prostitute Body.* Bloomington: Indiana University Press, 1994.

Bell, Laurie, ed. *Good Girls/Bad Girls: Feminists and Sex Trade Workers Face to Face.* Seattle, WA: Seal Press, 1987.

Benvenisti, Eyal. *The International Law of Occupation.* Princeton, NJ: Princeton University Press, 1993.

Bernstein, Elizabeth. "The Meaning of the Purchase: Desire, Demand and the Commerce of Sex." *Ethnography* 2, no. 3 (2001): 389–420.

———. *Temporarily Yours: Intimacy, Authenticity, and the Commerce of Sex.* Chicago: University of Chicago Press, 2007.

Best, Joel. *Controlling Vice: Regulating Brothel Prostitution in St. Paul, 1865–1883.* Columbus: Ohio State University Press, 1998.

Biddiscombe, Perry. "Dangerous Liaisons: The Anti-Fraternization Movement in the U.S. Occupation Zones of Germany and Austria, 1945–1948." *Journal of Social History* 34, no. 3 (2001): 611–47.

Bliss, Kathleen. *Compromised Positions: Prostitution, Public Health, and Gender Politics in Revolutionary Mexico City.* University Park: Pennsylvania State University Press, 2001.

Blussé, Leonard. *Bitter Bonds: A Colonial Divorce Drama of the Seventeenth Century.* Translated by Diane Webb. Princeton, NJ: Markus Wiener Publishers, 2002.

Bos, Pascale R. "Feminists Interpreting the Politics of Wartime Rape: Berlin, 1945; Yugoslavia, 1992–1993." *Signs: Journal of Women in Culture and Society* 31, no. 4 (2006): 995–1025.

Bourke, Joanna. *Rape: Sex, Violence, History.* London: Virago, 2007.

Bowers, Faubion. "The Late Great MacArthur, Warts and All." *Esquire*, January 1967, 91–95, 164–68.

Brandt, Allan. *No Magic Bullet: A Social History of VD in the United States Since 1880.* New York: Oxford University Press, 1985.

Brandt, Kim. "'There Was No East or West/When Their Lips Met . . .': A Movie Poster for Japanese War Bride (1952) as Transnational Artifact." *Impressions* 30 (2009): 119–27.

Bresnahan, Josephine Callisen. "Dangers in Paradise: The Battle Against Combat Fatigue in the Pacific War." Ph.D. diss., Harvard University, 1999.

Briggs, Laura. *Reproducing Empire: Race, Sex, Science, and U.S. Imperialism in Puerto Rico.* Berkeley: University of California Press, 2002.

Brownmiller, Susan. *Against Our Will: Men, Women, and Rape.* New York: Simon & Schuster, 1975.

Card, Claudia. "Rape as a Weapon of War." *Hypatia* 11, no. 4 (1996): 5–18.

Cary, Otis, ed. *Eyewitness to History, the First Asians in Postwar Asia.* New York: Kodansha International, 1975.

Chapkis, Wendy. "Trafficking, Migration, and the Law: Protecting Innocents, Protecting Immigrants." *Gender and Society* 17 (2003): 923–37.

Chung, Haeng-ja. "Performing Sex, Selling Heart: Korean Nightclub Hostesses in Japan." Ph.D. diss., University of California, Los Angeles, 2004.

Chung, Yuehtsen Juliette. *Struggle for National Survival: Eugenics in Sino-Japanese Contexts, 1896–1945.* New York: Routledge, 2002.

Clifton, Allen S. *Time of Fallen Blossoms.* New York: Alfred A. Knopf, 1951.

Cohen, Stanley. *Folk Devils and Moral Panics: The Creation of the Mods and Rockers.* New York: St. Martin's Press, 1972.

Cooley, Alexander. *Base Politics: Democratic Change and the U.S. Military Overseas.* Ithaca, NY: Cornell University Press, 2008.

Cornebise, Alfred Emile. *Ranks and Columns: Armed Forces Newspapers in American Wars.* Westport, CT: Greenwood, 1993.

Crockett, Lucy Herndon. *Popcorn on the Ginza: An Informal Portrait of Postwar Japan.* New York: W. Sloane Associates, 1949.

Davidson, Julia O'Connell. *Prostitution, Power, and Freedom.* Ann Arbor: University of Michigan Press, 1998.

Davies, George. *The Occupation of Japan: The Rhetoric and the Reality of Anglo-Australasian Relations, 1939–1952.* St. Lucia, Australia: University of Queensland Press, 2001.

Davis, Ann Marie. "Bodies, Numbers, and Empires: Representing 'The Prostitute' in Modern Japan (1850–1912)." Ph.D. Diss., University of California, Los Angeles, 2009.

De Becker, J. E. *The Nightless City, or, the History of the Yoshiwara Yūkwaku.* 5th ed. Rutland, VT: C. E. Tuttle, 1971.

Dern, Elizabeth A. "'For God, Home, and Country,' The Women's Christian Temperance Union and Reform Efforts in Meiji Japan." Ph.D. diss., University of Hawaii, 2003.

Dinan, Kelsey. *Owed Justice: Thai Women Trafficked into Debt Bondage in Japan.* New York: Human Rights Watch/Asia, 2000.

Domentat, Tamara. *Hallo Fräulein: Deutsche Frauen und Amerikanische Soldaten.* Berlin: Aufbau-Verlag, 1998.

Dower, John W. *Embracing Defeat: Japan in the Wake of World War II.* New York: W. W. Norton & Company/New Press, 1999.

———. *Empire and Aftermath: Yoshida Shigeru and the Japanese Experience, 1878–1974.* Cambridge, MA: Harvard University Press, 1979.

———. "Occupied Japan as History and Occupation History as Politics." *Journal of Asian Studies* 34, no. 2 (1975): 485–504.

————. *War Without Mercy: Race and Power in the Pacific War*. New York: Pantheon Books, 1986.

Doyle, Michael. *Empires*. Ithaca, NY: Cornell University Press, 1986.

Duggan, Lisa, and Nan D. Hunter. *Sex Wars: Sexual Dissent and Political Culture*. New York: Routledge, 1995.

Dworkin, Andrea. *Intercourse*. New York: Free Press, 1987.

————. *Pornography: Men Possessing Women*. New York: Dutton, 1989.

Dworkin, Andrea, and Catharine MacKinnon. *Pornography and Civil Rights: A New Day for Women's Equality*. Minneapolis: Organizing Against Pornography, 1988.

Ellis, Havelock. *Studies in the Psychology of Sex*. Vol. 2. 1906. Reprint, New York: Random House, 1936.

Enloe, Cynthia. *Bananas, Beaches, and Bases: Making Feminist Sense of International Politics*. Berkeley: University of California Press, 1989.

————. *Does Khaki Become You? The Militarization of Women's Lives*. Boston: South End Press, 1983.

Faier, Lieba. *Intimate Encounters: Filipina Women and the Remaking of Rural Japan*. Berkeley: University of California Press, 2009.

Fauci, A. S., et al. *Harrison's Principles of Internal Medicine*. 17th ed. www.access medicine.com.

Feldman, Eric. *The Ritual of Rights in Japan: Law, Society, and Health Policy*. Cambridge: Cambridge University Press, 2000.

Fish, Robert A. "The Heiress and the Love Children: Sawada Miki and the Elizabeth Saunders Home for Mixed-Blood Orphans in Postwar Japan." Ph.D. diss., University of Hawaii, 2002.

————. "Mixed-Blood Japanese: A Reconsideration of Race and Purity in Japan." In *Japan's Minorities: The Illusion of Homogeneity*, edited by Michael Weiner. New York: Taylor & Francis, 2009.

Fisher, Siobhan K. "Occupation of the Womb: Forced Impregnation as Genocide." *Duke Law Journal* 46, no. 1 (1996): 91–134.

Freud, Sigmund. "The Most Prevalent Form of Degradation in Erotic Life." In *Sexuality and the Psychology of Love*, edited by Philip Rieff. 1912. Reprint, New York: Collier Books, 1963.

Frühstück, Sabine. *Colonizing Sex: Sexology and Social Control in Modern Japan*. Berkeley: University of California Press, 2003.

Fujiki, Hideo. "Recent Trends of Juvenile Crime in Japan," *Journal of Criminal Law, Criminology, and Police Science* 53, no. 2 (1962): 219–21.

Fujime Yuki. "Japanese Feminism and Commercialized Sex: The Union of Militarism and Prohibitionism," *Social Science Japan Journal* 9, no. 2 (2006): 33–50.

————. "The Licensed Prostitution System and the Prostitution Abolition Movement in Modern Japan." Translated by Kerry Ross. *positions* 5, no. 1 (1997): 135–70.

Fujita, Taki. "Prostitution Prevention Law." *Contemporary Japan* 24 (1956): 484–97.

Garon, Sheldon. *Molding Japanese Minds: The State in Everyday Life.* Princeton, NJ: Princeton University Press, 1997.

Gayn, Mark. *Japan Diary.* Rutland, VT: Charles E. Tuttle, 1981.

Gelb, Joyce. *Gender Policies in Japan and the United States: Comparing Women's Movements, Rights, and Politics.* New York: Palgrave Macmillan, 2003.

Gerster, Robin. *Travels in Atomic Sunshine: Australia and the Occupation of Japan.* Melbourne: Scribe, 2008.

Gilfoyle, Timothy J. "Prostitutes in History: From Parables of Pornography to Metaphors of Modernity." *American Historical Review* 104, no. 1 (1999): 117–41.

Gleß, Sabine. *Die Reglementierung von Prostitution in Deutschland. Kriminologische und sanktionenrechtliche Forschungen.* Vol. 10. Berlin: Duncker and Humblot, 1999.

Goedde, Petra. "From Villains to Victims: Fraternization and the Feminization of Germany, 1945–1947." *Diplomatic History* 23, no. 1 (1999): 1–20.

———. *GIs and Germans: Culture, Gender, and Foreign Relations, 1945–1949.* New Haven, CT: Yale University Press, 2003.

Gordon, Beate Sirota. *The Only Woman in the Room: A Memoir.* New York: Kodansha, 1997.

Graham, Lloyd B. "The Adoption of Children from Japan by Individual Families, 1952–1955." Ph.D. diss., University of Toronto, 1958.

Grey, Jeffrey. *Australian Brass: The Career of Lieutenant General Sir Horace Robertson.* Cambridge: Cambridge University Press, 1992.

Grossman, Atina. "A Question of Silence: The Rape of German Women by Occupation Soldiers." In *West Germany Under Construction: Politics, Society and Culture in the Adenauer Era,* edited by Robert G. Moeller. Ann Arbor: University of Michigan Press, 1997.

Guy, Donna. *Sex and Danger in Buenos Aires: Prostitution, Family, and Nation in Argentina.* Lincoln: University of Nebraska Press, 1991.

Hastings, Sally Ann. "Women Legislators in the Postwar Diet." In *Re-Imaging Japanese Women,* edited by Anne E. Imamura. Berkeley: University of California Press, 1996.

Henriot, Christian. *Prostitution and Sexuality in Shanghai: A Social History, 1849–1949.* Cambridge: Cambridge University Press, 2001.

Hershatter, Gail. *Dangerous Pleasures: Prostitution and Modernity in Twentieth Century Shanghai.* Berkeley: University of California Press, 1997.

Hirano, Kyoko. *Mr. Smith Goes to Tokyo: The Japanese Cinema Under the American Occupation, 1945–1952.* Washington, DC: Smithsonian Institution Press, 1994.

Höhn, Maria. *GIs and Fräuleins: The German-American Encounter in 1950s West Germany.* Chapel Hill: University of North Carolina Press, 2002.

Hopper, Helen M. *A New Woman of Japan: A Political Biography of Katō Shidzue.* Boulder, CO: Westview Press, 1996.

Howard, Keith, ed. *True Stories of the Korean Comfort Women.* London: Cassell, 1995.

How the "Social Evil" Is Regulated in Japan. Tokyo: N.p., circa 1890s.

Hume, Bill. *Babysan: A Private Look at the Japanese Occupation.* Tokyo: Kasuga Boeki, 1953.

Inoue, Kyoko. *Macarthur's Japanese Constitution: A Linguistic and Cultural Study of Its Making.* Chicago: University of Chicago Press, 1991.

Ishimoto, Shidzue. *Facing Two Ways: The Story of My Life.* New York: Farrar & Rinehart, 1935.

Itoh, Mayumi. *The Hatoyama Dynasty: Japanese Political Leadership Through the Generations.* New York: Palgrave Macmillan, 2003.

Jaggar, Alison. "Prostitution." In *The Philosophy of Sex: Contemporary Reading*, 2nd ed., edited by Alan Soble. Savage, MD: Rowman & Littlefield, 1991.

James, D. Clayton. *The Years of MacArthur: Triumph and Disaster 1945–1964.* Vol. 3. Boston: Houghton Mifflin, 1985.

Japan and the United Nations: Report of a Study Group Set up by the Japanese Association of International Law. New York: Manhattan Publishing Company, 1958.

Jeffrey, Leslie Ann. *Sex and Borders: Gender, National Identity, and Prostitution Policy in Thailand.* Honolulu: University of Hawai'i Press, 2002.

Jenness, Valerie. *Making it Work: The Prostitute's Rights Movement in Perspective.* New York: Aldine de Gruyter, 1993.

John, Arthur. *Uneasy Lies the Head that Wears a Crown: A History of the British Commonwealth Occupation Force Japan.* Melbourne: Gen Publishers, 1987.

Johnson, Carmen. *Wave-Rings in the Water: My Years with the Women of Postwar Japan.* Alexandria, VA: Charles River Press, 1996.

Johnson, Chalmers. *Blowback: The Costs and Consequences of American Empire.* New York: Metropolitan Books, 2000.

———. *The Sorrows of Empire: Militarism, Secrecy, and the End of the Republic.* New York: Metropolitan Books, 2004.

———. "Three Rapes: The Status of Forces Agreement and Okinawa." *Tom's Dispatch.* www.commondreams.org/scriptfiles/views03/1207-07.htm.

Kadokura, Takashi. "Chapter 4. Total Value of Boryokudan Activities and the Enjo Kosai Market." *Japanese Economy* 34, no. 2 (2007): 62–87.

Kaname Yukiko. "Sex Workers' Movement in Japan." In *Another Japan Is Possible: New Social Movements and Global Citizenship Education*, edited by Jennifer Chan. Stanford, CA: Stanford University Press, 2008.

Kempadoo, Kamala, and Jo Doezema, eds. *Global Sex Workers: Rights, Resistance, and Redefinition.* New York: Routledge, 1998.

Keyso, Ruth Ann. *Women of Okinawa: Nine Voices from a Garrison Island.* Ithaca, NY: Cornell University Press, 2000.

Kimoto, Kinuko. "Barriers to Safer Sex Practices Among Commercial Sex Workers in Osaka, Japan: Scope for Prevention of Future HIV Epidemic." www.hsph.harvard.edu/takemi/RP181.pdf. Accessed on July 11, 2004.

Kleinschmidt, Johannes. *"Do Not Fraternize": Die schwierigen Anfänge deutsch-amerikanischer Freundschaft 1944–1949.* Trier: Wissenschaftler Verlag Trier, 1997.

Koikari, Mire. *Pedagogy of Democracy: Feminism and the Cold War in the U.S. Occupation of Japan.* Philadelphia: Temple University Press, 2008.

———. "Rethinking Gender and Power in the US Occupation of Japan, 1945–1952." *Gender and History* 11, no. 2 (1999): 313–35.

Koshiro, Yukiko. *Trans-Pacific Racisms and the U.S. Occupation of Japan.* New York: Columbia University Press, 1999.

Kovner, Sarah. "Base Cultures: Sex Workers and Servicemen in Occupied Japan." *Journal of Asian Studies* 68, no. 3 (2009): 777–804.

———. "Prostitution in Postwar Japan: Sex Workers, Servicemen, and Social Activists, 1945–1956." Ph.D. diss. Columbia University, 2004.

Leheny, David. *Think Global, Fear Local: Sex, Violence, and Anxiety in Contemporary Japan.* Ithaca, NY: Cornell University Press, 2006.

Leigh, Carol. "Inventing Sex Work." In *Whores and Other Feminists*, edited by Jill Nagle. New York: Routledge, 1997.

Levine, Phillipa. "Rereading the 1890s: Venereal Disease as Constitutional Crisis in Britain and British India." *Journal of Asian Studies* 55, no. 3 (1996): 585–612.

Lie, John. "The State as Pimp: Prostitution and the Patriarchal State in Japan in the 1940s." *Sociological Quarterly* 38, no. 2 (1997): 251–64.

Lilly, J. Robert. *Taken by Force: Rape and American GIs in Europe During World War II.* New York: Palgrave Macmillan, 2007.

Lindstrom, Nicole. "Regional Sex Trafficking in the Balkans: Transnational Networks in an Enlarged Europe." *Problems of Post-Communism* 51, no. 3 (2004): 45–52.

Long, Lynellyn D. "Trafficking in Women and Children as a Security Challenge in Southeast Europe." *Journal of Southeast European and Black Sea Studies* 2, no. 2 (2002): 53–68.

Mackey, Thomas C. *Pursuing Johns: Criminal Law Reform, Defending Character, and New York City's Committee of Fourteen, 1920–1930.* Columbus: Ohio State University Press, 2005.

Mackie, Vera. *Feminism in Modern Japan: Citizenship, Embodiment, and Sexuality.* New York: Cambridge University Press, 2003.

MacKinnon, Catharine. *Feminism Unmodified: Discourses on Life and Law.* Cambridge, MA: Harvard University Press, 1987.

———. *Toward a Feminist Theory of the State.* Cambridge, MA: Harvard University Press, 1989.

Manderson, Lenore, and Margaret Jolly, eds. *Sites of Desire, Economies of Pleasure: Sexualities in the Pacific.* Chicago: University of Chicago Press, 1997.

Månsson, Sven-Axel. "The Man in Sexual Commerce." Translated by Vernon Boggs and Birgitta Borafia, Report, School of Social Work, Research Division, Lund University, Sweden, 1987.

Marchetti, Gina. "Contradiction and Viewing Pleasure: The Articulation of Racial, Class, and Gender Differences in Sayonara." In *Multiple Voices in Feminist Film Criticism*, edited by Diane Carson, Linda Dittmar, and Janice R. Welsch. Minneapolis: University of Minnesota Press, 1994.

———. *Romance and the "Yellow Peril": Race, Sex, and Discursive Strategies in Hollywood Fiction.* Berkeley: University of California Press, 1993.

Marshall, Phil, and Susu Thatun. "Miles Away: The Trouble with Prevention in the Greater Mekong Sub-Region." In *Trafficking and Prostitution Reconsidered: New Perspectives on Migration, Sex Work, and Human Rights*, edited by Kemala Kempadoo, 43–61. Boulder, CO: Paradigm Publishers, 2005.

Mast, George W. "Venereal Disease Control in the U.S. Navy." *Journal of Social Hygiene* 33, no. 6 (1947): 273–78.

McClintock, Anne. "Screwing the System: Sexwork, Race and the Law." *boundary 2* 19, no. 2 (1992): 70–95.

———. "Sex Workers and Sex Work: Introduction." *Social Text* 37 (1993): 1–11.

McNinch, Colonel Joseph H. "Recent Advances in Medicine and Surgery (19–30 April 1954): Based on Professional Military Experiences in Japan and Korea 1950–1953." In *Medical Science Publication No. 4*. Vol. 2. Washington, DC: U.S. Army Graduate School, Walter Reed Army Medical Center, 1954. http://history.amedd.army.mil/bookdocs/korea/recad2/ch4-2.htm. Accessed on November 20, 2003.

Meyer, Leisa D. *Creating GI Jane: Sexuality and Power in the Women's Army Corps During World War II*. New York: Columbia University Press, 1996.

Michener, James A. *Sayonara*. New York: Random House, 1954.

Mihalopulos, Vassilos Bill. "Finding Work Through Sex: Transforming Pre-war Japanese Female Migrant Labourers into Prostitutes 1870–1930." Ph.D. diss., New York University, 2001.

———. "Mediating the Good Life: Prostitution and the Japanese Woman's Christian Temperance Union, 1880s–1920s." *Gender and History* 21, no.1 (2009): 19–38.

———. "Ousting the Prostitute, Retelling the Story of the Karayuki-san." *Postcolonial Studies* 4, no. 2 (2001): 169–87.

Ministry of Health and Welfare. *Statistics on Communicable Disease: Japan, 1998, 1999*. Tokyo: Ministry of Health and Welfare, 1999.

Ministry of Justice. "The Administration of the Anti-Prostitution Law in Japan." Tokyo: Ministry of Justice, 1960.

———. "Materials Concerning Prostitution and Its Control in Japan." Tokyo: Ministry of Justice, 1957.

Mochizuki, Mike. "Managing and Influencing the Japanese Legislative Process: The Role of Parties and the National Diet." Ph.D. diss., Harvard University, 1982.

Mock, John. "Mother or Mama: The Political Economy of Bar Hostesses in Sapporo." In *Re-Imaging Japanese Women*, edited by Anne Imamura. Berkeley: University of California Press, 1996.

Molasky, Michael. *The American Occupation of Japan and Okinawa: Literature and Memory*. New York: Routledge, 1999.

Moon, Katherine H. S. *Sex Among Allies: Military Prostitution in U.S.-Korea Relations*. New York: Columbia University Press, 1997.

Morden, Bettie J. *The Women's Army Corp, 1945–1978*. Washington, DC: Government Printing Office, 1990.

Morrison, Andrew D. "Teen Prostitution in Japan: Regulation of Telephone Clubs Note." *Vanderbilt Journal of Transnational Law* 31 (1998): 457–97.

Muroi, Hisae, and Naoko Sasaki. "Tourism and Prostitution in Japan." In *Gender, Work, and Tourism,* edited by M. Thea Sinclair. New York: Routledge, 1997.

Murphy, U. G. *The Social Evil in Japan and Allied Subjects: With Statistics, Social Evil Test Cases, and Progress of the Anti-Brothel Movement,* 4th ed. Tokyo: Methodist Publishing House, 1908.

Murphy-Shigematsu, Stephen."Multiethnic Lives and Monoethnic Myths: American-Japanese Amerasians in Japan." In *The Sum of Our Parts: Mixed-Heritage Asian Americans,* edited by Teresa Williams-León and Cynthia L. Nakashima. Philadelphia: Temple University Press, 2001.

Nagle, Jill, ed. *Whores and Other Feminists.* New York: Routledge, 1997.

Naimark, Norman M. *The Russians in Germany: History of the Soviet Zone of Occupation, 1945–1949.* Cambridge, MA: Harvard University Press, 1995.

Nalty, Bernard C. *Strength for the Fight: A History of Black Americans in the Military.* New York: Simon & Schuster, 1989.

National Public Opinion Research Institute. *The Japanese People Look at Prostitution.* Tokyo: Public Opinion and Sociological Research Division, 1949.

"The Navy Provides Social Protection for Servicemen in Japan." *Journal of Social Hygiene* 32, no. 2 (1946): 82–89.

Ngai, Mae M. *Impossible Subjects: Illegal Aliens and the Making of Modern America.* Princeton, NJ: Princeton University Press, 2004.

Nikolic-Ristanovic, Vesna. *Women, Violence and War: Wartime Victimization of Refugees in the Balkans.* Budapest: Central European University Press, 1999.

Norgren, Tiana. *Abortion Before Birth Control: The Politics of Reproduction in Postwar Japan.* Princeton, NJ: Princeton University Press, 2001.

Ogai, Tokuko. "The Stars of Democracy: The First Thirty-Nine Female Members of the Japanese Diet." *U.S.-Japan Women's Journal, English Supplement* no. 11 (1996): 81–117.

Olujic, Maria B. "Embodiment of Terror: Gendered Violence in Peacetime and Wartime in Croatia and Bosnia-Herzegovina." *Medical Anthropology Quarterly* 12, no. 1 (1998): 31–50.

Ōoka Shōhei and Dennis C. Washburn. *The Shade of Blossoms, Michigan Monograph Series in Japanese Studies.* No. 22. Ann Arbor: Center for Japanese Studies, University of Michigan, 1998.

Overall, Christine. "'What's Wrong with Prostitution?' Evaluating Sex Work." *Signs* 17, no. 4 (1992): 705–24.

Packard, George R. *Protest in Tokyo: The Security Treaty Crisis of 1960.* Princeton, NJ: Princeton University Press, 1966.

Pan, Liang. *The United Nations in Japan's Foreign and Security Policymaking, 1945–1992: National Security, Party Politics and International Status.* Cambridge, MA, and London: Harvard University Asia Center, 2005.

Parreñas, Rhacel Salazar. *The Force of Domesticity: Filipina Migrants and Global-ization*. New York: New York University Press, 2008.

Pateman, Carole. *The Sexual Contract*. Stanford, CA: Stanford University Press, 1988.

Petty, Bruce M. "Yap and Tinian: The Flemings from Yap, Alfred Flores and Rosalia Aldan Fleming." In *Saipan: Oral Histories of the Pacific War*. Jefferson, NC: McFarland, 2002.

Pflugfelder, Gregory M. *Cartographies of Desire: Male–Male Sexuality in Japanese Discourse, 1600–1950*. Berkeley: University of California Press, 1999.

Pheterson, Gail. *The Prostitution Prism*. Amsterdam: Amsterdam University Press, 1996.

———, ed. *A Vindication of the Rights of Whores: The International Movement for Prostitutes' Rights*. Seattle, WA: Seal Press, 1989.

Pivar, David. *Purity and Hygiene: Women, Prostitution, and the "American Plan," 1900–1930*. Westport, CT: Greenwood Press, 2002.

Prieur, Annick, and Arnild Taksdald. "Clients of Prostitutes: Sick Deviants or Ordinary Men? A Discussion of the Male Role Concept and Cultural Changes in Masculinity." *Nordic Journal of Women's Studies* 2, no. 2 (1993): 105–14.

Ramseyer, J. Mark. "Indentured Prostitution in Imperial Japan: Credible Com-mitments in the Commercial Sex Industry." *Journal of Law, Economics, and Organization* 7, no. 1 (1991): 89–116.

Raymond, Janice, and Donna Hughes. "Sex Trafficking of Women in the United States: International and Domestic Trends." Kingston, RI: Coalition Against Trafficking in Women, 2001.

———. "Sex Trafficking of Women in the United States: Links Between International and Domestic Sex Industries." North Amherst, MA: Coalition Against Trafficking in Women, 2001.

Renda, Mary A. *Taking Haiti: Military Occupation and the Culture of U.S. Imperialism, 1915–1940*. Chapel Hill: University of North Carolina Press, 2001.

Roberts, Mary Louise. "The Price of Discretion: Prostitution, Venereal Disease, and the American Military in France, 1944–1946." *American Historical Review* 115, no. 4 (2010): 1002–30.

Robertson, Jennifer. "Blood—in All of Its Senses—as a Cultural Resource." In *Cultural Resources*, Asian Anthropologies Series, edited by Shinji Yamashita and Jerry Eades. Oxford: Berghahn Press, forthcoming.

Robinson, Ronald. "Non-European Foundations of European Imperialism: Sketch for a Theory of Collaboration." In *Imperialism: The Robinson and Gallagher Controversy*, edited by William Roger Louis. New York: New Viewpoints, 1976.

Rowley, G. G. "Prostitutes Against the Prostitution Prevention Act of 1956." *U.S.-Japan Women's Journal, English Supplement* 23 (2002): 39–55.

Rubin, Gayle. "Thinking Sex: Notes for a Radical Theory of the Politics of Sexuality." In *Pleasure and Danger: Exploring Female Sexuality*, edited by Carole Vance. Boston: Routledge & Kegan Paul, 1984.

Rubin, Jay. "From Wholesomeness to Decadence: The Censorship of Literature Under the Allied Occupation." *Journal of Japanese Studies* 11, no. 1 (1985): 71–103.

"Sailors and Sex: Prostitution Flourishes in Japan." *Newsweek*, November 12, 1945.

Sams, Crawford. *Medic: The Mission of an American Military Doctor in Occupied Japan and Wartorn Korea.* Armonk, NY: M. E. Sharpe, 1998.

Sanders, Holly. "Prostitution in Postwar Japan: Debt and Labor." Ph.D. diss., Princeton University, 2005.

Sandos, James A. "Prostitution and Drugs, the United States on the Mexican-American Border, 1916–1917." *Pacific Historical Review* 49, no. 4 (1980): 621–45.

Saveliev, Igor R. "Rescuing the Prisoners of the Maria Luz: The Meiji Government and the 'Coolie Trade,' 1868–75." In *Turning Points in Japanese History,* edited by Bert Edström. Avon, United Kingdom: Japan Library, 2002.

Sayonara. Directed by Joshua Logan. 147 minutes. Metro Goldwyn Mayer, 1957.

Scambler, Graham, and Annette Scambler. *Rethinking Prostitution: Purchasing Sex in the 1990s.* London: Routledge, 1997.

Schaller, Michael. *The American Occupation of Japan: The Origins of the Cold War in Asia.* New York: Oxford University Press, 1985.

Seidensticker, Edward. *Tokyo Rising: The City Since the Great Earthquake.* Cambridge, MA: Harvard University Press, 1991.

Seigle, Cecilia Segawa. *Yoshiwara: The Glittering World of the Japanese Courtesan.* Honolulu: University of Hawai'i Press, 1993.

Shafer, Jack. "Sex Slaves, Revisited." *Slate,* June 7, 2005. www.slate.com/id/ 2120331. Accessed on August 17, 2009.

Sharlach, Lisa. "Rape as Genocide: Bangladesh, the Former Yugoslavia, and Rwanda." *New Political Science* 22, no. 1 (2000): 89–102.

Sheldon, Walt. *The Honorable Conquerors.* New York: Macmillan, 1965.

Shibusawa, Naoko. *America's Geisha Ally: Reimagining the Japanese Enemy.* Cambridge, MA: Harvard University Press, 2006.

Shiga-Fujime, Yuki. "The Prostitutes' Union and the Impact of the 1956 Anti-Prostitution Law in Japan." *U.S.-Japan Women's Journal English Supplement,* 5 (1993): 3–27.

Shin Young-Sook and Cho Hye-Ran. "On the Characteristics and Special Nature of the Korean 'Military Comfort Women' Under Japanese Rule." *Korea Journal* 36, no. 1 (1996): 50–78.

Sievers, Sharon L. *Flowers in Salt: The Beginnings of Feminist Consciousness in Modern Japan.* Stanford, CA: Stanford University Press, 1983.

Silverberg, Miriam. "The Café Waitress Serving Modern Japan." In *Mirror of Modernity: Invented Traditions of Modern Japan,* edited by Steven Vlastos. Berkeley: University of California Press: 1998.

———. *Erotic, Grotesque, Nonsense: The Mass Culture of Japanese Modern Times.* Berkeley: University of California Press, 2009.

———. "The Modern Girl as Militant." In *Recreating Japanese Women,* edited by Gail Lee Bernstein. Berkeley: University of California Press, 1991.

Social Department National Christian Council of Japan. *The System of Licensed Prostitution in Japan: The Report of an Investigation*. Tokyo: July 16, 1925.

Soh, C. Sarah. *The Comfort Women: Sexual Violence and Postcolonial Memory in Korea and Japan*. Chicago: University of Chicago Press, 2008.

Sone Hiromi. "Conceptions of Geisha: A Case Study of the City of Miyazu." In *Gender and Japanese History*, edited by Wakita Haruko, Anne Bouchy, and Ueno Chizuko. Osaka: Osaka University Press, 1999.

——. "Prostitution and Public Authority in Early Modern Japan." Translated by Akiko Terashima and Anne Walthall. In *Women and Class in Japanese History*, edited by Hitomi Tomomura, Wakita Haruko and Anne Walthall. Ann Arbor: Center for Japanese Studies, University of Michigan, 1999.

Song, Youn-ok. "Japanese Colonial Rule and State-Managed Prostitution: Korea's Licensed Prostitutes." *positions* 5, no. 1 (1997): 171–217.

Spongberg, Mary. *Feminizing Venereal Disease: The Body of the Prostitute in Nineteenth-Century Medical Discourse*. New York: New York University Press, 1997.

Stanley, Amy. "Pinning Down the Floating World: Prostitution in Provincial Japan, 1600–1868." Ph.D. diss., Harvard University, 2007.

Stansell, Christine. *City of Women: Sex and Class in New York, 1789–1860*. New York: Alfred A. Knopf, 1986.

"State of the Union Regarding Commercialized Prostitution." *Journal of Social Hygiene* 35, no. 4 (1949): 146–66.

Stein, Michael. *Japans Kurtisanen: Eine Kulturgeschichte der japanischen Meisterinnen der Unterhaltungskunst und Erotik aus zwölf Jahrhunderten*. Munich: Iudicium, 1997.

Stoler, Ann Laura. "Carnal Knowledge and Imperial Power: Gender, Race, and Morality in Colonial Asia." In *Gender at the Crossroads of Knowledge: Feminist Anthropology in a Postmodern Era*, edited by Micaela di Leonardo. Berkeley: University of California Press, 1991.

——. "Sexual Affronts and Racial Frontiers: European Identities and the Cultural Politics of Exclusion in Colonial Southeast Asia." In *Tensions of Empire: Colonial Cultures in a Bourgeois World*, edited by Frederick Cooper and Ann Laura Stoler. Berkeley: University of California Press, 1997.

Sturdevant, Saundra Pollock, and Brenda Stoltzfus. *Let the Good Times Roll: Prostitution and the U.S. Military in Asia*. New York: New Press, 1992.

Suh, Alexandra. "Movie in My Mind: American Culture and Military Prostitution in Asia." Ph.D. diss., Columbia University, 2001.

Sullivan, Barbara Ann. *The Politics of Sex: Prostitution and Pornography in Australia Since 1945*. New York: Cambridge University Press, 1997.

Takemae, Eiji. *Inside GHQ: The Allied Occupation of Japan and its Legacy*. Translated and adapted from the Japanese by Robert Ricketts and Sebastian Swann. New York: Continuum, 2002.

Tamura, Keiko. *Michi's Memories: The Story of a Japanese War Bride*. Canberra: Research School of Pacific and Asian Studies, Australian National University, 2001.

Tanaka, Yuki. *Hidden Horrors: Japanese War Crimes in World War II*. Boulder, CO: Westview Press, 1996.

———. *Japan's Comfort Women: Sexual Slavery and Prostitution During World War II and the US Occupation*. New York: Routledge, 2002.

Tatsuhiro, Ōshiro and Mineo Higashi. *Okinawa: Two Postwar Novellas*. Translated by Steve Rabson. Japan Research Monograph 10. Berkeley, CA: Center for Japanese Studies, 1989.

Tipton, Elise. "Pink Collar Work: The Café Waitress in Early Twentieth Century Japan." *Intersections* 7 (March 2002). wwwsshe.murdoch.edu.au/intersections/issue7/tipton.html. Accessed August 8, 2009.

Trafficking of Women and Children in the International Sex Trade. Washington, DC: Government Printing Office, 2000.

Truong, Thanh-Dam. *Sex, Money and Morality: Prostitution and Tourism in Southeast Asia*. London: Zed Books, 1990.

United Nations, *International Review of Criminal Policy* 13 (October 1958).

U.S. Strategic Bombing Survey. "The Effects of Bombing on Health and Medical Services in Japan, Medical Division," June 1947.

———. *Summary Report (Pacific War)*. Washington, DC: Government Printing Office, 1946.

Vance, Carole, ed. *Pleasure and Danger: Exploring Female Sexuality*. London: Pandora Press, 1989.

Verdugo, Naomi. "Crimes and Punishment: Blacks in the Army's Criminal Justice System." *Military Psychology* 10, no. 2 (1998): 107–25.

Walkowitz, Judith R. *City of Dreadful Delight: Narratives of Sexual Danger in Late-Victorian London, Women in Culture and Society*. Chicago: University of Chicago Press, 1992.

———. *Prostitution and Victorian Society: Women, Class, and the State*. New York: Cambridge University Press, 1980.

Ward, Robert Edward, and Yoshikazu Sakamoto, eds. *Democratizing Japan: The Allied Occupation*. Honolulu: University of Hawai'i Press, 1987.

Warren, James Francis. *Ah Ku and Karayuki-san: Prostitution in Singapore, 1870–1940*. Singapore and New York: Oxford University Press, 1993.

Watt, Lori. *When Empire Comes Home: Repatriation and Reintegration in Postwar Japan*. Cambridge, MA: Harvard University Press, 2009.

Weitzer, Ronald. *Sex for Sale: Prostitution, Pornography, and the Sex Industry*. New York: Routledge, 2000.

———. "The Social Construction of Sex Trafficking: Ideology and Institutionalization of a Moral Crusade." *Politics & Society* 35, no. 3 (2007): 447–75.

West, Mark D. "Japanese Love Hotels: Legal Change, Social Change, and Industry Change." November 26, 2002. Michigan Law and Economics Research Paper No. 02-018. http://ssrn.com/abstract=357000.

————. *Lovesick Japan: Sex, Marriage, Romance, Law.* Ithaca, NY: Cornell University Press, 2011.

White, Luise. *The Comforts of Home: Prostitution in Colonial Nairobi.* Chicago: University of Chicago Press, 1990.

Willoughby, John. *Remaking the Conquering Heroes: The Social and Geopolitical Impact of the Post-War American Occupation of Germany.* 1st ed. New York: Palgrave, 2001.

Wood, James. *The Forgotten Force: The Australian Military Contribution to the Occupation of Japan, 1945–52.* St. Leonards, Australia: Allen and Unwin, 1998.

Yang Sunyoung. "The Movement for Abolishing Licensed Prostitution." Ph.D. diss., Tokyo University of Foreign Studies, 2005.

Yoda, Tatsuro. "Japan's Host Nation Support Program for the U.S. Japan Security Alliance: Past and Prospects." *Asian Survey* 46, no. 6 (2006): 937–61.

Yokoyama, Minoru. "Emergence of Anti-Prostitution Law in Japan—Analysis from Sociology of Criminal Law." *International Journal of Comparative and Applied Criminal Justice* 17 (1993): 213–18.

Yoshida, Takashi. *The Making of the "Rape of Nanking": History and Memory in Japan, China, and the United States.* New York: Oxford University Press, 2006.

Yoshimi Yoshiaki. *Comfort Women.* Translated by Suzanne O'Brien. New York: Columbia University Press, 2000.

Japanese-Language Sources

Akamatsu Keisuke. *Yobai no minzokugaku.* Tokyo: Meiseki Shoten, 1994.

Akasen chitai (Streets of Shame). Directed by Mizoguchi Kenji. 87 minutes. Daiei, 1956.

Baishun Kinshihō Seitei Sokushin Iinkai. *Baishun kinshi kisei daiikkai zenkoku fujin taikaiki.* Tokyo: Baishun Kinshi Hō Seitei Sokushin Iinkai, 1954.

Baishun Shobatsuhō Sokushin Iinkai. *Nihon kara baishun o nakushimashō: tadashii danjo kankei no kakuritsu no tameni, akarui shakai no kensetsu no tame ni.* Tokyo: Baishun Shobatsuhō Sokushin Iinkai, 1953.

Baishun Taisaku Shingikai. *Baishun taisaku no genkyō.* Tokyo: Okurashō Insatsu Kyoku, 1959.

Buta to gunkan (Pigs and Battleships). Directed by Imamura Shohei. 106 minutes. Nikkatsu, 1962.

Duus Masayo. *Haisha no okurimono: kokusaku ianfu o meguru senryoka hishi.* Tokyo: Kodansha, 1979.

Etō Jun. "Senryōgun no ken'etsu to sengo Nihon." *Shokun* 14, no. 2 (1982): 34–109.

Forman, Leonard. "Gaikokujin to Nihon musume." *Kaizō*, November 1951.

Fujime Yuki. Higashi Ajia reisen to jendā. Self-published report, Osaka, 2003.

————. *Sei no rekishigaku.* Tokyo: Fuji Shuppan, 1997.

Fujino Yutaka. *Sei no kokka kanri: baibaishun no kin-gendaishi.* Tokyo: Fuji
Shuppan, 2001.

Fujiwara Akira, Awaya Kentaro, and Yoshida Yutaka, eds. *Shōwa 20–nen,
1945–nen.* Tokyo: Shōgakukan, 1995.

Fukushima Jūrō. *Sengo zasshi hakkutsu.* Tokyo: Yōsensha, 1985.

Gendai yōgo no kiso chishiki. Tokyo: Jiyū Kokuminsha, 1949.

Gotō Tsutomu. *Zoku Nihon no teisō.* Tokyo: Sōjusha, 1956.

Hanzai Tōkeisho. Tokyo: Kokka Chihō Keisatsu Honbu Keijibu Chōsa Tōkeika,
1950.

Hatoyama Haruko. *Fujin seikatsu no kaizen,* edited by Yamazaki Tomoko.
Tokyo: Senshidō, 1920. Reprint, Tokyo: Ōzorasha, 1996.

Hatoyama Ichirō. *Kaoru nikki,* edited by Itō Takashi and Suetake Yoshiya.
Tokyo: Chūō Kōron, 2005.

Hirai Kazuko. "Nihon senryō o 'sei' de minaosu." *Nihonshi kenkyū* 500 (2004):
107–30.

————. "RAA to 'akasen' Atami ni okeru tenkai." In *Senryō to sei: seisaku, jittai,
hyosho,* edited by Keisen Joshigakuen Daigaku Heiwa Bunka Kenkyūjō,
79–118. Tokyo: Impakuto Shuppankai, 2007.

Hirata Tadamichi and Morita Shōheji. *Gaishō to kodomotachi: toku ni Yokosu-
kashi no genjo no bunseki.* Tokyo: Keio Gijuku Daigaku Shakai Jigyō
Kenkūkai, 1953.

Hiroshima-ken Keisatsu-shi Henshū Iin-kai. *Shinpen Hiroshima-ken keisatsushi.*
Hiroshima: Hiroshima-ken Keisatsu Renraku Kyōgi-kai, 1954.

Honda Mitsurō, ed. *Furusato no omoide shashinshū: Meiji Taishō Shōwa Sasebo.*
Tokyo: Kokusho Kankōkai, 1979.

Ideoka Manabu. "Karikomi to seibyōin—sengo Kanagawa no seiseisaku." In
Senryō to sei: seisaku, jittai, hyosho, edited by Keisen Joshigakuen Daigaku
Heiwa Bunka Kenkyūjō. Tokyo: Impakuto Shuppankai, 2007.

Ino Kenji, ed. *Tōkyō yamiichi kōbōshi.* Tokyo: Futabaraifu Shinsho, 1999.

Inomata Kōzō et al. *Kichi Nihon: ushinawareyuiku sokoku no sugata.* Tokyo:
Wakōsha, 1953.

————. *Kichi no ko: kono jijitsu o dō kangaetara yoi ka.* Tokyo: Kyōbunsha, 1953.

Inoue Setsuko, *Senryō ianjo: kokka ni yoru baishun shisetsu haisen.* Tokyo: Shin
Hyōron, 1995.

Ishiguro Keishō. *Meijiki no porunogurafi.* Tokyo: Shinchōsha, 1996.

Ishii Ryōsuke. *Edo no yūjo.* Tokyo: Akashi Shoten, 1989.

Kamichika Ichiko. *Kamichika Ichiko jiden.* Tokyo: Nihon Tosho Sentaa, 1997.

Kanagawa-ken Keisatsu Hensan Iinkai. *Kanagawa-ken keisatsu-shi.* Vol. 2.
Yokohama: Kanagawa-ken Keisatsu Honbu, 1974.

Kanō Mikiko. "'Konketsuji' mondai to tan'itsu minzoku shinwa." In *Senryō to
sei: seisaku, jittai, hyosho,* edited by Keisen Joshigakuen Daigaku Heiwa Bunka
Kenkyūjō hen. Tokyo: Impakuto Shuppankai, 2007.

Kanzaki Kiyoshi. *Musume o uru machi: Kanzaki repōto.* Tokyo: Shinkō Shuppan-
sha, 1952.

―――. *Sengo Nihon no baishun mondai*. Tokyo: Shakai Shobō, 1954.

Katsuo Ryōzō. *Jitsumu chūshin: baishun bōshi hō chikujō kaisetsu*. Tokyo: Keisatsu Jihōsha, 1957.

Kawamoto Yoshikazu. *Kaiko ianfu to hisabetsu buraku: sengo RAA ianfu e no kiseki*. Tokyo: San'ichi Shobō, 1997.

Kawamura Kunimitsu. *Sekushuariti no gendai*. Tokyo: Kōdansha, 1996.

Kimura Satoshi. *Akasen ato o aruku: kieru yume no machi o tazuneru bunko*. Tokyo: Chikuma Shobō, 2002.

Kobayashi Daijirō and Murase Akira. *Minna wa shiranai kokka baishun meirei*. Tokyo: Yūzankaku, 1992.

Kokuritsu Yoron Chōsasho. *Yoron chōsa hōkokusho: fūki ni kansuru yoron chōsa, baishun tō shobatsu hōan ni taisuru*. Tokyo: Kokuritsu Yoron Chōsasho, 1949.

Koyano Atsushi. *Nihon baishunshi: yūgyō nyofu kara sōpurando made*. Tokyo: Shinchō Senso, 2007.

Kubushiro Ochimi, *Haishō hitosuji*. Tokyo: Chūō Kōronsha, 1982.

Kusama Yasoo, Isomura Eiichi, and Yasuoka Norihiko. *Kindai kasō minshū seikatsu shi II: shōfu*. Tokyo: Akashi Shoten, 1987.

Maki Hidetoshi and Fujiwara Akihisa. *Nihon hōsei shi*. Tokyo: Seirin Shoin, 1995.

Media View. *1946–1999 Uretamono arubamu*. Tokyo: Tōkyō Shoseki, 2000.

Mihashi Osamu. *Meiji no sekushuariti: sabetsu no shinseishi*. Tokyo: Nihon Editaa Sukūru Shuppanbu, 1999.

Mitani Kazuma. *Edo yoshiwara zushū*. 7th ed. Tokyo: Chūō Kōronsha, 2001.

Nagai Yoshikazu. *Fūzoku eigyō torishimari*. Tokyo: Kōdansha, 2002.

Naikakufu Danjo Kyōdō Sankaku Kyoku. "Baibaishun kankei jihan kenkyo kensū tō gurafu." www.gender.go.jp/danjo-kaigi/boryoku/siryo/b013-1.pdf. Accessed on August 11, 2004.

Nihon Kirisutokyō Fujin Kyōfukai. *Nihon Kirisutokyō Fujin Kyōfukai hyakunen-shi*. Tokyo: Domesu Shuppan, 1986.

Nihon Shakaitō Seinen Fujin Kyoku Fujin Taisakubu. *Baishun o nakusanakereba ikenai*. Tokyo: Nihon Shakaitō Seinen Fujin Kyoku Fujin Taisakubu, 1955.

Nihon Tōkei Kyōkai. *Nihon chōki tōkei sōran*. 5 vols. Tokyo: Nihon Tōkei Kyōkai, 1987.

Nikutai no mon (Gates of Flesh). Directed by Seijun Suzuki. Nikkatsu, 90 minutes. 1964.

Nishi Kiyoko. *Senryōka no Nihon fujin taisaku: sono rekishi to shōgen*. Tokyo: Domesu Shuppan, 1989.

Nishino Rumiko. *Jūgun ianfu: moto heishi no shōgen*. Tokyo: Akashi Shoten, 1992.

Nora inu (Stray Dog). Directed by Kurosawa Akira. 122 minutes. Toho, 1949.

Ōizumi Shirō, Ōtsuka Eiju, and Nagasawa Michio. *Wasurete wa naranai gendai shigo jiten*. Tokyo: Asahi Sonorama, 1993.

Okawa Kazushi, Takamatsu Nobukiyo, Yamamoto Yūzō. *Chōki keizai tōkei*. Vol. 8. Tokyo: Tōyō Kei Shinpōsha, 1967.

Ōtani Susumu. *Ikite iru: Ueno chikadō no jittai*. Tokyo: Sengo Nihon Shakai Settaishi, 1948.

Ōya Sōichi. "Batafurai bitaishi." *Kaizō* (Spring 1953): 36–40.

Rōdōshō Fujin Shōnen Kyoku. *Baishunfu narabi ni sono aitekata ni tsuite no chōsa.* Fujin Kankei Shiryō shiriizu. Chōsa shiryō no. 12. Tokyo: Rōdōshō Fujin Shōnen Kyoku, 1953.

———. *Baishun ni kansuru hōrei kaiteiban.* Fujin kankei shiryō shiriizu. Hōki kankei no. 11. Tokyo: Rōdōshō Fujin Shōnen Kyoku, 1955.

———. *Baishun ni kansuru shiryō kaiteiban.* Fujin kankei shiryō shiriizu. Ippan shiryō no. 31. Tokyo: Rōdōshō Fujin Shōnen Kyoku, 1955.

———. *Baishun o nakusu tame ni.* Panfuretto no. 26. Tokyo: Rōdōshō Fujin Shōnen Kyoku, 1953.

———. *Fūki ni tsuite no yoron.* Fujin kankei shiryō shiriizu. Chōsa shiryō no.11. Tokyo: Rōdōshō Fujin Shōnen Kyoku, 1953.

———. *Sengo arata ni hassei shita shūshō chiiki ni okeru baishun no jitsujo ni tsuite.* Fujin kankei shiryō shiriizu. Chōsa shiryō no.16. Tokyo: Rōdōshō Fujin Shōnen Kyoku, 1953.

Sasama Yoshihiko. *Zuroku: sei no Nihonshi.* Tokyo: Yūzankaku Shuppan, 1996.

Sasebo Joseishi no Kai. *Sasebo no joseishi 3.* Sasebo: Sasebo Joseishi no Kai, 1996.

———. *Sasebo no joseishi 4.* Sasebo: Sasebo Joseishi no Kai, 1998.

Shiina Takashi. *Daijūni tokubetsu kokkai baishun mondai.* Tokyo: Yōyōsha, 1955.

Shimizu Ikutarō, Miyahara Seiichi, and Ueda Shōjirō. *Kichi no ko: kono jijitu o dō kangaetara yoika.* Kobunsha, 1953.

Shimokawa Kōshi. *Gokuraku shōbai: kiki kaki sengo seisōshi.* Tokyo: Chikuma Shobō, 1998.

Sone Hiromi. "Baijo: kinsei no baishun." In *Nihon josei seikatsushi: kinsei*, edited by Josei Sei Sōgō Kenkyūkai. Vol. 3. Tokyo: Tokyo Daigaku Shuppankai, 1990.

Suzuki Yūko. *Jūgun ianfu, naichō kekkon: sei no shinryaku, sengo sekinin o kangaeru.* Tokyo: Miraisha, 1993.

Takahashi Keiji. *Gendai onna ichiba.* Tokyo: Sekirōkaku Shobō, 1931.

Takemura Tamio. *Haishō undō: kuruwa no josei wa dō kaihō saretaka.* Tokyo: Chūō Kōronsha, 1982.

Takeuchi Chieko. *Shōwa yūjo kō.* Tokyo: Miraisha, 1990.

Takigawa Masajirō. *Yūjo no rekishi*, Nihon Rekishi Shinsho. Tokyo: Shinbundō, 1967.

Tamura Taijirō. *Nikutai no mon*; *Nikutai no akuma.* Tokyo: Shinchōsha, 1968.

Tōkyōto Taitō Kuyakusho. *Shin Yoshiwara shikō.* Tokyo: Tōkyōto Taitō Kuyakusho, 1960.

Toyoshita Narahiko. *Nihon seibyō kanri taisei no seiritsu.* Tokyo: Iwanami Shoten, 1992.

Tsubota Itsuo, ed. *Senchū sengo no josei.* Tokyo: Akatsuki Kyōiku Tosho, 1983.

Uchida Fumio. *Paradaisu dōri no onna tachi.* Sasebo: Hotaru Shoten, 1989.

Uesugi Chitoshi. *Kenshō jūgun ianfu: jūgun ianfu mondai nyūmon.* Zōhoban. Tokyo: Zenbōsha, 1996.

Watanabe Kenji, *Edo yūri seisuiki.* Tokyo: Kōdansha, 1994.

Yamada Meiko. *Senryōgun ianfu: kokusaku baishun no onnatachi no higeki.* Tokyo: Kōinsha, 1992.

Yamamoto Akira. *Kasutori zasshi kenkyū: shinboru ni miru fūzokushi.* Tokyo: Shuppan Nyūsusha, 1976.

Yamazaki Tomoko. *Ajia josei kōryūshi: Meiji Taishō ki hen.* Tokyo: Chikuma Shobō, 1995.

Yoon Chong-ok et al. *Chōsenjin josei ga mita: "ianfu mondai."* Tokyo: San'ichi Shinsho, 1993.

Yoru no onnatachi (Women of the Night). Directed by Mizoguchi Kenji. Shochiku, 73 minutes, 1948.

Yoshida Hidehiro. *Nihon baishunshi kō: hensei to sono haikei.* Tokyo: Jiyūsha, 2000.

Yoshimi Kaneko. *Baishō no shakaishi: zōho kaitei.* Tokyo: Yūzankaku Shuppan, 1992.

Yoshimi Yoshiaki and Hayashi Hiroshi. *Kyōdō kenkyū: Nihongun ianfu.* Tokyo: Ōtsuki Shoten, 1996.

Yunomae Kazuko. "Baibaishun." In *Joseigaku jiten*, edited by Inoue Teruko et al. Tokyo: Iwanami Shoten, 2000.

Index

Page numbers set in italic denote a table or figure.